QUESTIONS & ANSWERS

Family Law

Questions and Answers Family Law
A0047036

QUESTIONS & ANSWERS SERIES

Other titles in preparation

QUESTIONS & ANSWERS

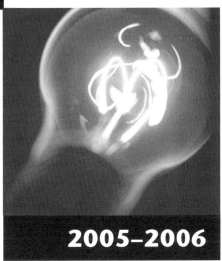

2005–2006

Family Law

FOURTH EDITION

Chris Barton
LLB
Honorary Visiting Professor of Family Law, Staffordshire University

Mary Hibbs
LLB, Solicitor
Honorary Visiting Fellow in Law, Staffordshire University

OXFORD
UNIVERSITY PRESS

OXFORD

UNIVERSITY PRESS

Great Clarendon Street, Oxford OX2 6DP

Oxford University Press is a department of the University of Oxford.
It furthers the University's objective of excellence in research, scholarship,
and education by publishing worldwide in

Oxford New York

Auckland Cape Town Dar es Salaam Hong Kong Karachi Kuala Lumpur
Madrid Melbourne Mexico City Nairobi New Delhi Shanghai Taipei Toronto

With offices in

Argentina Austria Brazil Chile Czech Republic France Greece
Guatemala Hungary Italy Japan South Korea Poland Portugal
Singapore Switzerland Thailand Turkey Ukraine Vietnam

Oxford is a registered trade mark of Oxford University Press
in the UK and in certain other countries

Published in the United States
by Oxford University Press Inc., New York

First published by Blackstone Press 1994
Second edition 1998
Third edition 2003

© Chris Barton, Mary Hibbs, 2005

British Library Cataloguing in Publication Data

Data available

Library of Congress Cataloging in Publication Data

Data available

ISBN 0–19–927652–8

3 5 7 9 10 8 6 4 2

Typeset by RefineCatch Limited, Bungay, Suffolk
Printed in Great Britain by
Ashford Colour Press Limited, Gosport, Hampshire

Contents

The Q&A Series

Key features

The Q&A series provides full coverage of key subjects in a clear and logical way. This new edition contains the following features:

- Question
- Commentary
- Bullet point list
- Suggested answer
- Further reading
- Diagrams

Preface

The first edition of this book appeared over a decade ago when the Children Act 1989 was bedding down, divorce reform was in the air, and the law was coming to terms with increases in cohabitation, parenthood outside marriage, and one-parent families. Today, the courts continue to work at the Children Act 1989, divorce reform has gone quiet, and the law is still struggling with the continuing growth in non-marital families.

Additionally, many fresh matters have arisen even since the third edition, e.g., legal recognition of same-sex partnerships and of gender re-assignment, enhanced protection from domestic violence, a Ministry for Children, the Proceeds of Crime Act 2002—and the publicity given to 'Fathers' Rights'.

Yet because of the essential permanence of the family, these developments have generated more changes to answers than they have to questions, and family law students continue to be assessed in pretty much the same manner, i.e. by examination or by examination and coursework. Those students continue to earn our admiration, as do our own respective families—the grandchild ratio has now risen to 2:0—who are surely grateful for our seasonal disappearances from the living room generated by the production of new editions of this book

Chris Barton
Mary Hibbs
Semester 2, 2004

Table of Cases

Table of Statutes

Table of Rules And Regulations

Introduction: technique for exams and coursework

Hints (j) and (oo) (below) are the gold cards.

Most students enjoy family law—they are likely to be finalists studying it from choice—but hardly anyone enjoys being assessed. The authors like family law too, and *Questions and Answers* represents a (joint) lifetime's experience of teaching or examining the subject, internally or externally, at eight different universities of varying modernity. Our book shows candidates how to display their learning (and/or how to disguise their ignorance). Although the means of converting a year's study into good marks can be mastered far more easily than the year's study itself, even senior students can be surprisingly reluctant to devote time to it. So even though this opening chapter is particularly valuable to them, we have kept it short (and, hopefully within limits, entertaining).

This chapter starts with three lists of exam hints. Where relevant, the assumption is that the exam is to be set internally. The first list consists of preparation advice whilst the second covers the exam itself. Some of the points made in these two lists are obviously applicable to any exam, law or otherwise. The third list is exclusively concerned with *family law* exams. Even third year students may gain from the first two lists, if only by way of a refresher course. Indeed, we suspect that some people will be encountering some of the points for the first time; we have certainly marked a number of scripts which make us think so. This saddens us because we respect the dedication which law students increasingly bring to their work and do not wish to see it wasted by easily-avoided errors. So many students fail to do themselves (or indeed their tutors) justice.

Before embarking on these lists, you should take note of our advice about coursework, now commonly a part of the assessment process.

The advice is that the *minimum* the markers want in return for the extra time and the ability to consult the books and each other which coursework affords, is that you *do the basics properly*. (See the postscript at the end of the chapter.)

We will avoid patronising references about not working the night before, getting there in plenty of time and bringing a spare pen, etc. (although those with poor handwriting should remember that the better the pen, the greater the aid to legibility).

Do's and don't's before exams

(a)   Get the time and place right; check that noticeboard again and do not rely on your classmates (for this or for anything else).

(b)   Know the form; i.e. duration, degree of choice, any reading time. Is the exam in parts? Is the exam 'open book'? 'Seen'?—we suspect we have had at least one student who sat down to the exam unaware of that fact. Is anything compulsory? Are marks for all questions equal?

(c)   Don't believe what your classmates say about how little work they are doing. There is no substitute for thorough learning: it is the only way you can approach an exam with (justifiable) confidence.

(d)   Look at past papers. We regret to say that some examiners actually recycle material, attempting to salve their consciences by changing dates and names etc. Be particularly suspicious if there are no past papers in the library or on the net. That apart, problems, in particular, are a bit like crossword puzzle clues in that you become familiar with the examiners' style.

(e)   Take note of the examiners' (and the externals') views, particularly if published. Revision classes are likely to be rich in implicit—or even express—hints.

(f)   Work out the time at which you should be starting the second and subsequent questions. If the arithmetic is complicated, e.g. the exam starts at 9.15, with ten minutes reading time with five questions to do in three hours, then it is easy to lose track of time. (One of the writers was a long-distance runner who attributed his regular failures to an inability to divide time left by miles remaining.) Remember to allow for reading time in this.

(g)   The last topic taught is a good bet; similarly, anything new, e.g. Law Commission recommendations, etc.

(h)   Claim any allowance to which you may be entitled, e.g. extra time, amanuensis, word-processor, private room, etc.

(i)   If the exam is open book, make sure you have everything you are allowed and know your way around it. Check how best to deploy it all within the limited confines of an exam hall desk. (The other author, *qua* invigilator, was once approached by a distressed candidate who eventually admitted to having mislaid the exam paper within her own detritus.) Remember that the examiners will want something extra from you in return for their munificence (more so, of course, if they have also given advance notice of the questions). Do not forget that, as in all exams, you are required to answer the question set, and that an open book exam is particularly unlikely to be of the 'Tell me all about . . .' variety, so you will not be able to answer simply by 'lifting' from the book.

(j)   Prepare an opening-paragraph-length statement of the structure of each topic; definition(s); place within the subject as a whole; an out-of-the-way quote from the wilds of the further reading; and some thought of your own. On the day, however, do remember to tailor it to the actual question, of course.

(k) If you have, or you think you have, weaknesses in your exam technique, go to your college's student counsellors. They are free, accessible and private. There is no shame involved and you cannot lose; they tend to know a lot about exam worries, rational and otherwise.

Do's and don't's during exams

Before you start writing

(l) Check the rubric, despite (b) above.

(m) Read the whole paper with the object of deciding which questions you can, and ideally will, do. (This applies whether or not there is any formal 'reading time', but if there is, then scribble notes on the paper itself if permitted.) Make sure you have read all the paper—turn the page over!

(n) Achieve this object (i.e. (m) above) by deciding which areas of the subject are invoked by which questions.

(o) In doing this, you might read the essay questions, or part-questions, first. That way—essay questions having less bulk and less potential for concealment than problems—early inroads may be made more quickly. Then look at the problems, starting with those which are the other part(s) of the half-essay questions, and remember that a two-part question may involve different topic(s) in each part. Remember also that all this may take some time, and involve reading several sides of A4 paper.

(p) The golden rule, particularly with problems, is not to panic if the penny doesn't drop on first reading—read it again and the ideas should start to come. If they do not, take your law into the question, i.e. check off the topics covered in the course. If in doubt, do not do it—always assuming you can do the required number without it.

(q) Ready to start? Think (see (j) above) and note the time (see (f) above). Do not start before you are ready just because everyone else appears to be scribbling furiously.

Answering: pointers common to both essays and problems

(r) Use a conventional essay style with paragraphs and a beginning, middle and end: *not* note form other than where you are desperate for time, i.e. at the end of the last question.

(s) Spelling and general literariness will pay, so at the very least make sure you can spell 'Matrimonial Causes' and 'Cretney' and the like. (Do not call it 'the Children's Act' and, on a related issue, start your preparation for the resit now, if you have referred to extra-marital cohabitation as 'common law marriage'.) If you have 'good cause' for any writing or spelling difficulties, then you should already have acted on (h) above; if not see (ee) and (ff) below.

(t) Use (j) above.

(u) Cite authority for your propositions. As ever in law exams, the more relevant authority you cite properly, the better your answer. So far as cases are concerned, the principle and the facts are the most important; names if you can remember them; with dates a poor fourth (unless they are significant, e.g. for modernity). Underline, or otherwise emphasise, the name. This is not merely for cosmetic reasons: it is the handwritten equivalent of the italics used in print. If you cannot remember the name, use some such phrase as 'in a decided case'. In child law, many cases are known by a single capital letter.

(v) Spell out the name of a statute the first time you use it ('Family Law Act 1996', but 'FLA' thereafter)—as a finalist, you will know too much to want to pad out your answers unnecessarily. Try to recall the section numbers if you can, particularly the key ones (e.g. s. 8, Children Act 1989 orders); more so if it is open book.

Answering: essays

(w) As a very general principle, essays are easier than problems in that there is less scope to display technique (see (z)–(dd) below); it follows (equally generally) that the same amount of knowledge may be deployed to greater effect in a problem.

(x) Use your knowledge in the manner required of you, i.e. if the question is: 'The Adoption and Children Act 2002 represents a missed opportunity for unmarried fathers and their children', then there are few marks to be had for discussing the Act generally. Do not just describe the material concerned—judge it in the way asked of you. Answer the question set, not the question you wish had been set.

Yet in this respect, remember you have been on a course, and are not being asked to spout extempore as if you were in the back bar of *The Ferret and District Judge*; subjective opinion is not enough. Ground your analysis in the academic materials you have been studying, and remember that if the essay attributes a view to someone or something prominent, be it *Bromley's Family Law* or the Law Commission, there is likely to be something to be said for it.

(y) Say what you are going to say, say it, and say what you have said. This is easy enough in coursework, but do not panic in the exam if, halfway through an answer, you change your mind. The examiners see many such changes of direction.

Answering: problems

(z) ISAC!—Identify (the relevant area of law). State (the relevant law). Apply (the law to the facts of the problem). Conclude.

(aa) Note the question, i.e. what you are being asked to do with the data. Often, it will be to advise one or more of the parties; e.g. would she succeed in her application for/resistance to: a residence order, financial relief, or occupation order? The answer may well be qualified—examiners like their creations to be evenly balanced. The point of law may be unclear, or its application to the declared facts debatable. (Implicitly praise the question for being so darned clever.) So debate the issues—do not just raise them.

(bb) Make sure that you have grasped the legal significance of all the data. There will be little in the way of superfluous material. If your initial analysis leaves parts of the story untouched, read them again. You could use a highlighting pen for this purpose, thus giving you a cumulative visual check.

The examiners started by thinking, 'Q. 3(a). We will make it a nullity problem . . . er . . . duress, lot of cases there . . . non-consumation, ditto . . . good, three-year bar for the first, but not the second . . . so the marriage can be coming up to three years old and we will make the non-consummation part the less likely to work . . .'. If you decode the story and start by telling the examiners where they started, they will be impressed from the outset and expect to read what should be there.

(cc)   Deal with each area in turn, after you have set the scene (see (j) and (bb) above). So far as choice of sequence is concerned, there are a number of possibilities. Use any one of them, but make sure you announce it (never give the examiners the chance to miss how clever you—and they—are). Two easy alternatives are, respectively, the order in which: (i) the facts appear in the question; or (ii) the relevant law appears in the statute. Another way, particularly if you are running out of time, is in descending order of volume of material, so you deal first with those points which are worth the most marks. Perhaps the best sequence—and hardest (but see (y) above)—is in ascending order of importance, so that each point carries an increasingly heavier punch.

(dd)   If you are 'defending', one weak area in the other's case may do the trick overall, although the story will never be structured so as to permit you to kill the whole thing off by dealing with one item only. When you are 'attacking', you will need to be satisfied, on balance, with all the links in your chain.

After the exam

It is much better (and ultimately easier, probably) to have done the work, rather than to have recourse to these next two, however:

(ee)   File your medical certificate/statement of extenuating circumstances before the deadline. Also see your personal tutor, the more susceptible of your other tutors ('I knew you'd understand') and student counsellor, if you have not done so pre-emptively (see (h) and (s) above).

(ff)   Appeal.

Family law exams in particular

(gg)   Be modern. The bad news about family law for teachers and practitioners, i.e. that it changes more in a month than jurisprudence does in a decade, can be turned to your advantage. An hour with the most recent Family Law Reports during the revision period might milk you a case a question.

(hh)   Be aware of the potential for mixed-topic questions. In the good old 'real world' the client may well want a divorce, ancillary relief and a residence order as well as immediate protection from violence; it is sometimes thus in the exam as well. Consider the significance of this when you are considering what topics to drop during revision—with a bit of luck, you can hawk beneficial interests round three exams, i.e. land law, equity and trusts and family law.

(ii)   Remember that different topics attach different degrees of priority to the welfare (of children) principle—e.g. occupation orders, financial relief, and s. 1 of the Children Act (CA) 1989. Know chapter and verse in each case.

(jj)   Be sensitive as to whether the partnership is marital or not—and whether it is different-sex or not.

(kk)   Be ready to make choices between/amongst a number of possible courts and remedies, e.g. divorce or magistrates' court, say.

(ll)   Be ready to use some statistics, e.g. numbers of divorces and the children involved; one-parent families; wedding rates; pre-marital cohabitation rates; number of same sex couples; number of fixed-term financial relief orders made etc. Essays (law reform etc.) can make particular use of this and other social data, but you can slip them into problems in half a sentence.

(mm)   Note dates and times, e.g. when the parties married, how long they have lived apart, how old the children are. Virtually all family law problems contain data which is time-significant. The length of the relationship may involve bars in nullity; how much of it was merely pre-marital may affect financial relief. The age of children can always be used; e.g. the weight to be attached to their views, whether they can be given leave to apply for a CA 1989, s. 8 order, or be treated as '*Gillick* [spelling] competent'.

(nn)   Be right-on! Family lawyers, at least those who teach, tend to an attitude of 'social responsibility'. Get a copy of the Solicitors Family Law Association Code of Practice (see **www.//sfla.co.uk**) and trot out its contents as appropriate.

(oo)   Europe and the UN. You should be ready and able to slip appropriate Articles from the European Convention on Human Rights (ECHR) 1957 or the United Nations Convention on the Rights of the Child (UNCRC) 1989 into your assessments

If you read the first line of this chapter—of this book, in fact—you know that we trumpet this paragraph as one of our two gold cards. Here is a check list of some of the articles, and their concomitant rights, which bear repeated playing. ECHR 1957: 6 (a fair hearing); 8 (respect for private and family life); 12 (marry and found a family); 14 (prohibition of discrimination); and article 5 of the 7th protocol (equality of rights of spouses). Almost by definition, homes can be found in the answer to almost any child law question for at least one article from the UNCRC. A core selection might include: 3 (child's best interests); 5 (parental guidance appropriate to child's evolving capacities); 9 (right to contact with both parents); 12 (child's opinion to be taken into account); 18 (joint parental responsibility); 19 (state obligation of protection from abuse) and 21 (child's best interests in adoption). Be sure you know the differing weights attached to each Convention by our domestic law.

Postscript—coursework

A lawyer who 'did it for real' the way it is done in exams might well be guilty of professional negligence: i.e. a number of inadequately summarised matters (probably chosen for their difficulty) being dealt with in handwriting in a ridiculously short time without reference or consultation.

Coursework—now often used as a mid-year assessment device contributing up to 50 per cent of the total marks available—examines skills which cannot otherwise be tested properly, or sometimes even at all. It is a medium by which a person's capacity for research and reflection can properly be measured at appropriate length. It encourages recourse to word-processing and allows for peer discussion without prejudice to individual responsibility. It provides an opportunity for self-managed time and to anticipate (other) postgraduate skills. In particular—and you may care to remember this—it removes pretty well every excuse for getting the basics wrong. Although coursework was used in over 70 per cent of family law courses by as early as 1997, some places gave it up after one go, ostensibly because of plagiarism, but in fact due to their disinclination to set and mark more than once per year. Worse, they actually had to correct the stuff: make sure your tutors don't get away with not doing that.

But enough of such negativity. Not surprisingly, most students get more marks in coursework than they do in the exam. On which point, do check the weighting between the two, and measure your commitment accordingly. Your rapture on reaching a coveted First in the first limb—coursework is usually a mid-academic year device—should be modified if it contributes a mere 25 per cent of the total, although such niggardliness should also be reflected in the quantity (not quality) required of you. In a modern Law School all such information, including the coursework questions themselves and what you get your marks for, should be contained in the Module Study Guides distributed in the first lecture: and be permanently available—and updated—on the internet. Maximise your exploitation of such rubrics, and your advance knowledge of the question. Let them both marinate in your consciousness as the course unfolds, and as you make the connections between your growing knowledge and what is asked of you. If you discuss it with your classmates, avoid collusive plagiarism, of which more below. Tailor your tutorial preparation with the coursework in mind.

High marks in word-limit coursework, and this also applies to exams, where it is much harder to do, are achieved by demonstrating a depth of understanding available only those to those who have mastered the rudiments—which such people may therefore safely go light on. (To put it another way, missing the opportunity to go beyond the student texts will limit the rewards available.) The three steps involved in this may be stated very simply. Firstly, raid the primary sources for stuff not in the main texts. Quotations from judgments are an easy example. Secondly, ransack the relevant academia—journals and books. Electronically, the titles are quickly found, at which point (with the help of the abstracts and conclusions) gut them quickly, fishing out a relevant quote. Thirdly, keep pondering: what does the question *mean*?: and what do *you* think about it?, remembering that the more you read, the more you'll get out of yourself. One specific tip: if the question contains a quotation, then look it up, milk the whole of the material, and see if you can find any response to it elsewhere.

This is a good point at which to discuss plagiarism: passing off other people's work as your own, be it your classmate's (whether s/he knows it or not) or someone more august. The authors are sensitive folk and dislike facing their trembling charges at Disciplinary Hearings for academic dishonesty. And it's all so easily avoided. If you find some good stuff in the books or on the net, use it happily—just attribute it. Paying some dubious supplier, or even sweet-talking your aunt the judge, to do the whole thing? On your own head be it if you get caught: resit limited to a Third and no reference to the Law Society are just two of the likely outcomes. Many places are getting wise to such ploys and use secret countering devices, although anonymous tip-offs from—understandably resentful—classmates remain a prolific source. Their graduation will be so much the sweeter for them in your absence, itself a difficult manner to explain to your family.

Conclusion

This chapter has been shorter, and of more immediate value to you, than chapter 1 of *An Introduction to Family Law*, 2nd edn (Oxford: Oxford University Press, 2004) (Douglas), currently the best—if already dated—conceptual introduction to our subject. Final tip: read, enjoy, and be inspired by the Hon Mr Justice Wilson's 'The Misnomer of Family Law' [2003] Fam Law p. 29, which is a thrilling, plain language, account of the subject, and one which crushes the sometimes-heard *canard* that it is 'Third Division' in nature.

Our answers are 'suggested', rather than 'model'.

Further reading on studying (family) law

Barton, C., 'Family Law in the Classroom' [2004] Fam Law 264.

Burton, F., Martin Clement, N., Standley, K., and Williams, C., *Teaching Family Law* (National Centre for Legal Education, 1999).

Williams, G., *Learning the Law*, ed. A. T. H. Smith, 12th edn (London: Sweet & Maxwell, 2002).

. . . and here are some of the best recent texts, and a source book, on family law:

Black, J., and Bond, T., *A Practical Approach to Family Law*, 7th edn (Oxford: Oxford University Press, 2004).

Cretney, S., *Family Law in the Twentieth Century: a History* (Oxford: Oxford University Press, 2003).

Cretney, S., Masson, J., and Bailey-Harris, R., *Principles of Family Law*, 7th edn (London: Sweet & Maxwell, 2002).

Douglas, G., *An Introduction to Family Law*, (Oxford: Oxford University Press, 2001).

Hale, B., et al., *The Family, Law and Society: Cases and Materials*, 5th edn (London: Butterworths, 2002).

Probert, R., *Cretney's Family Law*, 5th edn (London: Thomson, 2003).

Family law: cohabitation, weddings and marriage

Introduction

Text books often start with overviews which may be better read at the end of the course, when you are more capable of understanding them. They usually contain a smattering of history, an assurance of the radical changes which have taken place since the last edition, and some attempt to explain the rationale of the subject. Yet family law books have only recently begun to discuss this 'family' that their 'law' is about. In 1957, in the first edition of *Bromley's Family Law* an opening passage entitled 'The Scope of Family Law' barely manages to make the second side of the first page. Although the coverage is doubled in the ninth edition (1998), a GCSE sociology student would be expected to have a better extra-legal knowledge of the family unit.

Yet family law LLB students are increasingly expected to know about these matters. Social policy drives legal reform in this area harder than ever before. Parts of the course may well be taught by people from other disciplines. The need to make coursework assignments more challenging than examination questions has also necessitated a broader-based approach, requiring knowledge not available in the standard set books (except, perhaps, such as Hale, Pearl, Cooke and Bates, *The Family, Law and Society*, 5th edn, London: Butterworths, 2002). Less loftily, examiners are often keen to find a general, all-embracing essay when they run short of substantive topics on which to base their final question. What better than something along the lines of 'Does family law do more for lawyers than it does for families?' or, 'The law is primarily interested in the nuclear marital family only. Discuss.' The first question (below) falls into this category.

Some old-fashioned practitioners would scoff at such 'academic' stuff. They might have a similar reaction to any study of the marriage ceremony and its preliminaries. Even today, despite the interest in pre-marital contracts and the like, there is not much client interest in the opening ceremony, which is why it is unlikely to be covered in a legal practice course. But weddings are fun—and fashionable—and so is their legal content, at least for those prepared to see beyond the dreary lists of residence conditions, etc. It has the benefit, highly prized by examiners, of recommendations for reform which currently remain on the table. It is the *sine qua non* of the law's preferred form of domestic partnership. The second question in this chapter, or at least its suggested answer, demonstrates how the prepared student can capitalise on that.

Both these questions are in the form of essays, as is the final one, which concerns extra-marital cohabitation. No family law paper set in the last thirty years or more, will have failed to acknowledge the rise in this social phenomenon—if that is what it still is—and many of them are now shot through with this issue ('How, if at all, would your answer differ if H and W were not married to one another?'). You will see many examples of this in our chapters on domestic violence and property and, of course, in those chapters which deal with child law. There is always room, however, for what might be termed the new chestnuts, i.e. the questions which invite an overall consideration of the legal policies with regard to informal domestic partnership, including same-sex coupledom.

Q Question 1

In which members of the family is family law interested?

Commentary

At the beginning of this chapter we said that 'overviews' might be better dealt with at the end; perhaps the same applies to this question. Wherever dealt with, it should only be asked if the course has been suitably imaginative and enquiring, as many are these days. Even without that, a cool candidate should be able to make something of it from scratch. Mentally survey the chapters and you quickly see that they involve rather more than the husband, wife and children of the nuclear marital family. For example: restrictions on choice of partner (the prohibited degrees of marriage and prohibitions on sex with an adult relative); rights of intestate (and tenancy) succession; surrogacy; right to apply for residence orders 'over' children; 'relative' adoption; 'children of the family'; stepchildren; non-marital children, etc. We're into brothers, sisters, aunts, in-laws, step-parents and grandparents straight away. You should also be able to make use of the perennial debate about family form, i.e. single parent, non-marital, etc.

Although this question is apparently descriptive in scope, it provides room for debate as to what constitutes 'family' and as to the meaning of 'interest' in this context. Elementary contextual knowledge, such as the meaning of 'nuclear' and 'extended' can be pressed into service, as can anthropological definitions of the family unit—does it include non-marital and 'childfree' partnerships?—and sociology's categories of primary, secondary and tertiary relatives. Do not forget Art. 8 of the European Convention on Human Rights 1957, 'the right to respect for . . . family life'.

In this answer, we aim to show how the student with a good overall knowledge of the subject can scan that knowledge to good effect.

- The most important members are the nuclear family—on division

- The most important of those are partners, parents and children

- Unmarried partners (incl. 'same-sex')

- Grandparents, step-parents and in-laws

- Net most widespread on death!

:Q: Suggested answer

Had the question asked about the family members with which the law is most *frequently* concerned, it would not be necessary to venture far beyond the nuclear family, marital or otherwise. Domestic partners (husbands and wives; cohabitants—increasingly including same-sex pairings) and children (marital and non-marital) take up most, if not all, of the time of the family lawyer. Of those, the extra-marital group had little legal significance, particularly so far as the adult partners were concerned, until the early 1970s (e.g., the fate of the family home in *Cooke* v *Head* [1972] 1 WLR 518). Had the question been about *when* the law is most interested, it would have been necessary to limit the enquiry to the division, or at least the straining, of relationships. We should note at the outset that the very word 'family''... must be given its popular meaning at the time relevant to the decision in the particular case' (*Dyson Holdings* v *Fox* [1975] 2 All ER 1030, 1035–6 *per* James LJ). Nearly twenty years later, in 1993, 27 per cent of all households in England and Wales consisted of one person living alone and 31 per cent consisted of two people living together without children—and at the end of the millennium the House of Lords held that a homosexual couple could constitute a 'family' for the purposes of tenancy succession under the Rent Act 1977 (*Fitzpatrick* v *Sterling Housing Association* [2000] 1 FCR 21). Section 62(3) of the Family Law Act 1996 had already included within its definition of 'associated persons' those who 'live or have lived in the same household', thus permitting a same-sex partner to obtain a 'non-molestation' order. Now, all three of the Gender Recognition Act 2004, the Civil Partnership Bill 2004 and the Domestic Violence, Crime and Victims Bill 2003 extend, actually or prospectively, the domain of 'family' law. The first introduces 'gender recognition certificates' which grant the bearer 'acquired' gender status, the second affords quasi-marital status to registered same-sex couples,—and the third extends the definition of 'associated persons' (FLA 1996, above) to 'intimate personal relationships', i.e. those which have never involved marriage, cohabitation, or even engagement. The incorporation into English law of the European Convention of Human Rights by the Human Rights Act 1998—Art. 8 requires respect for family life—has considerable potential here: *Re R (a child)* [2003] EWCA Civ 182 has already held that whilst genetic fatherhood does not always produce family life, social parenthood may.

We may at least start with the law's acknowledgement of the seven 'primary' relatives (mother, father, sister and brother from the 'family of orientation', and partner, son and daughter from the 'family of procreation'). It seems that the latter group of three attract the most, and the most-invoked, law. So far as financial support for the children is concerned, it now makes very little difference whether the parents are married or not. With regard to child support legislation, the Child Support Act 1991 requires a 'non-resident parent' (s. 1(2)) to meet her or his 'responsibility to maintain' if she/he is '. . . in law the mother or father of the child' (s. 54). The non-marital father is, however, not equated with his married brother in so far as the *prima facie* vesting of parental responsibility is concerned. Section 2(1) of the Children Act (CA) 1989 treats the married father in the same way as his wife, i.e. automatic parental responsibility, but the unmarried father needs a court order or the mother's agreement (s. 4)—plus, also under s. 4 but as amended by s. 111 of the Adoption and Children Act 2002, joint registration of the birth. Most importantly, it should not be forgotten that, should the child's upbringing become a matter for the court, then 'its' welfare becomes 'the paramount consideration' under s. 1(1) of the 1989 Act, a criterion which may bring into play adults from outside the family.

So far as the unmarried partners themselves are concerned, we may identify three different attitudes. At one extreme, there is no duty to maintain, no divorce, and no financial relief, whatever popular misunderstandings may still obtain about the wrongly named 'common law marriage'. At the other extreme, the position of cohabitants approaches assimilation with that of marrieds. An example is to be found in s. 2(2) of the Law Reform (Succession) Act 1995. It amended the Inheritance (Provision for Family and Dependants) Act 1975 to permit claims by a surviving cohabitant where the deceased died after 1995, provided the cohabitation lasted for a continuous period of at least two years immediately before the deceased's death (s. 1(1A) of the 1975 Act). (Even then, a surviving cohabitant is less well placed than a spouse in that the former's financial provision is limited to an amount sufficient for his or her 'maintenance' (s. 1(2)(b)).) In the middle, there are many circumstances where the cohabitational relationship is recognised but not afforded the same weight, such as in the legal response to family violence. An example is Part IV of the Family Law Act 1996. Although a cohabitant may obtain an occupation order against her partner, it is limited in duration to one year if she has no existing right to occupy. (Under the Domestic Violence, Crime and Victims Bill 2004 same-sex couples, and couples who never cohabited, would receive improved preotection from harrassment.)

In that 'family of orientation', does the law retain any interest after the child comes of age at 18 (s. 1, Family Law Reform Act 1969)? Precious little continuing duty is owed by the parents; indeed on divorce, the court's duty under s. 41 of the Matrimonial Causes Act 1973 to consider whether its Children Act 1989 powers should be exercised is limited to children of the family under 16, unless the court directs otherwise (s. 41(3)(b)). The corollary is that until such time as the state off-loads responsibility for the elderly, adult children owe little if any legal duty to their parents. It is in the area of succession, particularly the intestate variety, that the law is most concerned with adult parent-child relationships. Siblings and the extended family are also involved, as seen below.

This leads us to the 33 'secondary' relatives as the sociologists call them (we will not be considering the 151 'tertiaries'!). We might start with grandparents, who might well be given leave to apply for a s. 8 CA 1989 order under s. 10(1)(a)(ii) of the latter Act—as in *Re W (Contact Application by Grandparent)* [1997] 1 FLR 793. In *Re W* [1988] 1 FLR 175, an adoption order was made in favour of the child's grandparents when their mentally handicapped daughter, the child's mother, had failed to form a satisfactory relationship with the child.

We encounter even more branches of the family tree by way of the incest taboo, and even more through the prohibited degrees of consanguinity and affinity. Under Sch. 1 of the Marriage Act 1949, the prohibited degrees of consanguinity cover parents, grandparents, children, grandchildren, brothers, sisters, half-brothers, half-sisters, uncles, aunts, nephews and nieces—a list which ss. 64 and 65 of the Sexual Offences Act 2003 now duplicate in its entirety for the purposes of criminalising familial carnal knowledge. Apart from these consanguinity bars there still remains, even today, the possibility that a marriage contracted between certain affines would be invalid. Although the Marriage (Prohibited Degrees of Relationship) Act 1986 now permits marriage between in-laws, and between step-relatives, there are two cases where certain conditions apply.

First, marriage to a stepchild will only be valid if: (a) both parties are 21 or over; and (b) the stepchild had never been a child of the step-parent's family at any time whilst the stepchild was under 18. The policy is that marriage should not be permitted where one of the parties has effectively acted as the other's mother or father during the stepchild's childhood, yet sexual intercourse and cohabitation remain available, of course. Secondly, marriage to a son- or daughter-in-law. A woman, for example, may only marry her son-in-law if both parties are 21 or over, and the son-in-law's spouse (the woman's daughter) and her father (the woman's former husband) are both dead. Incidentally, under s. 112 of the Adoption and Children Act 2002 (inserting s. 4A into the CA 1989) a *married* (only) step-parent will be able to obtain parental responsibility. The parent-spouse will need to have PR, and to consent, as will the other parent with PR. Failing that the step-parent may apply for a court order.

Perhaps the legal net is at its most widespread on death. Should the deceased leave no surviving spouse or issue then, under the Administration of Estates Act 1925, all goes to the parent (in equal shares if they both survive), then brothers and sisters of the whole blood (the issue of any predeceased siblings taking their share), then brothers and sisters of the half blood, then grandparents equally, then (finally) uncles and aunts, with their issue taking their predeceased parents' share(s) on the statutory trusts.

In view of the ramifications of step, half-blood, in-law, non-marital and same-sex possibilities involved in many of the above, perhaps it is fortunate that the question does not require us to *count* the number of family members in which family law is interested!

Q Question 2

'The law is not understood by members of the public or even by all those who have to administer it' (Law Commission No. 53, Annex, para. 6, Report on Solemnisation of Marriage (1973)).

In the light of this remark, consider how far the current law provides a suitable start to marriage.

Commentary

This is the sort of question which should leave the examinee in no doubt as to whether it is 'on' or not. The subject matter is immediately clear, even in the heat of an exam; similarly, the (sometimes not so clear) matter of how the material is to be deployed. It is about the idea that wedding law is unduly complicated, which does not make for a good send off for the ship of marriage, and that it may not match up in other ways, either. You would have realised that even before you started the course, even before you had the knowledge to address it. Do note that you can make a good fist of it even though you have not read the Law Commission Report, which few students will have done.

One note of caution. It concerns the danger, almost always present in essay questions, of adopting an over-descriptive approach. It should be easy to show why so few of those involved in weddings can have much idea of the legal content, but a good answer will also need to address the harder issue of whether the ceremony and its preliminaries (do not forget those) are capable of influencing the success of the marriage.

Two mistakes to avoid. It is the register, not the registry, office, and the major division (as regards the preliminaries, at least) lies between Anglican weddings and the rest, not between Church and civil. Finally, try to be lively. Weddings are fun.

- Weddings on the wane

- Anglicans v the rest

- Preliminaries

- Place and nature of ceremony—increased choice

- 2002 White Paper

- Limited potential for helping marriage succeed

:Ọ: Suggested answer

2001 saw the lowest number of weddings in England and Wales—249,227—since 1897 (*Social Trends 33*, 2003). Furthermore, only those who comply with the Marriage Acts 1949–1996 may normally achieve a legally valid union, a fact probably known only to a much smaller number of the population. Such compliance ensures the formal validity of the marriage by satisfying the *lex loci celebrationis*. In further reliance on the analogy with contract, the parties must also have had capacity to marry by their respective *lex domicilii*. Only if these requirements are satisfied will the relation-ship qualify as one of 'marriage', and the 'spouses' enjoy the law's preferred form of partnership. In *Rignell* v *Andrews* [1991] 1 FLR 332, the couple had lived together for 11 years and she had used his surname, but he was not thereby permitted to claim the higher rate of personal allowance for income tax purposes available to a man whose 'wife' was living with him. There is, at least superficially, a right to wed. Article 12 of the European Convention on Human Rights so provides, but only 'according to national laws governing [its] exercise'. So no further restrictions may be imposed, and in *Rota CPS* v *Registrar-General of Births, Deaths and Marriages* [2002] EWCA Civ 1661, the Crown Prosecution Service failed in its application to prevent a marriage which would have prevented the bride from giving evidence against the groom. So superintendent registrars have no innate power to refuse 'marriages of convenience' provided the former have no reason to doubt the capacity of the parties.

This popular misunderstanding, that cohabitation produces something called 'common law marriage', has had no basis in reality since Lord Hardwicke's Marriage Act in 1753 (although it survived in Scotland until the Marriage Act of 1939). Until then, consent (Roman law) and consummation (the early Church) were the only requirements. The disadvantages were those of ill-considered marriage and uncertainty; the adventurer could too easily lay claim to the heiress's fortune. Our wedding law can only be properly understood in the light of its history, i.e. the search for certainty and openness, and the supremacy of the Church of England. Yet there is scope for optimism. At the very least the increased choice of civil location since the Marriage Act 1994 (below) has made weddings more fashionable.

Nonetheless, the supremacy of the Church of England still underpins the present choice—at least so far as the preliminaries are concerned—which is not between civil and religious but between the Church of England and everything else. It has been so since the Marriage Act 1836 and, leaving aside the special arrangements available for Jews and Quakers, the law lumps together non-Anglican Christians not only with all other believers, but with non-believers as well. It is a mark of the comparative modesty of the 2002 proposals for reform (see below) that they barely touch the established Church. The scope for ignorance, to paraphrase the Law Commission's remark, is perhaps most marked in the preliminary formalities. This is ironic because their original purpose was to ensure openness. Anglicans and the others each have a number of (different) choices, some of which can be paired.

The famous banns, used for some 90 per cent of Anglican weddings, are probably the preliminary with which the public is most conversant. 'Three Sundays preceding the solemnisation' (s. 7(1), Marriage Act 1949) rings a bell with most of us. Since the 1973 remark mentioned in the question, s. 160 of the Immigration and Asylum Act 1999 has gone some way towards simplifying the non-Anglican complexities by abolishing the old superintendent registrar's certificate (SRC,) with licence (which permitted a wedding after one day's wait). Now, all non-Anglicans will usually obtain an SRC, and must (normally) wait for at least 15 days before the wedding. In addition, s. 161 makes it compulsory for both affianced to present themselves to the Registrar. Furthermore, in 2001, the Archbishop of Canterbury's Working Group floated the suggestion that the 'civil' preliminaries be used for all couples, which would do away with the 'common licence' which is the Anglican equivalent of the old SRC with licence—just as the Banns are twinned with the superintendent registrar's certificate *simpliciter*. So we may have some sympathy with The Law Commission's 1973 assertion!

At first sight, the final pairing, special licence and the Registrar General's licence, seems ill-matched: the one seems to be for the well-off and the other for the sick. The romantic-sounding special licence, which some of those using the Superintendent Registrar's certificate with licence thought they were employing, is obtained from the Master of Faculties, an officer of the Archbishop of Canterbury. It permits marriage at any hour in any place and demand is likely to be much reduced under the government's 2002 proposals (below). The civil equivalent is supplied by the Marriage (Registrar General's Licence) Act 1970 and permits non-Anglicans to avoid a register office, or registered place of worship. It is normally used for the so-called 'deathbed marriage'. Duplication, and possibly further complication, is provided by the Marriage Act 1983 which permits the use of Superintendent Registrar's certificates for the house-bound and the imprisoned.

The wedding ceremony is surely what matters most, both to the parties and to everyone else—we all go to them. Perhaps the most important factor is the location. Disregarding marriages of members of the armed forces under the Marriage Act 1949, the choices available until the Marriage Act 1994 were: a place of worship; a govern-ment building; a prison; or a sickbed. What constitutes a place of worship can be controversial; in *R v Registrar General ex parte Segerdal* [1970] 2 QB 697, the Court of Appeal upheld the Registrar General's refusal to register a chapel of the Church of Scientology. The 'take-up rate' of mosques, Sikh and Hindu temples, and other places of ethnic worship, has been surprisingly low: so weddings in such non-registered places of worship are of 'merely' religious significance.

The Green Paper, 'Registration; a Modern Service' (Cm. 531, 1988) said that many register offices '. . . fail to meet the public's expectations of a suitable place for a marriage'. The 1994 Marriage Act now frees the secularly-inclined from having to wed in the district of residence of one or both of them (s. 2) and, more importantly, from having to marry in a register office (s. 1). Section 2 allows a redistribution of business from hard-pressed, inner city register offices to other less-used, but perhaps more agreeable, sites. Under s. 1 the Secretary of State for Health has made regulations permitting local authorities to approve—for a fee—sites other than their own register offices. The regulations require the local authority to satisfy itself that the premises provide a 'seemly and dignified venue' with no connection with any religion. No food or drink may be served in the room during the ceremony nor for one hour before-hand. *Selfridges*, HMS *Warrior* and Newcastle United Football Club have all been authorised under the Act. That the 1994 de-regulation appeals to the affianced may be seen in its growing share of the market; over 45,000 couples availed themselves of it in 2000. Since the Marriage Ceremony (Prescribed Words) Act 1996, the ceremony in a register office can be extremely simple. After the parties have declared that they are legally free to marry, the minimum form of words is: 'I, AB, take you [or thee], CD, to be my wedded wife [or husband]'. Encouraged by the 'reception', as it were, of the 1994 Act, the Government intends to take further de-regulatory measures. The 2002 White Paper, *Civil Registration: Vital change; Birth, Marriage and Death Registration in the 21st Century*, Cm. 5355, presages a system based on the appointment of celebrants who would be responsible for the solemnisation of either religious or civil marriages as in, eg, Scotland or New Zealand (para. 3.16). The time and place of ceremonies will be a matter of negotiation between the celebrant and the parties, although national standards for civil ceremonies will ensure that 'the solemnity and dignity of the occasion are not compromised' (para. 3.17).

Even the best wedding formalities we could design would hardly produce so 'suitable a start' as to eliminate unhappy marriages altogether. Yet on the 'harder to marry, less likely to divorce' principle, some other possibilities do suggest themselves. Information, suitability testing, counselling (if only optional) might all prove inexpensive investments for society, for the couple, and for their children. (On a related issue, whilst suspected cases of sham marriages are to be reported to the immigration authorities under SI 2000/3164, it is believed that many such abuses are taking place.) Some of the member states of the United States, for example, require certification of freedom from venereal disease as a necessary preliminary to marriage. Here, following Governmental recommendations in the 1998 White Paper *Supporting Families*, registrars are making marriage preparation packs available, thus facilitating informed discussions between the couple in advance of the ceremony. So, whilst there is a limit to what even the most accessible wedding law can do to ensure success in marriage, perhaps matters have improved since 1973.

Q Question 3

Do you approve of the legal differences between marriage and cohabitation?

Commentary

It is 30 years or so since the marriage/cohabitation essay-type question started to appear in family law exams. Today, any family law course is likely to keep a running total of the score between the two forms of marital partnership, and the examination candidate is likely to have to economise, rather than maximise, in order to do well. It has become a 'scan and summarise question'. Although now very dated in content, the structure of the comparison tables in chapter 2 of *Cohabitation Contracts* (C. Barton, 1985), might still prove a good starting point for a coursework answer. In an exam, it will not be possible to deal with every relevant incident, but your examples should be representative. Roam over the entire subject, e.g.: violence, the home, property, money, succession and children. Perhaps this is best done chronologically, working through the history of the partnership from its inception onwards. Do use some statistics.

Leaving aside the subject matter, please note that this question is a very good example of the need for analysis. You are not asked just for a statement of the differences but for a value judgment about them. Most examiners will be reluctant to hand out as much as a lower second without it. An early, wrong, but still stimulating source of opinion, is Ruth Deech's 'The Case Against Legal Recognition of Cohabitation' in J. M. Eekelaar and S. M. Katz (eds), *Marriage and Cohabitation in Contemporary Societies* (1980). But what do you think? You must have an opinion—everyone else does. Just base yours in the law.

- Increased cohabitation and changed social attitudes

- Incidents of partnership law

- Differentials

- Same-sex couples

- Proposals for reform: closing the gap

:Q: Suggested answer

The 249,227 weddings in 2001 represented a 7 per cent decline on the previous year, and the lowest number since 1987. In contrast, about a quarter of all unmarried adults aged between 16 and 59 are cohabiting, and a similar proportion of births are to such couples (*Social Trends* 33, 2003). (Perhaps these developments are to do with the fact that, according to surveys, many people believe that informal pairing produces marriage-like status.)

Both of these last two ratios have risen sharply over the last 20 years, during which period the legal recognition of extra-marital cohabitation has grown with its social acceptability. It may be helpful, in deciding whether to 'approve' of the 'legal differences', to consider the likely reasons for this trend. 'Our' cohabitants might be categorised as: 'informed' (avoiding responsibility), 'uninformed' (living in ignorance); 'reluctant' (one wishes to marry but the other does not); and 'forced' (one or both married to someone else, or of the same sex)—see *Cohabitation—The Case for Clear Law* (2002), The Law Society. It should not be forgotten that living together can be achieved at will, and without expense, and that the declining social disapproval has been increasingly self-fulfilling. Times have changed. Cohabitation is a socially acceptable alternative to marriage, rather than a mere prelude to it (the latter is now the case with over 50 per cent of marriages).

The legal differentials can be considered under a number of heads, e.g. choice of partners, during the functioning relationship, after death, the failing relationship, ending it, and afterwards.

The status of domestic partnership contracts has become more clear recently. In so far as a 'pre-marital contract' might purport to deal with the post-marital financial arrangements, it could not be guaranteed as binding, because the parties may not contract out of the divorce court's powers of financial relief under the MCA 1973 (although such agreement might be seen as one of 'all the circumstances' under s. 25: *M* v *M (Prenuptial Agreement)* [2002] FLR 655, and in *K* v *K (Ancilliary Relief: Prenuptual Agreement)* [2003] 1 FLR 120, the court held that an injustice would be done to the husband by ignoring the agreement insofar as capital was concerned). So far as cohabitation contracts are concerned, it is now clear from *Sutton* v *Mishcon de Reya and Gawor and Co* [2004] EWHC 3166, that they can 'stick' provided there is a manifested intent to create legal relations, there is no promise of payment for sexual services, and none of the vitiating factors apply. Perhaps couples—and others—who hanker for pre-emptive private ordering are better served by cohabitation, rather than pre-marital, contracts, given that the former involve a comparatively blank legal canvass. The Government Discussion Paper *Supporting Families* (1998) suggests a template for the marital variety which provides, e.g., that the court could ignore them if they would occasion 'significant injustice': but would not the affianced be put off by such a threat to their deal? To add to the confusion, the Law Society in its 2002 paper (above) recommends that the evidential value of cohabitation contracts should be the same as 'pre-nups' and that they should not be given legal force.

Where differences do still exist, the more stringent law, if any, is to be found in marriage. A refusal of sex, or infidelity, may give rise to matrimonial causes or domestic proceedings, whereas no such rights or duties arise from a 'mere' cohabit-ation, no matter how long-standing.

Generally, the question of who owns the home is a matter of standard principles of contract, conveyancing, equity and trusts: *Pettit* v *Pettit* [1970] AC 777; *Gissing* v

Gissing [1971] AC 886. It follows that as the law was not prepared to give anything to a wife, there was nothing to take away from a cohabitant. Yet it must be remembered that a spouse has the safety net of the courts' discretionary powers of property adjustment in matrimonial causes (see the MCA 1973) and that recently (since the retirement of Lord Denning, some would say) the declaratory principles have been applied less liberally. There are hard cases like *Burns* v *Burns* [1984] FLR 216 (19-year cohabitation, the woman took the man's name and gave up her job to look after him), and *Lloyds Bank plc* v *Rosset* [1990] 2 FLR 155 (wife's supervision of renovation), in both of which cases the court has refused to draw the inference from her indirect contribution that the beneficial interest be shared. Despite their (normally) lesser need of them, wives are slightly better served by the declaratory principles than are cohabitants, e.g. the presumptions of advancement and resulting trust (now much weakened in this gender-conscious age); and s. 37 of the Matrimonial Proceedings and Property Act 1970 (a share of the beneficial interest by virtue of substantial contribution to an improvement in the home). Finally would-be reformers should remember that in its 2002 Discussion Paper 'Sharing Homes', the Law Commission concluded that it was not possible to devise a universally fair system for the determination of shares in a co-occupied home.

Death provides a variety of legal responses. No rights for a cohabitant on intestacy under the Administration of Estates Act 1925 as amended, and different rights from those of a spouse under the Inheritance (Provision for Family and Dependants) Act 1975 (a cohabitant can only qualify as of right if he or she had been living with the deceased at the time of the death and for at least two years beforehand).

During the failure of the relationship, rights of protection from violence and of occupation in the home are again available to both sorts of partner under Part IV of the Family Law Act 1996 (which sometimes does more for the spouse than for the cohabitant; s. 41, for example, requires the court, when considering an application for an occupation order by a non-entitled (i.e. non-owning) cohabitant, 'to have regard to the fact that the parties have not given each other the commitment involved in marriage'). (Under the Domestic Violence, Crime and Victims Bill 2004, same-sex couples, and even couples who never cohabited, would receive improved protection from harrassment.)

Many people would say that legal differences require the greatest scrutiny where they concern a person's capacity as a parent; children have no say about the nature of their parents' relationship. Section 1(1) and (2) of the Children Act 1989 grants *prima facie* 'parental responsibility' (PR) for marital children to each parent, but to the mother only for non-maritals. (A putative father may obtain this 'responsibility' under s. 4 either by court order or agreement with the mother, the latter made in a prescribed form and filed in the Principal Registry of the Family Division.) In not granting *prima facie* 'responsibility' to the 'unmarried' father irrespective of whether he is a rapist (as a husband could equally well be), a one-night stander, or a better man/partner/father than the average husband, the law may well be depriving large numbers of children (by 2000, 80% of births outside marriage were registered by both parents and in 75% of those cases the parents were co-habiting) of a vital right. Consequently, the Adoption and Children Act 2002 amends s. 4 of the 1989 Act to give him PR on joint registration of birth.

In moving to the ending of the partnership, we may remain in the area of child law. The Child Support Act 1991, in requiring each parent of qualifying children to maintain them, is even-handed between marrieds and others; s. 15 of the Children Act 1989 provides almost the same opportunities of financial relief for non-marital children as does Part 2 of the MCA 1973 for spouses and children on divorce. Where divorcing parents have 'children of the family', then, under s. 41(2) of the MCA 1973 the court may, exceptionally, delay the decree absolute if Children Act 1989 orders are contemplated.

This survey demonstrates that the law oscillates between no recognition of cohabitation (e.g. no divorce), and (in other contexts) near equation with marriage. Some argue that this selective policy is probably appropriate in that the parties must be taken to have rejected the trappings of marriage in their decision not to wed—yet surveys suggest that people's perceptions of the legal consequences, accurate or not, play little part in their decisions as to family form. This approach is surely inappropriate, however, so far as their children are concerned; many people are coming round to the view that it is family function not form that should be recognised, and that even as regards the adults, some monitoring is necessary in order to avoid injustice to, e.g. women who have mixed their labour in the family home. Proposals have included assimilation, opting in/out by registration and removing the same-sex complication—a large anomaly but which involves only a very few pairs—by offering them the knot, if not the sacrament. All these possibilities have been explored further in various other legal systems, e.g. France and Canada, and there appears to be a certain historic inevitability that we will join them. The Law Society's July 2002 Paper 'Cohabitation: the Case for Clear Law; Proposals for Reform' recommends that same-sex partners should, on registration, be given rights and responsibilities 'analogous' to those for married couples, and that all unmarried partners of two or more years duration (or who have had a child together) should be given rights to protect them from economic disadvantage at the end of the relationship. The reference to children is consistent with the statement in the Government's Consultation Document 'Supporting Families' (1998) at para. 7: '. . . the interests of children must be paramount . . . The Government's interest in family policy is primarily an interest in ensuring that the next generation gets the best possible start in life'. But for the moment parity is limited to giving same-sex couples registration rights under the Civil Partnership Bill. Whilst not allowing them to wed—or, e.g., divorce for adultery—it gives such pairs quasi-marital status in both public and private law. The Government declined to extend this to different-sex couples (because they, unlike their 'gay' counterparts, may choose to marry) or indeed to other sorts of people who live together. Those homosexual couples who do not register may at least be assured that, under *Ghaidan* v *Godin-Mendoza* [2004] UKHL 30 (21 June 2004) they must not be treated differently to heterosexual cohabitants. Perhaps it would have been easier (if displeasing to certain best-selling newspapers) had the former simply been permitted to wed. After all, since the Adoption and Children Act 2002 (s. 50) both they and different-sex unmarried couples are now eligible to adopt, although—unlike married couples—the statute requires them to be 'in an enduring family relationship' (s. 144(b)).

Further reading

Barlow, A. and James, J., 'Regulating Marriage and Cohabitation in 21st Century Britain' MLR Vol. 67 (2004) 145.

Barton, C., 'White Paper Weddings—the Beginnings, Muddles and Ends of Wedlock' [2002] Fam Law 431.

'Civil Registration: Vital Change; Birth Marriage and Death Registration in the 21st Century', Cm. 5355 (2002).

'Cohabitation: The Case for Clear Law; Proposals for Reform' (London: The Law Society, 2002).

Gibson, C., 'Changing Family Patterns in England and Wales over the Last Fifty Years', in *Cross Currents: Family Law and Policy in the US and England* eds. S. Katz, J. Eekelaar, and M. Maclean (Oxford: Oxford University Press, 2000).

Hale, B., 'Unmarried Couples in Family Law' [2004] Fam Law 419.

Hibbs, M., Barton, C., and Beswick, J., 'Why Marry?—Perceptions of the Affianced' [2001] Fam Law 197.

Probert, R., 'When are we Married? Void, Non-existent and presumed marriages' Legal Studies (2002) 22(3) 398.

'Sharing Homes', Law Commission Discussion Paper (2002).

'Supporting Families: a Consultation Document', (London: HMSO, 1998).

Websites

www.dca.gov.uk/family/cohabit/htm

Nullity

Introduction

Nullity is a good bet for the exam. It is a comparatively brief, settled, and compact subject, yet popular with examiners because it lends itself to easily made-up stories of doubtful outcome which test analytical skills. It contains a fair amount of established case law within a statutory setting, and has a number of grounds and defences to inter-relate. Additionally, its conceptual significance has considerable theoretical importance within family law. So it attracts both problems and essays, although the former tend to be more common. It comes early in the course when there is time to do it in full detail. (Incidentally, we have seen exams where the questions have appeared in the order in which the topics were taught—a practice which was very helpful to the student, although no doubt inadvertently so.)

Those are some of the reasons why nullity questions are probably more common than nullity petitions. Beware of confusing the nullity question with the divorce question, or of overlooking a divorce aspect. They both involve failed marriages from which at least one party wishes to be freed by the court. A nullity problem can also open the door to wedding law, in that some formal irregularities may invalidate the marriage. The latter type of question is particularly appropriate in open book exams or coursework, because of the close attention to detail required. Look out also for ancillary relief, which can always be included within any question on nullity or divorce.

As always, use your revision period to understand and summarise the structure of the topic. Nullity is concerned with marriages legally blemished from the outset. That is why books often deal with it near the start of the subject, with weddings and capacity, rather than with divorce. The really spectacular flaws, which give rise to the void *ab initio* grounds such as incapacity and informality, are specified in s. 11 of the Matrimonial Causes Act (MCA) 1973. They are unlikely to fill a question on their own because they have attracted less case law, are virtually bereft of bars, and do not require a decree (although you will normally suggest that one be obtained anyway, in order to dispel doubt and obtain ancillary relief). In more recent times, they have attracted a bit more substance by way of: (i) the Marriage (Prohibited Degrees of Relationship) Act 1986, which deals with in-law and step-relation unions; and (ii) the marriage rights of transsexuals.

The eight voidable heads in s. 12(a) to (h), MCA 1973, as amended by the Gender Recognition Act 2004, provide more scope. Look out particularly for: sexual problems (non-consummation), but remember that same-sex 'unions' will be void (however, under the Gender Recognition Act 2004, a person with a full Gender Recognition Certificate (GRC) will be entitled to a new birth certificate reflecting the acquired gender (provided a UK birth register entry already exists for the person) and will be able to marry someone of the opposite gender to his or her acquired gender); and duress (lack of consent) both of which are easily spotted. 'Arranged' marriages in the ethnic communities have recently breathed some new life into the latter. Make sure you know which of the three s. 13 bars apply to which grounds.

Be ready to distinguish the effects of void and voidable marriages respectively; see *De Reneville* v *De Reneville* [1948] P 100 and s. 16, MCA 1973.

Q Question 1

Four years ago Robin married Pauline, his ex-wife's mother, but quickly realised that she was too old for him and left her.

Two years ago he met and fell in love with Heidi, an Austrian woman who had just arrived in the country and spoke little English. Robin persuaded her to go through a ceremony of marriage at a register office, but Heidi thought it was merely a ceremony of betrothal.

Because of an hereditary illness, it would be unwise for Robin to have children, yet Heidi refuses to use any form of contraception as to do so would be contrary to her religious beliefs. Consequently the marriage has never been consummated.

Now, Robin has recently met Alice and intends to marry her next month despite the fact that she was born male and has undergone a 'sex-change' operation.

Discuss the validity of Robin's marriages to Pauline and Heidi and advise him with regard to his intended union with Alice.

Commentary

As a well-prepared student, you will have heard the data screaming 'nullity' at you even before the word 'validity' in the instruction gave the game away. From the data, you should deduce that the basic marks lie in prohibited degrees, lack of consent (mistake as to ceremony), non-consummation and transsexual marriage. The instruction, as ever, contains express guidance, i.e. 'discuss' and 'advise', as to how to deploy your knowledge in order to maximise those marks.

To achieve the maximum marks you will also need to link the separate issues into an overall analysis. It is important to avoid an episodic treatment. What, if anything, has to be done before Robin can validly marry Alice?

(a) (Only) if the Pauline marriage is void *ab initio* will it be unnecessary to obtain a decree in order to dispose of it.

(b) If the Pauline marriage is valid or even voidable then the Heidi ceremony must be void and the principle in **(a)** above applies to it.

(c) If examination shows both these 'unions' to be void (for whatever reason) then there is no strict reason for any petition.

(d) Yet whatever the embarrassment to Robin it may well be that the truth should out and decrees be sought, in order to avoid uncertainty.

Finally it should be realised that the question is riddled with uncertainty, thus providing potential, in a problem question, for marks. On the facts given, for example, the mother-in-law marriage with Pauline is wide open, and the law on transsexual weddings may soon become so.

Answer plan

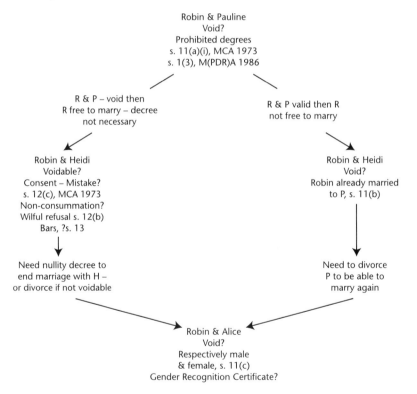

- Relevant area of law—nullity. Define void/voidable marriages. Grounds—void s. 11, Matrimonial Causes Act 1973—voidable s. 12—or if nullity unavailable/uncertain consider divorce MCA 1973.

- Apply relevant cases and statutes to facts—Pauline—void marriage? Section 11, Matrimonial Causes Act 1973. Prohibited degrees of relationship s. 11(a)(i),

MCA 1973. 'In-laws'—s. 1(3), Marriage (Prohibited Degrees of Relationship) Act 1986.

- If Pauline marriage void—consider Heidi marriage—voidable?—lack of consent—mistake—ceremony s. 12(c)? Non-consummation—wilful refusal s. 12(a).

- If Pauline marriage valid or voidable (s. 12) note, s. 16—then marriage to Heidi void, s. 11(b).

- Voidable—Bars—'approbation' s. 13(1), time bars, s. 13(2), 'ignorance' only applies to s. 12(e), (f) or (h) (as amended by the Gender Recognition Act 2004).

- Valid marriages—then Robin would need a divorce. Voidable—need nullity decree. Void—nullity decree not strictly necessary but advisable for certainty and ancillary financial relief (see chapter 13).

- Marriage to Alice—Robin must not be lawfully married to anyone else, s. 11(b) and parties must be respectively male and female, s. 11(c). Cases. Human Rights Act 1998. Gender Recognition Act 2004.

:Q: Suggested answer

The difficulties which beset Robin arise from his desire to marry Alice despite his existing unions, if such they are, with Pauline and Heidi respectively. Clearly the matter must involve either annulment (the voiding of a marriage for innate legal invalidity) or dissolution (termination of a valid marriage by a divorce order following irretrievable breakdown). Generally speaking, the distinction is mainly historical in that the ecclesiastical courts could only annul, and not dissolve, marriages. There is a functional connection in that a 'decree' of nullity and a divorce 'order' will each 'open the gate' both to ancillary financial relief and to orders with regard to children.

Sections 11–16 of the Matrimonial Causes Act 1973 deal with nullity. They consolidate the substantive reforms instituted by the Nullity of Marriage Act 1971.

Here it is surely nullity we are concerned with: the question specifically directs us to 'validity'. We can see some particular grounds which may be invoked: the capacity issue of 'prohibited degrees', s. 11(a)(i), MCA 1973, together with the requirement that the parties must be 'respectively male and female' (s. 11(c)). Added to these may be 'non-consummation' under s. 12(a) and (b) and, finally, 'consent' under s. 12(c). Although these matters are specified here in statute order it will be necessary to follow a different sequence in our analysis.

Before embarking upon that analysis, it is necessary to draw a distinction between marriages void *ab initio* (void) and those which are merely voidable. In *De Reneville* v *De Reneville* [1948] P 100; Lord Greene MR said:

A void marriage is one that will be regarded . . . as never having taken place and can be so treated by both parties to it without the necessity of any decree annulling it: a voidable marriage is one that will be regarded as . . . valid . . . until a decree annulling it has been pronounced . . .

The current void grounds are enumerated in s. 11 and the voidable ones in s. 12. We will also need to know that the latter set, and only the latter set, is variously subject to a series of bars specified in s. 13. We must also note at the outset that, by virtue of s. 16, a decree annulling a voidable marriage leaves the marriage valid 'up to that time'.

'Four years ago Robin married Pauline, his ex-wife's mother . . .' We will start here, not just because it is the first thing we are told, but because if this marriage is either valid or voidable then the Heidi marriage will be void *ab initio* without need for further examination! The answer lies in the 'prohibited degrees of relationship'. English marriage is 'exogamous', i.e. a partner must be chosen from outside a specified group. That group includes affines, based upon the theological idea that as husband and wife were one, marriage to a sister-in-law was as incestuous as marriage to a sister. The numbers of 'in-laws', etc., involved have been steadily reduced by statute, culminating in the Marriage (Prohibited Degrees of Relationship) Act 1986.

Robin's and Pauline's case falls under one of the two heads (the other is step-relatives) retained by the Act. Section 1(3), however, permits marriage between 'a man and a woman who is the mother of a former spouse of his' provided that it 'is solemnised after the death of both that spouse and the father of that spouse and after both parties to the marriage have attained the age of 21'. As the data does not inform us about these matters, we must continue our analysis on the alternative hypotheses that this marriage either was, or was not, void *ab initio*.

If the latter obtains, then it becomes necessary to examine the intrinsic legal merits, if any, of Robin's marriage to Heidi, who 'spoke little English' and who thought the register office event 'merely a ceremony of betrothal'. Is this sufficient to avoid the marriage under s. 12(c), 'that either party . . . did not validly consent to it, . . . in consequence . . . of . . . mistake'?

It is clear from the decided cases that mistake is operative (*Bromley's Family Law*, 9th edn, 1998, p. 92) 'in two cases only'. The first, mistake as to person, is clearly unhelpful here. Perhaps the second, mistake as to ceremony, will run. The criterion is strict; the party must have been unaware that he/she was contracting a marriage. A mistake about the legal consequences of matrimony, for example, is insufficient as in *Way* v *Way* [1950] P 71, where the husband wrongly assumed that his Russian wife would be allowed to leave the Soviet Union and live with him. Here, however, the data may well provide sufficient support. In *Valier* v *Valier* (1925) 133 LT 830, also involving a register office ceremony, the Italian husband had a poor command of English. He obtained his decree. If that were not enough, Heidi's predicament is further reflected in *Mehta* v *Mehta* [1945] 2 All ER 690 which involved a mistaken belief that a Hindu marriage ceremony was one of religious conversion. How could

Heidi have been aware that she was contracting marriage—the requirement for valid consent—if she thought that she was merely 'contracting' an engagement?

One difficulty arises so far as the bars are concerned. Although this marriage is within the three-year bar applied to s. 12(c) to (h) by s. 13(2), it may be that the 'statutory approbation' bar found in s. 13(1) (which applies to all voidable grounds) may present more of a problem. We will return to the matter after considering s. 12(a) and (b) to which s. 13(1) is also relevant.

The bald statement that Heidi and Robin's marriage has 'never been consummated' pre-empts any debate; it is self-evident that there has been no sexual intercourse at all, let alone anything which qualifies as, in Dr. Lushington's famous phrase from *DE* v *AG* (1845) 1 Rob Eccl 279, 298, 'ordinary and complete, and not partial and imperfect'. Non-consummation *per se* is not, however, sufficient to mount a petition. It must be due to either 'the incapacity of either party' (s. 12(a)) or 'the wilful refusal of the respondent' (s. 12(b)). There is no suggestion of incapacity here but can one of them, preferably Robin, petition on the basis of the other's wilful refusal?

In *Baxter* v *Baxter* [1948] AC 274, the House of Lords held that a wife's refusal to allow intercourse unless her husband used a condom did not qualify. *Bromley's Family Law* (8th edn) states (p. 89) that this:

> . . . raised a difficulty which cannot be easily solved. Suppose the marriage is never consummated because the husband, H, refuses to use a contraceptive and the wife, W, refuses to let him have intercourse unless he does. It is difficult to see how either of them can be said to have refused to consummate . . .

Turning the above quote around, this would seem to apply to the present case. Neither's motive—Robin's fears or Heidi's religion—would seem easy to impugn and, in any case, there is no evidence that Heidi is prepared to petition. Furthermore his petition might fail by virtue of s. 13(1) in that he might be said to have 'conducted himself in relation to the respondent as to lead (her) reasonably to believe that he would not seek to do so; and that it would be unjust to the respondent to grant the decree'. (This would only apply (see s. 13(1)(a)) if he had known his rights at the time of such conduct.) Other than that, the first leg would seem to be satisfied by his implied attempts to persuade her to have sex and the second by his wishing to discard her in favour of Alice.

It may be (we are not told) that Heidi would not defend. Were she to do so on a 'mistake as to ceremony' petition (see above) then s. 13(1) would seem even more likely to apply, given that it was her, not his, mistake. We may conclude that nothing less than her petition on this ground is likely to invalidate the Robin-Heidi nuptials.

What of Robin's wish to marry Alice? If his marriage to Pauline is not void, then his marriage to Heidi must be. He might be able to divorce Pauline, or she him. If that marriage is void, then his marriage to Heidi (which is more than a year old, so s. 3 MCA 1973 will not bar) could ultimately be dissolved.

Even if he is free of earlier marriage(s) he and Alice do not have the capacity to marry one another in that they are not 'respectively male and female' (s. 11(c)). We are told that 'she was born male and has undergone a sex-change operation'. In *Corbett* v *Corbett* [1971] P 83, April Ashley was denied marrying as a female despite her work as a female model and recognition as a woman for such as national insurance purposes. More recently (*Rees* v *UK* [1987] 2 FLR 111; *Cossey* v *UK* [1991] 2 FLR 492) the European Court of Human Rights declined to hold that the right to marry protected by the European Convention on Human Rights applies to transsexuals in their chosen gender.

As recently as *J* v *S-T (formerly J) (Transsexual: Ancillary Relief)* [1997] 1 FLR 402, the English court has annulled a marriage in which one party had previously undergone a degree of gender reassignment treatment.

However, in *W* v *W (Nullity: Gender)* [2001] 2 WLR 674 the court came to a sensible conclusion when it held, dismissing the application for a decree of nullity, that the respondent was female for the purposes of her marriage to the applicant even though due to her indeterminate sex at birth she was registered as a male. In 2002 there was a significant development in this area. In two transsexual cases, *Goodwin* v *UK* (Application No. 28957/95) [2002] 2 FLR 487, *I* v *UK* (Application No. 25680/94) [2002] 2 FLR 518, the European Court of Human Rights held unanimously that there had been violation of the right to respect for private and family life and the right to marry and found a family as guaranteed respectively by articles 8 and 12 of the European Convention on Human Rights. It was thought that such matters are no longer regarded as controversial and that the lapse of time is no longer required to cast clearer light on the issues. Domestic recognition of that view can be found in the report of the Interdepartmental Working Group on transsexual people and the House of Lords' declaration of incompatibility under s. 4 of the Human Rights Act 1998 in *Bellinger* v *Bellinger* [2003] 1 FLR 1043.

To rectify the incompatibility the Gender Recognition Act 2004 was enacted on 1 July 2004. The Act provides that a person of either gender who is at least 18 may make an application, to a Gender Recognition Panel (GRP), for a gender recognition certificate (GRC). This is on the basis of living in the other gender, or having changed gender under the law of a country or territory outside the United Kingdom (s. 1(1)). The GRP must grant the application if satisfied that the applicant—

(a) has or has had gender dysphoria (that is—gender dysphoria, gender identity disorder and transsexualism),

(b) has lived in the acquired gender throughout the period of two years ending with the date on which the application is made (in the first six months of the Act coming into force, the two-year period will be increased to six, to deal with the anticipated backlog of applications. Gender dysphoria is estimated to affect 1 in 10,000 people. It is believed that there are some 5,000 people in the

UK who could qualify for GRCs under the new legislation, see Hanson, N., 'It's Law in the Genes' (2004) 101(21) *LSG* 30) , and

(c)   intends to continue to live in the acquired gender until death (s. 2(1)).

The applicant must provide the information by way of a statutory declaration and medical evidence in support (s. 3).

If a GRP grants an application it must issue a GRC to the applicant. Unless the applicant is married, the certificate is to be a full GRC. On the issue of a full GRC, the person will be entitled to a new birth certificate reflecting the acquired gender (provided a UK birth register entry already exists for the person) and will be entitled to marry someone of the opposite gender to his or her acquired gender.

A married applicant will receive an interim GRC, which would make the existing marriage voidable (s. 12(g) Matrimonial Causes Act (MCA) 1973 (as amended by Gender Recognition Act (GRA) 2004)). A decree would not be granted on the s. 12(g) ground unless proceedings are instituted within six months of the issue of the interim GRC (s. 13(2A) MCA 1973 as amended by GRA 2004)).

The court granting the nullity decree under s. 12(g) must issue a full GRC. If the marriage ends for any other reason, i.e. divorce, nullity on any other ground or death, the applicant with an interim GRC may apply, within a six months of the end of the marriage, for a full GRC. The fact that a person's gender has become the acquired gender will not affect the status of the person as the father or mother of a child.

Robin and Alice are, of course, free to cohabit together and to make such private arrangements as the law may permit. This applies irrespective of Robin's (and Alice's) matrimonial status. Best advice to the uxorious Robin would be to obtain the appropriate decree(s) with regard to his existing marital entanglements and hope that his feelings with regard to Alice are unchanged when she has a full GRC.

Q Question 2

Should nullity proceedings be abolished and replaced by divorce?

Commentary

Even in the heat of the exam, this sort of question can be accurately assimilated at a glance. Or can it? This one may certainly seem attractive to the weak student who has done enough to write about 'nullity' and 'divorce' for 45 minutes or so. Unfortunately, even a good-ish answer will need to deploy some knowledge of history, statistics, proposals 'on the table' and what the writers think about it all. A pessimistic view would be that it is a question for weak students to do badly, average students to avoid, and for good students to prove it.

More positively, the issue is comparatively static at the moment, at least by family law standards. There is even some consensus in the standard texts (see *Principles of Family Law*,

Cretney, Masson, and Bailey-Harris, 7th edn, 2002) as to the answer; i.e. 'no' for void marriages, 'yes' for voidable ones. Even a good answer can use some account of the staple fare of non-consummation, duress and 'irretrievable behaviour'. Most examiners, *qua* teachers, will only set questions like this if their course has directed you towards the relevant materials. Here, they would be such as the historical development of nullity, Judicial Statistics and Law Commission Report No. 33, Nullity of Marriage (1970). A good secondary source would be: Hale, Pearl, Cooke and Bates, *The Family Law and Society*, 5th edn, pp. 57–70.

Answer plan

• **Brief history of nullity and divorce.**

• **Current law.**

• **Define and explain difference between void and voidable.**

• **Statistics.**

• **Effects of decrees.**

• **Published recommendations for reform.**

• **Own views/recommendations.**

:Q: **Suggested answer**

Since the (first) Matrimonial Causes Act in 1857, petitions of divorce and nullity have provided the only means whereby the civil court can end a marriage (divorce) or declare it invalid (nullity). To understand this question properly it is necessary to delve even further back into the history of 'family' law.

Until the Reformation, English law followed the canonical law in not permitting divorce, in any modern sense at least. This Catholic view of marriage as a sacrament also gave the ecclesiastical courts exclusive jurisdiction over marriage law and, whilst these courts could not dissolve marriages, there was nothing to prevent them from declaring that some impediment had prevented the parties from acquiring the status of husband and wife.

Until the middle of the nineteenth century the only means of divorce was by private Act of Parliament, with an average of two a year, and a total of four only on the wife's petition. So historical and religious influences produced radical differences of both concept and forum between the two 'remedies'. The 1857 Act removed the latter distinction by vesting the existing jurisdiction of the ecclesiastical courts in a new statutory Divorce Court (transferred to the High Court by the Judicature Acts 1873 and 1875) and by permitting divorce '*a vinculo matrimonii*' (which permitted the parties to remarry) by judicial process.

Today, of course, both decrees serve much the same social purpose; i.e. to permit the parties to escape failed unions, and annulments are now far outnumbered by dissolutions. Judicial Statistics for 2003 (Cm. 6251) (Table 5.5) show that 148,164 decrees of divorce were made absolute as opposed to just 167 for nullity. There was a particularly sharp reduction in nullity petitions following the Matrimonial and Family Proceedings Act 1984 which reduced the waiting period for divorce from three years to one. Since the Divorce Reform Act 1969, virtually all marriages can now be dissolved if one party so desires—whereas previously the petitioner had to prove that the respondent had committed a 'matrimonial offence'. If not, then the only way out (at least in theory) was nullity. In *A v J (Nullity Proceedings)* [1989] FLR 110, 111, Anthony Lincoln J said:

> Nullity proceedings are nowadays rare, though not wholly extinct. It is unfortunate that these had to be fought out . . . there would have been no difficulty in pronouncing mutual decrees nisi, dissolving the marriage, if the necessary consent (to a decree) had been forthcoming.

Furthermore, nullity and divorce afford the courts virtually identical powers of financial relief as regards children of the family. Quite apart from that, even void marriages now attract many of the legal consequences of marriage. Since 1959, in a principle now enshrined in s. 1(1) of the Legitimacy Act 1976, the children of such a marriage will be treated as their parents' legitimate offspring if at the time of conception (or marriage ceremony if later) both or either of the parents reasonably believed the marriage to be valid. Similar recognition is to be found in what is now s. 1(1)(a) of the Inheritance (Provision for Family and Dependants) Act 1975, which enables a person who entered a void marriage in good faith with a person since deceased to apply to the court for reasonable provision out of his estate, just as if the applicant were his widow.

So far as the respective decrees are concerned, the effect of a nullity decree on a voidable marriage is now very close to that of divorce on a valid marriage. Since the Nullity of Marriage Act 1971, 'the marriage shall, notwithstanding the decree, be treated as if it had existed up to that time' (s. 16, Matrimonial Causes Act (MCA) 1973).

Can the subsuming of nullity within divorce therefore be represented as the next, and final, step in an inevitable historical development? It seems essential to distinguish between void (*ab initio*) and voidable marriages. There seems to be no lobby in favour of assimilating the first within divorce. Such dramatic, inescapable, flaws as are specified in s. 11, MCA 1973, i.e. incapacity (age, gender, prohibited degrees, existing marriage) and serious, guilty failures to comply with the required form, must surely be kept separate from the 'mere' dissolving of a subsequently unsuccessful union. A void marriage, unlike the merely voidable, can never become valid (other, perhaps, than by certain forms of estoppel).

Many see a stronger case for including voidable marriage within divorce (as is now the case in Australia under the Family Law Act 1975) even though the Law Commission, admittedly nearly 30 years ago, decided against such recommendation (Nullity of Marriage, Law Com. No. 33, 1970), giving several reasons (at para. 24) in support of this attitude. Although the conceptual divide may no longer mean much to the lawyer, it remains essential to the Christian Church, which attaches particular importance to consent as a prerequisite to marriage. This latter includes consent to sex, so impotence is regarded as vitiating consent.

The Law Commission felt in 1970 that many people, whether they are Christian or not, associate divorce with stigma and would prefer to see illnesses such as mental disorder and impotence treated differently. Those who do not appreciate the existing difference between divorce and nullity and who would not, presumably, oppose assimilation, should not be given greater credence than the 'substantial minority' who would be offended by such change. The Commission's final argument was that the (then) bar on divorce petitions being mounted before the marriage was three years old would be quite inappropriate in nullity cases.

Should these arguments obtain today? The final one is, perhaps, the easiest to dispose of, in that the bar is now one year only and remedies such as judicial separation decrees (which carry virtually the same ancillary redress) are available within that time. Perhaps, also, the all-important conceptual distinction is not as watertight as has been assumed. Wilful refusal to consummate, which accounted for 360 out of 410 decrees in the last year for which such figures were collated (Judicial Statistics for 1986, Cm. 173), is clearly *ex post facto*. Since 1971, annulment is now permitted for the respondent's mental illness known to the petitioner at the wedding; the reason given for this reform was that the sickness may have worsened during the marriage.

Many would argue that any Anglican objection should be disregarded now that the civil law has parted from religious doctrine; any individual who so chooses is free to seek church approval.

The likelihood today is that nullity proceedings will involve the unpleasantness inherent in medical examination(s) and a full hearing. It is submitted that little would be lost, and much gained, by an affirmative answer to this question so far as voidable marriages are concerned. Dr Cretney for one has consistently urged such reform (*Principles of Family Law*). Many of the legal consequences of marriage have now been applied even to void 'unions', and virtually all marriages are open to dissolution even if only one spouse wishes it. However, nullity has proved durable; particularly for those who wish to end their marriage yet do not wish to be excluded from their birth families and cultural communities (see *P v R (Forced Marriage: Annulment: Procedure)* [2003] 1 FLR 661).

Further reading

Baker, M., 'Nullity Proceedings in the 21st Century: a case for reform?' [2002] NLJ 942–943.

Barton, C., 'Bigamy & Marriage—Horse and Carriage?' [2004] Fam Law 517.

Law Commission, *Report on Nullity of Marriage*, LC Report 33 (1970) (London: HMSO).

Probert, R., 'When are we married? Void, non-existent and presumed marriages' [2002] Legal Studies, 398–419.

Judicial Statistics, Annual Report 2003, Department for Constutional Affairs.

Singer, S.L.C., 'Transsexual Marriages' [2004] J Soc Wel & Fam L 79–87.

Websites

www.dca.gov.uk/judicial/jsar01
www.statistics.gov.uk

Divorce and judicial separation

It is a symptom of the recent history of divorce law that this chapter has more in common with what appeared in the 1st (1993) edition of this book than with the version found in the 2nd (1998) version. This is because of the Lord Chancellor's 2001 announcement that Part II of the Family Law Act 1996, which would have given us a new divorce law, was not, after all to be implemented. So this chapter reverts to the 'old' law of Part I of the Matrimonial Causes Act 1973 whilst nodding in the direction of the 1996 'reform' which was found wanting even before implementation.

Questions on the current substantive divorce law tend to take the form of problems, the student usually being asked to advise a party to a marriage on whether proceedings would be successful. You should be aware that in practice the emphasis in divorce has shifted from the process whereby a marriage can be ended to the ancillary matters. The introduction of the 'special' procedure meant that decisions of the courts interpreting the technical law were rendered largely 'academic', though still relevant in defended cases (which are very rare indeed). Nevertheless you will still be expected to be aware of the academic niceties of each of the five 'facts' and to be able to apply them making full and effective use of relevant case law, particularly any recent decisions: even though the district judge does not test—try—the evidence filed in the petition, she must be satisfied that the allegations merit a decree as they stand.

This topic may well overlap with other topics. The facts presented in a problem question may invite you to discuss the possibility of a petition in nullity, or to consider the likely financial settlement, but if you are required to discuss more than the ground for divorce, it will be clear from the question that this is the case. (See questions 1 and 2 in chapter 16.)

Questions on divorce tend to be popular with students—although the topic is not as 'big' as it used to be—and the well-prepared student should have no fear: a good 2:1 mark is quite accessible. However, such questions are sometimes answered badly, often because the answers lack any logical structure. Do remember, for example, that the sole ground for divorce is irretrievable breakdown: the five 'facts' are not grounds (though they are, of course, for judicial separation). Dates are also likely to be important in terms of bars and defences. Approach the question with an open mind and be prepared to consider all the options, thereby ensuring that the person being advised knows exactly where he stands. Perhaps there are three things to consider before you embark on your final analysis. One, consider ALL of the five 'facts'. Two, that (to use the shorthand expressions) 'adultery' and 'unreasonable behaviour' effectively permit immediate divorce by consent, and therefore may be the most preferable. Three, never apply a fact without playing it past the bars, defences and elaborations to be found between ss. 2 and 10 of the MCA 1973. Table 4.1 should help with those bars, etc, and in explaining that the question of whether the parties are 'living with each other in the same household' (s. 2(6)) can apply to any one of the five 'facts'.

As ever, essays are the tool for discussions as to the value of the substantive law, and we include here two such: one on mediation, and the other on the reform that never saw the light of day, Part II of the Family Law Act 1996. Why did the Government change its mind and to what extent is the old, retained, law still unsatisfactory? Such questions are often hung on quotations from the mighty ('Mediation is an anodyne word but the lot of the fearful and intimidated wife in the mediation process will not be a happy one', Lord Irvine of Lairg, HL 30 November 1995. Discuss.)—although, for a year or two, you might be asked to supply alternative analyses ('Add a brief explanation of how your advice would have differed under Part II of the Family Law Act 1996').

Table 4.1 **Divorce—bars/defences and amplifications**
Allocate the following to the appropriate 'fact(s)'. Indicate * those which are designed to encourage reconciliation: MCA 1973, Sections 1(3), 1(4), 2(1–7), 3, 4, 5, 6, 7, 8, 9, 10, and 41.

Generally Applicable	'Fact'	*Specifically* Applicable
1(3), 1(4) 2(6) 3,* 4, 6,* 7, 8, 9, 10A 41	1(2)(a)	2(1), 2(2)*
	1(2)(b)	2(3)*
	1(2)(c)	2(4)
	1(2)(d)	2(7), 10(1)
	1(2)(e)	5

$$\left.\begin{array}{c} 2(4) \\ 2(7),\ 10(1) \\ 5 \end{array}\right\} 10(2{-}4) \left.\vphantom{\begin{array}{c}2(4)\\2(7)\\5\end{array}}\right\} 2(5)$$

Q Question I

Advise the following spouses:

(a) Andrew

He is a successful businessman and six years ago married Barbara, a divorcee. Barbara is a very selfish and lazy woman and as soon as they were married made it clear to Andrew that she was really only interested in him because of his money. Andrew's business is not doing very well at the moment but although he has told her that she must curtail her spending, Barbara spends vast sums on designer clothes and has run up high bills on credit cards. She insists on employing someone to do all the domestic chores, although she does not work herself. For the past few months she has refused all his attempts at sexual intercourse. Andrew is so worried about their financial position that he is taking tranquillisers prescribed by the doctor. Two weeks ago during a row about money, Barbara admitted that she was having an affair with a man 15 years her junior whom she has met at a health club. Andrew does not really mind about the adultery but objects to her attitude towards him and his friends and colleagues.

Andrew seeks advice as to whether he has grounds for divorce.

(b) Charlotte

She married David two years ago. They still live in the same house although since April this year they have occupied separate bedrooms and have rarely eaten together.

Charlotte has been having an affair with Edward since Christmas last year and intends to go and live with him as soon as his divorce comes through. David has committed adultery on numerous occasions since their marriage, the last occasion Charlotte remembers being at a New Year's Eve party in the early hours of this year. Neither of them really minded about the other's adultery until recently. David still does not really care and says he has no intention of divorcing Charlotte.

Charlotte wants a divorce.

Commentary

This question is an example of a two-part problem question, where you have to advise two spouses in different situations, whether they can establish the ground for divorce and end their respective marriages. The first part of the question focuses on behaviour and the second on adultery; though in each part it may be necessary and advisable to consider other facts. Have the confidence to be selective in what you include in your answer and avoid falling into the trap of writing 'all you know' about the ground for divorce. If, as is likely, in your answer to this question you find yourself referring to the adultery 'fact' in both parts, there is no need to produce the same detailed analysis of the fact twice: simply refer the examiner to your response to the other part of the question as and where relevant. Could you instead integrate your answers to the two questions, thus economising on the basics, permitting greater depth, and impressing the examiner with your ability to perform synthesised analyses? For all but the—justifiably—confident student, such a demanding approach is probably better left to coursework. Impress with a linking sentence, which is much easier to do.

Plan your answers, remembering that your task is to find the list of issues on which your examiner wishes to test you and which have been temporarily 'hidden' in the given scenario. Avoid at all costs referring to adultery and behaviour as grounds for divorce: avoidance of such errors is what distinguishes the good answer from the poor one.

- One ground—'irretrievable breakdown'

- Demonstrable only by the five 'facts'

- Adultery and 'intolerability'—causally connected?

- What constitutes sufficient 'behaviour'?

- 'Living with each other in the same household'

ⵟ Suggested answer

(a) Andrew

Section 3(1), Matrimonial Causes Act (MCA) 1973 provides that a petition for divorce can only be presented after one year from the date of marriage. As Andrew and Barbara have been married for six years, Andrew could commence divorce proceedings immediately, provided that he can establish the ground for divorce.

By s. 1(1), MCA 1973 the ground for divorce is irretrievable breakdown of marriage. Irretrievable breakdown can only be proved by establishing one of five facts, namely (and in summary) adultery, behaviour, desertion, two years' separation with consent and five years' separation (s. 1(2), MCA 1973). Proof of any one of the facts raises a presumption of breakdown (s. 1(4)) and although s. 1(3) puts a duty of enquiry on the court, the reality is that the 'special procedure' involves no testing of the evidence. The facts which seem to be of relevance to Andrew are behaviour and adultery—the two which are most commonly used in practice as providing an immediate way out of a broken marriage: by 2000 they accounted for over 61% of all petitions (*Annual Abstract of Statistics*, No. 138, 2002).

From the information given, the behaviour fact merits detailed discussion here. This fact requires the petitioner to establish that the respondent has behaved in such a way that the petitioner cannot reasonably be expected to live with the respondent (s. 1(2)(b), MCA 1973). There are two elements to this fact. Firstly, Andrew must establish that Barbara has behaved in a certain way. Behaviour has been defined in *Katz* v *Katz* [1972] 1 WLR 955 as action or conduct by one spouse which affects the other. It may take the form of acts or omissions, it may be a course of conduct but it must have some reference to the marriage. Secondly, Andrew must show that as a result of Barbara's behaviour, he cannot reasonably be expected to live with her. The test is objective, but in assessing whether this is the case, the particular parties, i.e., Andrew and Barbara, will be considered and not 'ordinary reasonable spouses'. Hence the test could be said to be objective/subjective.

In *Ash* v *Ash* [1972] Fam 135 the test was enunciated by Bagnall J:

> Can this petitioner with his/her character and personality with his/her faults and other attributes, good and bad, and having regard to his/her behaviour during the marriage, reasonably be expected to live with this respondent.

A similar approach was taken by Dunn J in *Livingstone-Stallard* v *Livingstone-Stallard* [1974] 2 All ER 776 and more recently by the Court of Appeal in *Birch* v *Birch* [1992] 1 FLR 564, where it was confirmed that the characters and personalities of the parties are relevant in deciding what conduct they should be expected to bear.

This needs to be applied to the facts of the problem. Barbara is selfish and lazy, she has refused sexual intercourse for the past few months and she has admitted to an affair with a man 15 years her junior. In addition her attitude towards their finances in the circumstances is unreasonable and irresponsible and is adversely affecting Andrew's health.

In *Carter-Fea* v *Carter-Fea* [1987] Fam Law 130 the husband's financial irresponsibility over a six-year period had affected his family and caused stress to his wife impairing her health. In the wife's words she 'lived in a world of unpaid bills, bailiffs at the door and second mortgages'. The Court of Appeal said that although running into financial difficulties which upset the other spouse would not form the basis of a petition, if one spouse was financially irresponsible and generally unable to manage his affairs, particularly if his attitude had an adverse effect on the other spouse, then this could be classed as behaviour with which the petitioner should not be expected to live. From the information provided and using the authority of *Carter-Fea* it would seem that Andrew could use Barbara's behaviour as the basis of a petition. Clearly his health is impaired and he has been prescribed tranquillisers. Applying the objective/subjective test (*Ash*) therefore, Andrew will be able to show that as a result of her behaviour, he cannot reasonably be expected to live with Barbara.

Andrew should be advised to commence divorce proceedings immediately, relying on the behaviour fact.

In addition, however, as we are told that Barbara has admitted that she is having an affair, Andrew should also be advised on the possibility of using the alternative fact of adultery: that the respondent has committed adultery and the petitioner finds it intolerable to live with the respondent (s. 1(2)(a), MCA 1973).

This fact will be examined in more detail in part (b) of this answer.

For this fact to be established, there has to be adultery. Here Barbara has admitted this, and all that is necessary is for her to respond positively to the question, 'Do you admit the adultery alleged in the petition', and sign the form (Appendix 1, FPR 1991). In addition, there must be intolerability. It has been decided by the Court of Appeal in *Cleary* v *Cleary* [1974] 1 WLR 73 that the two requirements for the fact are independent and that no causal link is required between the adultery and the intolerability. Therefore, the fact that Andrew does not mind about the affair but finds it intolerable to live with Barbara because of her attitude towards him and his friends and colleagues, will not prevent him relying on this fact, provided that the intolerability is genuine. Hence it would appear that Andrew may successfully petition for divorce on the basis of either adultery or behaviour. Both involve (in the absence of an—almost unheard-of in modern times—defence to the petition) a quick divorce by consent. By courtesy of the 'special procedure', the petitioner need, again, merely answer the question, 'Do you find it intolerable to live with the respondent' (Appendix 1, FPR 1991).

Before proceeding to (b), we should note that whilst we are not told about Barbara's attitude, we know that David 'has no intention of divorcing Charlotte'. Even David's attitude by no means implies resistance to divorce. (Defended petitions are extremely rare, being expensive and discouraged by the courts because of their futility and corrosive effect on family division.) Recourse to the 'special procedure' therefore seems likely in each case: so if the district judge is satisfied that the ground for divorce is made out on the face of the petition, then a decree nisi will be pronounced (as part of a batch) in open court, and will be automatically made absolute six weeks thereafter.

(b) Charlotte

As Charlotte and David have been married for two years, divorce proceedings could, on establishing the ground, be commenced immediately (s. 3, MCA 1973).

To obtain a divorce Charlotte must establish the sole ground for divorce: irretrievable breakdown as evidenced by one of the five facts. From the information given, the fact which Charlotte is most likely to want to rely on is adultery: that the respondent has committed adultery and the petitioner finds it intolerable to live with the respondent (s. 1(2)(a), MCA 1973).

Adultery is voluntary or consensual sexual intercourse between a married person and a person of the opposite sex, not being the other's spouse. We are told that David has committed adultery on numerous occasions, the last occasion remembered by Charlotte being in the early hours of New Year's Day this year. The onus of proving the fact of adultery and that she finds it intolerable to live with David, rests with Charlotte, the petitioner, the generally accepted standard being on a balance of probabilities. One assumes however, that David is likely to admit the adultery.

However, in cases involving adultery, the parties must not continue to cohabit for more than six months after the petitioner discovers the respondent's adultery (s. 2(1), MCA 1973). If they do, the petitioner cannot rely on that particular act of adultery as evidence of irretrievable breakdown. This is an absolute bar.

Since April this year, Charlotte and David have occupied separate bedrooms and have rarely eaten together. It is possible for a couple to be living apart although in the same house. The test is whether two separate households have been established (s. 2(6), MCA 1973). There must be no common domestic life. If Charlotte can establish that she and David have been living apart since April this year, she will be able to rely on the adultery on New Year's Day this year as evidence of irretrievable breakdown. In *Hollens* v *Hollens* (1971) 115 SJ 327 the unhappy couple were found to be living apart under the same roof when they did not speak, eat, or sleep together. Here, the estrangement has not been that extreme and a court might find it closer to *Mouncer* v *Mouncer* [1972] 1 All ER 289 where the spouses did talk and occasionally eat together. But all may not be lost if David has continued to 'stray'—the six months grace in 2(1) continues every time the other spouse discovers a new incident of such infidelity.

In addition to establishing the fact of adultery, the petitioner has also to show that she finds it intolerable to live with the respondent. The test here is subjective. In many cases the intolerability will be because of the adultery, but it has been established by the Court of Appeal that this does not have to be the case. There does not have to be a causal link: *Cleary* v *Cleary* [1974] 1 WLR 73 and *Carr* v *Carr* [1974] 1 All ER 1193. There is no House of Lords decision on this point.

In *Cleary* the intolerability was because of the wife's subsequent conduct and attitude after her husband had taken her back, and in *Carr* it was because of the husband's treatment of the children.

In the question we are told that neither David or Charlotte cared about each other's infidelity until recently and it seems that the reason why Charlotte finds it intolerable to live with David is her desire to be with Edward. The petitioner's intolerability does at least have to be genuine and Charlotte may have difficulty here, particularly as in *Cleary* Lord Denning MR suggested *obiter* that it would not be sufficient that the petitioner simply prefers to live with someone else. As Charlotte clearly wishes to marry and to be with Edward, she may not be able to show genuine intolerability. However, it should be noted that in practice, because of the special procedure, an affirmative answer to the question 'Do you find it intolerable to live with the respondent?' is likely to suffice, and the points raised above may thus not become determinative.

If Charlotte is unable to rely on the adultery fact, could she rely on any other? The only fact which would enable her to divorce David immediately is behaviour (s. 1(2)(b)). The elements were covered in detail in (a). From the information given, the only behaviour which Charlotte can rely on is David's infidelity. In applying the objective/subjective test to determine whether Charlotte, as a result of David's behaviour, can reasonably be expected to live with him, the courts will look for some disparity in the parties' behaviour.

In *Ash* v *Ash* [1972] Fam 135 it was stated that mutually bad spouses (i.e., spouses who are equally bad in similar respects) can reasonably be expected to live with each other. Here Charlotte has also been having an affair with Edward. Both spouses are 'flirtatious' and it is therefore unlikely that this fact could be successfully used to establish irretrievable breakdown.

The remaining facts involve a qualifying period of separation. Charlotte must be advised that if she is unsuccessful in establishing adultery or behaviour, she cannot commence proceedings immediately. Assuming, as mentioned earlier, that they have been living apart since April this year, then two years thereafter Charlotte will be able to petition on the basis that the parties have lived apart for a continuous period of two years immediately preceding the presentation of the petition and that David consents to the decree being granted (s. 1(2)(d)). Although David says he has no intention of divorcing Charlotte now, it is possible that in two years time he will be willing to consent. Should he refuse, then Charlotte will have to wait until they have lived apart for five years (s. 1(2)(e)).

Q Question 2

Robert and Edith were married 30 years ago. They have two grown up children both married and living away. Robert and Edith have not been happy for several years. They frequently have angry arguments because Edith wants Robert to give up his job as a law lecturer and accept one of the many lucrative offers he has received to go into private practice. Robert refuses to do this and Edith worries that they will have insufficient money to live on after retirement.

Edith and Robert's relationship had deteriorated to such an extent that seven years ago, Edith began to refuse to cook, clean or do the washing for Robert. By the start of the following year, they were sleeping in separate rooms and using the bathroom and kitchen at different times on a rota. They communicate by leaving notes for each other. On two occasions the couple have tried to resolve their differences and to live together normally but both attempts failed after just a few weeks. Edith continues to worry about Robert's meagre annual pay increase.

Robert now wants to divorce Edith. Edith is implacably opposed to divorce on religious grounds. She is an active member of the local church and fears divorce would prejudice her position there. She also fears losing the limited pension rights to which she would be entitled as Robert's widow.

Advise Robert.

Commentary

The facts of this problem question could lead to a discussion of a number of the five facts, but take the hint from the information given, that the emphasis is on separation. You are invited particularly to discuss the five-year separation fact and the defences or bars to such a petition.

Good marks will be obtained by a thorough analysis of the s. 5, Matrimonial Causes Act (MCA) 1973 defence, not simply by a brief mention of it.

In addition to looking at the five-year separation fact you will want to consider other facts, perhaps behaviour or desertion and you should do so, though briefly, to ensure that full advice is given. Although a petition based on two years' separation with consent appears irrelevant, remember that the passage of time, legal advice, and her bargaining position could well lead Edith to change her mind.

The situation in the problem is in fact such that in practice the desertion fact will still be relevant, because the petitioner will fear that the respondent will invoke the special defence to a five years' separation petition. Desertion was, however, alleged in less than .5 per cent of 2000 petitions and is generally regarded as being of little importance. It tends not to be the central issue in a problem question and you should avoid any detailed discussion here, not least of all because you will not have time.

- 'Irretrievable breakdown'—five 'facts'

- 'Behaviour'?

- Desertion?

- Five years' separation?

- Defence of 'grave hardship'?

⠿ Suggested answer

Robert wishes to divorce Edith. In order to obtain a divorce, he must establish that their marriage has broken down irretrievably (s. 1(1), MCA 1973).

To establish irretrievable breakdown, one of the five facts must be established. From the information given, there is no evidence of adultery (s. 1(2)(a)). It may though, be possible for Robert to rely on the behaviour fact, though he may be unwilling to rely on this in the circumstances, and the facts do seem to point us in the direction of a divorce based on separation.

However, looking briefly at the behaviour fact, i.e., that the respondent has behaved in such a way that the petitioner cannot reasonably be expected to live with the respondent (s. 1(2)(b)), Robert could point to the fact that their frequent arguments have been caused by Edith and her attitude towards his job and earning capacity, and that for the past seven years she has refused to cook, clean or do any washing for him. Applying the objective/subjective test enunciated by Bagnall J in *Ash* v *Ash* [1972] Fam 135, it is possible that Robert may establish that as a result of her behaviour, he cannot reasonably be expected to live with Edith. But less so today—if at all—than once: wives are no longer servants.

Another fact which Robert may consider relying on is desertion, as he may fear that if he chooses to rely on five years' separation, Edith will invoke the special defence under s. 5, MCA 1973 (see below). However, for this fact to be established he must show that Edith deserted him for a continuous period of two years immediately preceding the presentation of the petition (s. 1(2)(c)). This fact involves four technical elements: the fact of separation, intention to desert, lack of consent by Robert and lack of cause for desertion. There would be no problem in establishing the two-year period of separation (the issue of living apart will be discussed later) but the desertion must immediately precede the presentation of the petition and it would seem likely that Robert and Edith's separation has for some time, if not from the outset, been consensual. Any desertion on Edith's part is terminated by Robert agreeing to the separation.

A petition based on two years' separation with consent is not—at least as matters stand—practicable as Edith is implacably opposed to divorce and would not give the requisite consent to the decree being granted.

It seems therefore, that Robert should seek to rely on s. 1(2)(e): that the parties to the marriage have lived apart for a continuous period of at least five years immediately preceding the presentation of the petition. The use of this fact enables Robert to divorce Edith against her will. The parties must, however, have lived apart for five years. Robert and Edith still live in the same house. Section 2(6), MCA 1973 states that a husband and wife are treated as living apart unless living with each other in the household. Living apart involves both a physical and a mental element. We are told that seven years ago Edith began to refuse to cook, clean or to do the washing but the couple apparently still shared the same bedroom. It is likely therefore that at this stage there was still some 'sharing of domestic life', some matrimonial services being provided. From the following year, the couple slept in separate rooms and communication between them broke down. Hence from that time it would seem that Robert and Edith have been living apart and maintaining two separate households.

In *Mouncer* v *Mouncer* [1972] 1 WLR 321, the wife still did the cooking and cleaning and ate with her husband, but they slept apart. They were still sharing the same household, but were not living apart. In *Fuller* v *Fuller* [1973] 1 WLR 730, the husband moved in with his wife and her lover after he had suffered a heart attack. He paid for his food and laundry. The couple were held to be living apart: their relationship was that of a landlady and lodger only.

The mental element of living apart involves the recognition throughout the relevant period by one of the parties that the marriage is at an end (*Santos* v *Santos* [1972] Fam 247). This should not present Robert with any problems in practice: under the 'special procedure' (Form M7(e) of the FPR 1991) he will need merely to state the date he concluded that the marriage was over.

On two occasions, Robert and Edith attempted a reconciliation, on each occasion for just a few weeks. To encourage reconciliation, s. 2(5), MCA 1973 provides that no account is to be taken of a period or periods not exceeding six months of resumed cohabitation, but no such period will count towards the five years.

Robert and Edith have lived apart for six years and Robert could successfully rely on this fact as evidence of irretrievable breakdown. However, Robert must be advised that s. 5, MCA 1973, provides a special statutory defence available to the respondent to a petition based solely on five years' separation, and that in the circumstances, Edith may raise this defence. The defence, it should be pointed out, is very rarely raised successfully (but it was in *Julian* v *Julian* [1972] 116 SJ 763 and *Johnson* v *Johnson* [1981] 12 Fam Law 116, both cases decided very much on their own facts), but where it is, the divorce will not go through.

Section 5 provides that the respondent can oppose the decree nisi on the ground that (i) the divorce would result in grave financial or other hardship; and (ii) in all the circumstances it would be wrong to dissolve the marriage. Both limbs of the defence must be satisfied.

The petition must rely solely on five years' separation and the fact must be established. All the circumstances of the case will be considered, including the conduct of the parties and their interests and the interests of any children or other parties concerned.

Edith must show firstly that grave hardship will flow from the actual divorce, i.e., from the change in status from being a separated wife to a divorced woman (*Grenfell* v *Grenfell* [1978] 1 All ER 561). Loss of pension rights has been held to constitute grave financial hardship. Here, Robert will have an index-linked pension and therefore Edith can make out a case of grave financial hardship. However, it is possible for Robert to put forward proposals to offset this loss by, for example, a deferred annuity or insurance policy. He will need available capital to do this and particularly with an index-linked pension, the annuity or policy may prove not to be worth much by comparison. In *Le Marchant* v *Le Marchant* [1977] 1 WLR 559 the loss of an index-linked pension was held to constitute grave financial hardship. The husband made proposals to relieve the hardship including a life insurance policy and his offer was accepted by the court. Similarly in *Parker* v *Parker* [1972] Fam 116 the loss of a police pension to which the wife was contingently entitled on surviving her husband, was held to be grave financial hardship which the husband offset with an insurance policy. In some cases, the loss can be matched by an award of means tested income support which is likely to be relevant in Edith's case (*Reiterbund* v *Reiterbund* [1975] Fam 99). But today, the problem would probably be soluble by use of the divorce court's enhanced powers with regard to pension 'splitting' and pension 'sharing' under Part II of the MCA 1973 as (amended).

There will also be no grave financial hardship if the contingency for entitlement is too remote. Grave hardship other than financial is difficult to establish and there is no reported case where it has been. Merely to show that divorce is contrary to religious principles is insufficient (*Rukat* v *Rukat* [1975] Fam 63). There must be some evidence of specific hardship, e.g. ostracism as alleged but not substantiated by the Hindu wife-respondent in *Banik* v *Banik (No 2)* (1973) 117 SJ 874.

Even if Edith could establish grave financial hardship, she still has to establish that it would be wrong to dissolve the marriage. Here, the conduct of the parties and their respective interests are relevant. There do not seem to be any third parties involved here. It is necessary to weigh the relevant facts and balance the concern to uphold the sanctity of marriage and the desirability of ending empty ties. In *Brickell* v *Brickell* [1974] Fam 31 where the wife's conduct had caused the collapse of the family business and she had deserted her husband, the court held that it would not be wrong to dissolve the marriage. As many of Robert and Edith's problems have been caused by Edith's attitude, a similar decision would probably be reached in this case and the divorce would go through.

If the defence is rejected, or indeed if Edith chooses not to raise the defence, she may make an application under s. 10(2), MCA 1973. Where a decree is obtained on the basis of two years' separation with consent or five years' separation, the respondent can apply to the court for consideration of her financial position after the divorce. This is not a true defence and such an application merely delays the decree absolute. The court will consider all the circumstances including the age, health, conduct and financial resources and obligations of the parties and what Edith's financial position is likely to be after divorce if Robert should predecease her. The decree will not be made absolute unless the court is satisfied that no financial provision should be made for her or that the provision made is fair and reasonable or the best in the circumstances. In effect, this provision enables the court to make proper financial arrangements prior to the finalising of the divorce (*Archer* v*Archer* [1999] 1 FLR 327).

To summarise: the advice to Robert is to petition on the basis of five years' separation, should his wife not change her mind and 'give' him a divorce. Should Edith raise the s. 5 defence, she is most unlikely to be successful.

Q Question 3

'I believe that people flounce out of marriage too often, little recognising and seldom understanding the abiding consequences of dissolution. Divorce in haste, say I, and the consequences will be with you for the greater part of your life to come.' (Lord Hailsham, House of Lords, 21 November 1983.)

Consider Part II of the Family Law Act 1996 in the light of this remark.

Commentary

This question provides a good assessment vehicle, being both accessible and potent. It invokes a number of inter-related allegations: divorces which shouldn't happen at all; divorcers ignorant of the consequences; and divorced people who suffer because of the untimely speed of the process. Note the date and the passion ('flounce') of the remark and proceed to consider the matters raised in the light of the ill-fated Part II.

The passage selected by the examiner permits a fairly generic discussion of the discarded reform and good students can therefore legitimately rehearse points wisely mined—for this very purpose—from their 'further reading'. Such preparation (particularly when expressed in direct quotations) is inevitably more amenable to coursework, and below we use one device which should never be missed when a 'seen' question is itself based on a quotation—look it up, and air your new-found knowledge of the rest of the material.

Family law teaching and practice lean ever more heavily on data from other disciplines. This (sort of) question will only yield respectable marks to answers which explain something of the history, social causes, incidence and effects of divorce as well as its legal character.

Finally, and as ever, your answer must relate the *quotation* to the *question*.

- **The incidence of divorce**

- **'Matrimonial offences' and the special procedure**

- **The impact on children**

- **Part II—extending the process**

- **Mediation**

- **Part II—deterring both marriage and divorce?!**

☼ Suggested answer

Lord Hailsham, the then Lord Chancellor, expressed these convictions during the Parliamentary debate on what became the Matrimonial and Family Proceedings Act 1984. He was referring, in particular, to the reduction of the three-year bar to the commencement of divorce proceedings (with exceptions) to an (absolute) one-year period. This 'reform' would have been perpetuated by s. 7(6) of the Family Law Act 1996, which renders ineffective any 'statement of marital breakdown' given to the court prior to the first anniversary of the marriage concerned. Yet the relevance to the 'new' divorce law of Lord Hailsham's sentiments goes beyond the dangers of short marriages *per se*. His comments also cover such matters as the need to protect marriage, the general significance of divorce numbers, whether the wrong people are getting divorced, and the deleterious (and unanticipated by the parties) effects of dissolution on all concerned. Both the proponents and the opponents of the relevant areas (mainly Parts I, II and III) of the 1996 Act put these issues at the forefront of the debate on the Bill. Our task is to evaluate the ensuing legislation in the light of all these matters.

So far as numbers are concerned, it is perhaps surprising to discover (e.g. *Judicial Statistics*, annually) that since 1984—the year following Lord Hailsham's comment—the annual number of divorce decrees *nisi* has remained steady at about 150,000. Yet it is also true, as Ruth Deech points out at [1994] Fam Law 121, that all major divorce reforms, from the Matrimonial Causes Act 1857 onwards, have been followed by an increase in the number of dissolutions—a matter itself consistent with wider access to divorce. Perhaps such increases justify the reforms by improving the burial rate of dead marriages, but the reality is that were they to have happened again under the 1996 Act, they would have been attributed to it—with disapproval. (On the other hand, Martin Richards at [1996] Fam Law 153 claims that in the long view changes in divorce law have had little effect on the extent to which people have sought to escape their marriages.) Part I of the 1996 Act (in force) attempts to preclude an upward line on the graph by requiring the court, and any person exercising functions under the 'new' law, to have regard to such principles as, e.g. 'the institute of marriage is to be supported' (s. 1(a)) and that, 'the parties . . . are to be encouraged . . . to save the marriage' (s. 1(b)).

It certainly appears that the substance of the 'new' law, which is mainly to be found in Part II, was unlikely to have been responsible for any future increase in divorce numbers. True, it may have formally removed the need for one party to show that the other has committed a 'matrimonial offence'—adultery, 'unreasonable behaviour', desertion—or two years living apart when both parties want a divorce or five years when only one party does. But under the 'special procedure', applicable to all undefended divorces since 1977, the matrimonial offence had become the quickest (averaging six months from petition to decree) route to an effective divorce by consent: under the special procedure the allegations in the petition are not tried. Under Part II (as demonstrated below) it would have taken longer to obtain a divorce. This was to counter not merely over-hasty divorce, but also one of the other dangers deprecated by Lord Hailsham, i.e. that the parties may not appreciate the consequences of dissolution.

Divorce consequences which rightly excite particular concern are those which disadvantage the children (whose interests, as well as those of the parties, were also emphasised by Lord Hailsham in a further part of the speech cited in the question). Although it has been said that 'There is no indication that divorce is entered into lightly. Quite the reverse' (David Utting, *Family and Parenthood—Supporting Families, Preventing Breakdown*, Rowntree (1995 at p. 4), there is growing research evidence about the increased risk to the 'life chances' of such children. Utting refers to adverse possibilities for educational, health and behavioural outcomes, caused by the increased likelihood of father absence, poverty and parental conflict. Has this ended the debate as to whether children of divorce are worse served than those of merely separated, or even unhappy, partnerships?

So far as the adults are concerned, Utting warned that ill-health and decreased standards of living (possibly more enduringly so for women) are likely outcomes of divorce, with concomitant consequences for the public purse.

What does the 1996 Act 'do'—the Lord Chancellor famously announced in 2001 that Part II would not be implemented—for the pace and the informative nature of divorce proceedings, particularly where children are involved? So far as pace is concerned, the minimum time element stipulated for the divorce period was made up as follows. Three months from attending an information meeting to making a statement of marital breakdown. Then a further nine months as a 'period for reflection and consideration', to which a further six months was to be added if either (i) one party applied for more time (provided there was no order under Part IV (Family Homes and Domestic Violence)) or (ii) there was a child of the family under 16 (unless the court held that delay would be 'significantly' detrimental to the child's welfare). So the minimum time from initiating the process to applying for a divorce order was to be in excess of a year, or a year and a half.

This represented something like a doubling or tripling of the previous length, and raised the question of the intended quality of the experience: would it ensure that only the right marriages were dissolved and that the parties to them knew what to expect? Central to this was stage one, the prior attendance at an 'information meeting' by the party making a 'statement of marital breakdown'. Vital details about this meeting were to have been left to delegated legislation and pilot schemes, but s. 8(9) provided that such matters as marriage counselling, the needs of children, ancillary financial relief, mediation, legal aid and the nature of the divorce process must all be covered. Perhaps it would have brought home the truth to those whose marriages might yet be saved, whilst improving for others, through a knowledge of what to expect, the coming experience. On the other hand, perhaps it would have further exacerbated an inevitably painful period by starting with a perceivedly patronising and humiliating diatribe about matters of which the person concerned was only too well aware. And only the maker of the 'statement' had to attend: the other spouse only if he or she contested any application to the court with respect to a child of the family or certain financial matters (s. 8(5)). As Lord Hailsham also went on to say, 'Marry in haste, repent at leisure'—perhaps the affianced should also attend as a condition of wedlock.

The making of the ensuing 'statement', which was not to contain any allegations about responsibility for the breakdown and which started the period of reflection and consideration (PRC) running, could, unfortunately, be seen as confirming that spouse's determination to dissolve the union. Would the forthcoming year or more have saved the saveable and ensured a better-than-otherwise divorce outcome for the others? Stephen Cretney frequently suggested (e.g. at [1995] Fam Law 302) that 'some, at least, of those concerned seem likely to spend the time in the far more pleasurable activity of conceiving—necessarily illegitimate—babies'.

What did the Act itself require of the spouses during the PRC? Under s. 13 the court *may* direct them to attend a meeting to explain the mediation facilities available to them: the Act was founded on the premise that mediation will lower the temperature and produce better, more acceptable, more durable settlements produced by the parties for themselves and their children. Another central plank was the s. 9 requirement that arrangements concerning both children (normally only those under 16) and finances be settled before the marriage is dissolved. So far as the children are concerned, this apparently potent requirement was largely illusory. By s. 11 the court was merely to consider whether it should exercise any of its powers under the Children Act 1989; and even where the court thought it might have so to 'exercise', it was only in 'exceptional' circumstances that it might delay the divorce order.

The requirement about the 'financial arrangements' was rather more stringent. No divorce order could be made, subject to the exceptions specified in sch. 1, unless there was a previous court order, or a negotiated agreement, or a declaration by the parties that they had made their own arrangements. This was in marked contrast to the situation which prevails under the retained law, where the ancillary financial relief arrangements—and disputes about them—are well capable of rumbling on, or even starting, after the divorce itself has been finalised.

There was one final aspect of Part II which might well have assuaged Lord Hailsham's 1983 concerns. Under s. 10 (on application from the other spouse) the court could order the marriage not be dissolved if such would result in substantial financial hardship to that other party or to a child of the family *and* it would be wrong in all the circumstances to dissolve the marriage. This strengthened the existing law in two ways: it applied to all divorces, not just those based on five years' separation; and the hardship need not have been 'grave'.

Perhaps the new law would have gone a long way towards meeting Lord Hailsham's earlier worries about divorce: the process would certainly have been longer, more involved and less predictable. On the other hand, perhaps those very features would have deterred some couples from marrying, fearful of the risk of becoming involved in a disagreeable extrication process, whilst leading some disaffected marrieds to walk out of their relationships without bothering to divorce. The reason given in the Lord Chancellor's Department Press Department Notice (2001) for not implementing Part II should not be forgotten: '[It] does not meet Government objectives of saving marriages or helping divorcing couples to resolve problems with a minimum of acrimony'. This followed the pilot study which demonstrated that the information meetings came too late to save marriages, pushed waverers towards divorce, and were not tailored to individual needs. But perhaps Lord Hailsham would have been equally disapproving of the 'Family Advice and Information Network Services' which are now being set up to enable would-be divorcers to access a wide range of services through a single point of reference.

Q Question 4

Review the role of mediation in divorce proceedings in the light of the non-implementation of Part II of the Family Law Act 1996.

Commentary

No doubt what this is about. Mediation was set to play a big role in the theory and practice of divorce, and had quickly become the largest piece of 'non-legal' material in family law. Your tutors, like our legislators, were only just ahead of you—mediation was on the point of being institutionalised within the divorce process before anyone understood much about it. This ignorance was one reason for the delay in implementing the relevant parts of the Family Law Act 1996, and in the ultimate decision to scrap it.

Contemporary examination questions on mediation, whilst likely to be common, are also likely to be cautious. This is reflected in the instruction to 'review'. One dictionary defines this as 'to re-examine; to revise'. A broad enquiry is called for here.

The good answer requires a double, but integrated, approach. First, it is clearly necessary to define mediation, to say something about its history, particularly as applied to marriage break-up, and to consider the *a priori* hopes and doubts which have been expressed about its inclusion within our divorce system. (These matters are discussed in Barton and Douglas, *Law and Parenthood*, 1995, at pp. 378–95.) Secondly, this material should be seen in the light of the present law and practice of mediation within marital dissolution, and what led the government to have second thoughts about Part II.

Your conclusion can be as doubtful or as enthusiastic as you like about the wisdom of putting mediation at the centre of divorce law. Whilst many academic luminaries are cynical about it, many practitioners busily adopted a 'can't beat 'em, join 'em' approach.

- Meaning and history of mediation

- Its introduction to English divorce

- Part III, Family Law Act 1996 and public money

- 'Bargaining in the shadow of the law'

- Male dominance?

- Lawyers v mediators—a false dichotomy?

☼ Suggested answer

Although the Family Law Act 1996 contains many references to mediation, thereby integrating it within the divorce process, the statute offers no definition of the concept. Paragraph 5.4 of the White Paper, *Looking to the Future*, Cm. 2799 (1995) is one of a number of sources which describes it as '. . . a process in which an impartial third person, the mediator, assists couples considering separation or divorce to meet together to deal with the arrangements which need to be made for the future'. The reality of the matter is whether or not one mediator per couple will facilitate a better long-term exit from the marriage than the traditional 'one lawyer each' approach, better both for the couple and their children and at less public expense. It should also be remembered that mediation and law need not be stark alternatives, given, first, that matrimonial legal work is often geared towards settlement, and, secondly, that lawyers may well continue to play a role in mediated disputes. The Solicitors Family Law Association Code of Practice urges members to 'encourage clients to see the advantages to the family of a . . . non-confrontational approach as a way of resolving differences'.

Mediation in divorce proceedings was due to be institutionalised by the Family Law Act 1996. Yet as one method of alternative dispute resolution—arbitration is another—it has a long history. It was apparently the major forum for dispute-solving in ancient China, and amongst the Cheyenne Indians and the Ndendueli peoples of Tanzania.

In *Alternative Dispute Resolution—The Fundamentals of Mediation* (Old Bailey Press, 1993) at pp. 1–5 John Haynes identifies nine stages in the overall process: recognising the problem; choosing the arena; selecting the mediator; gathering the data; defining the problem; defining options; redefining positions; bargaining; and drafting the agreement. In the 'comprehensive', 'all issues', version, financial matters, as well as the future parenting arrangements, are subject to mediation.

Government thinking on the matter was developed in *Facing the Future, A Discussion Paper on the Grounds for Divorce* (Law Com. No. 170 (1988)), and *The Ground for Divorce* (Law Com. No. 192 (1990)). With an eye on the legal aid cost of publicly-funded divorce, the official view was that mediation might provide less expensive, as well as better, solutions to divorce problems.

The 1996 Act, which in some respects differs somewhat from the original Government Bill, nonetheless was laced with references to mediation. Perhaps it is implicit in s. 1(c) (in force) which requires that marriages that have irretrievably broken down must be ended with minimum distress, in a manner best conducive to continuing relations, and as inexpensively as possible.

The nature of mediation is—we will use the present tense as Part II has not actually been repealed—brought to the attention of a spouse contemplating divorce at the earliest possible stage. Section 8(9)(f) requires that such information be disseminated at the information meeting, attendance at which is a condition precedent to a divorce application: some commentators were worried that the detailed regulations to be made under s. 8 might 'over-sell' the concept. Section 12(2) continues this 'early exposure' policy by requiring legal representatives to inform their clients about mediation, to supply them with details of persons qualified to help with mediation, and to certify that they have done so. This is radically different from the requirement in the Divorce Reform Act 1969 which (in certain defined circumstances) requires solicitors to certify *whether or not* they had discussed the prospects of *reconciliation* with their 'petitioning' clients.

Moving on from the information meeting presenters and the lawyers, s. 13 enables the court itself to take a hand by directing that each party attend a meeting at which the facilities for mediation will be explained to them, and to provide an opportunity for them to agree to take advantage of it. The parties will be required to attend the same meeting unless one or both of them ask(s) for separate sessions, or the court itself thinks that such would be more appropriate. This does not oblige the spouses to use mediation, as it is generally—but, increasingly, not unanimously—accepted that compulsion would be a contradiction in terms and counterproductive. Perhaps this is particularly so where there has been domestic violence, and one early-expressed view, notably by Ann Bottomley ('Resolving Family Disputes: A Critical View' in Freeman (ed.) *State Law and the Family* (1984)), was that mediation disadvantages women generally. The fear is that it might conceal and continue pre-existing male dominance, thereby putting at risk the recent legal advances made by women in the context of violence and property. A more extensive objection, and possibly a more gender-neutral one, is that it may disadvantage a weak or inarticulate party, although it is claimed that the trained mediator can guard against this happening. (Other concerns about the value of mediation include the extent to which it can truly be impartial, that it can be in thrall to society's norms, and the extent to which the children themselves should be involved.) Perhaps these drawbacks have been countered by the current requirement in the Legal Services Commission's funding code that any contracts made by the Commission for the provision of mediation must require the mediator to comply with a code of practice. Such code must ensure that participation is restricted to willing parties, who are told that independent legal advice is available.

It is in the Act's final reference that, for better or worse, mediation is given its greatest prominence. ('We do not yet know whether that central plank will be made of teak or balsa wood': Elfyn Llywd MP, *Standing Committee E*, Report, 7 May 1996, col. 250.) Section 29 (repealed by the Access to Justice Act 1999, but part of the funding code (above)) enacts that whilst legal aid is to be available for mediation in certain circumstances, it may conversely be unavailable for legal representation. Although this represents a retreat from the degree of preference for mediation displayed in the original Bill, it raises one of the key objections to it—that initial Government enthusiasm was based more on the supposedly smaller dent mediation will make in the public purse than upon any improvement it may render to the parties' post-divorce arrangements. The essence of the matter is to be found in the funding code requirement that a person seeking legal aid for representation must first attend a meeting with a mediator to determine whether mediation would be suitable. Following that meeting the Commission decides whether mediation is, or is not, an appropriate use of public funds in the case.

It is certainly clear that mediation pervades the 1996 Act and that the corollary is the reduced role of lawyers in the divorce process. Is this an unwarranted reliance on a new, untested profession? Incompetent practice may become a coercive process in which both parties feign agreement in order to please the 'official', as they may perceive the mediator. The parties are 'bargaining in the shadow of the law' and the nature of ancillary relief, in particular, is such that it will often be difficult to identify even the parameters of the decision at which a court would otherwise arrive. And although the legal system may be able to force disclosure of, say, the other party's finances, the potential for mediation to produce informed settlements is correspondingly limited. Perhaps family mediation would have needed to make great strides to merit the trust placed in it by the 1996 Act. Most crucially—and this was one of the problems which led the Government to turn its back on Part II in 2001—it will need to win the trust of the divorcing classes. The pilot studies demonstrated, devastatingly, that only 7 per cent of those attending information meetings wanted to use mediation. Until that state of affairs changes, then the pro-mediation arguments: that there is no right answer to a particular dispute; that solutions arrived at by the parties themselves are more likely to stick; that it enables the parties to communicate more effectively, particularly with regard to the emotional issues, will be of no avail. The other problem was that, according to another pilot study, mediation was not cost-effective.
Nonetheless:

> Who said mediation was dead? Mediation has perhaps not taken off in the way anticipated by recent legislation and the government, but . . . it remains a useful way of enabling couples to resolve their children and financial arrangements and divorce . . . clients in mediation should report to their solicitors at key stages . . . This can still be done in a cost-effective way. E. Harte, 'Mediation—Help or Hindrance, and What of its Future' [2003] Fam Law 865.

Development opportunities for mediation may include, from America, 'collaborative' law, i.e. 'law without litigation, and mediation with advice, where the lawyers agree not to litigate' (Harte, above). Other possibilities might include *preparing* couples for domestic partnership—the skills needed are very similar, and might interest that large majority of the adult population who cohabit or marry: mediators are already helping two second families make a better start than might otherwise be the case. Finally, a word of caution. Mediators and family lawyers alike are still learning how to avoid embarrassment under the Proceeds of Crime Act 2002, which, when requiring advisers not merely to discontinue their work but also to 'shop' their advisees, can otherwise lead to the formers' imprisonment!

Further reading

Barton, C., 'The Mediator as Midwife—A Marketing Opportunity?' [2003] Fam Law 195.

Eekelaar, J., MacLean, M., and Beinart, S., *Family Lawyers* (Hart, 2000).

Freeman, M., *Divorce Gospel Style* [1997] Fam Law 413.

Hale, B., Conclusion, in M. Thorpe and E. Clarke (eds), *No Fault or flaw: the future of the Family Law Act 1996* (Family Law, 2002).

Harte, E., 'Mediation—Help or Hindrance and What of its Future?' [2003] Fam Law 865.

Walker, J., 'Information Meetings and Associated Provisions within the Family Law Act 1996', Lord Chancellor's Department (2001).

Walker, J., 'FAIns—A New Approach for Family Lawyers' [2004] Fam Law 436.

Domestic violence

Introduction

Family lawyers have to be adaptable creatures. It is not a subject specialism for the complacent or faint-hearted. Lord Irvine of Lairg, Lord Chancellor, as he then was, stated that divorce reform contained in the Family Law Act 1996 will not be brought into force—in fact it will be repealed at the earliest opportunity. However, so far as 'domestic violence' is concerned, the reforms in Part IV of the Family Law Act (FLA) 1996 were brought into force on 1 October 1997. The aim here, however, was rationalisation rather than complete change. The previous 'hotchpot of enactments', as described by Lord Scarman in *Richards* v *Richards* [1984] AC 174, is replaced by Part IV of the FLA 1996 which provides a single consistent set of remedies, available in all courts having jurisdiction in family matters. The new legislation has had a turbulent history. Proposals for reform and a draft Bill, the Family Homes and Domestic Violence Bill, were put forward by the Law Commission in a report *Domestic Violence and Occupation of the Family Home* (1992 Law Com. No. 207). Part IV FLA 1996 is a modified version of that draft Bill which was withdrawn by the Conservative Government following, said Lord Irvine of Lairg (*Official Report* HL 30 January 1996, vol. 573, col. 709), 'an uninformed campaign by a tabloid newspaper supported by a minority of Conservative members' who taking 'the spurious moral high ground' whipped themselves, and others, into a panic, claiming that the Bill undermined traditional family values.

The main aim of this area of civil law, in contrast with the criminal law (i.e. if the police were involved), is to regulate and improve matters for the future rather than making judgments or punishing past behaviour (Report on *Domestic Violence and Occupation of the Family Home* (Law Com. No. 207, 1992, para. 2.11)). In your examination, problem questions will be designed to allow you to demonstrate that you can find your way around the new legislation. The circumstances described in the question may be such that you are required to identify whether the persons involved fall within the categories covered by the FLA 1996. Alternatively, there may be little doubt that the persons are associated, but what may be in issue is whether they are entitled to any orders, and if so, which, and their duration. It is extremely unlikely that you would be expected to deal with all of the possible combinations of applicants in one question. However, should such a multi-applicant question be presented there may be consolation that in the limited time available to you very little depth of knowledge could be demonstrated of the complicated provisions (e.g. of the different types of orders for different types of applicants, the different factors which must be taken into account and whether the court has a discretion or is under a duty to grant an order).

There are four questions in this chapter: three problem questions and one essay in which you are asked to consider the recent reform of domestic violence legislation. This area of family law is of practical value, in addition to being of academic interest, reflecting the fact that a large proportion of a family lawyer's time is spent on issues of domestic violence (21,818 non-molestation order and 9,317 occupation orders made under Part IV FLA 1996 in 2003 (*Judicial Statistics* 2003, Cm. 6251, Table 5.9)). Do not assume that you will be asked always to advise the 'victim' (your client may be the alleged 'perpetrator'). Do not avoid issues. Be prepared to give advice about the likelihood of success in an application. Answer the question. Your aim should be to communicate clearly and concisely, therefore, do not make a forlorn attempt to impress the examiner by adorning your answers with inappropriate words and phrases (particularly in Latin) whose meanings—the examiner may suspect—you do not understand. You must not erect any barriers to communication.

Q Question 1

(a) Amanda began cohabiting with Barnaby when she moved into his house six years ago. After six months of cohabitation they married. Five years ago Amanda was confined to a wheelchair as a result of a riding accident. Barnaby had the house altered to make all areas accessible to Amanda in her wheelchair. New bathrooms and a new kitchen were fitted. Doors were widened and a lift installed. Amanda, who was a journalist before her accident, is now a successful author and has adapted her bestselling novels for television and cinema. Barnaby is editor of the local newspaper. With Amanda's success Barnaby has become more dissatisfied with his life and career. He has been drinking heavily for about six months and on a number of occasions he has lost his temper and hit Amanda, causing severe bruising. On the mornings following these events Barnaby is full of remorse and has promised Amanda he will give up alcohol. After the last incident, two days ago, he moved out of the house and slept on a camp bed in his office.

Advise Amanda. She does not want the police to be involved. She says that although she loves Barnaby, she is frightened of the injuries he may cause her. She wants immediate protection. [75 marks]

(b) Briefly highlight how your answer would differ if Amanda and Barnaby had never married. [25 marks]

Commentary

This problem question deals with the availability and range of civil remedies to protect family victims of domestic violence. You are required to display that you can find your way around Part IV of the Family Law Act 1996. Identify the orders available and the relevant sections under which the applications must be made. Discuss the principles on which the court will decide whether or not to make an order.

The advice is, as always, answer the question. Amanda has asked for immediate protection. The question does not state that Amanda wishes to end the marriage, therefore a detailed survey of the ground for divorce (MCA 1973) would not be expected here. A prolonged discussion of the law prior to the implementation of Part IV of the FLA 1996 would not be appropriate and, more to the point, would waste your time in the examination hall and raise very few marks, if any.

Part **(b)** of your answer should not repeat advice that is common to part **(a)**. One vital fact has been changed and you are urged to deal with that change as 'briefly' as possible—heed the instructions.

Answer plan

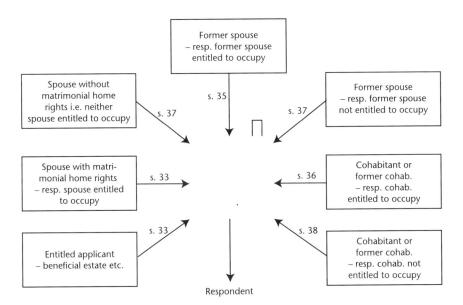

Occupation orders—Part IV, Family Law Act 1996.

- Identify relevant area of law—Domestic violence—Part IV, Family Law Act 1996

- Associated persons

- Orders available—non-molestation and occupation orders

- Molestation—meaning. Factors courts take into account when deciding to grant order.

- Apply relevant cases and statutes to facts. Occupation order—matrimonial home rights, s. 30. Application under s. 33. Factors courts take into account. Balance of harm test.

- Power of arrest, s. 47.

- Cohabitants. Occupation order, s. 36. Balance of harm test—court's discretion not duty. Duration of order.

☼ Suggested answer

(a) As Amanda wants 'immediate protection', but does not want the police to be involved, she can be advised that Part IV of the Family Law Act 1996 (FLA 1996) empowers courts which have jurisdiction in family matters to make two types of order, one which can provide protection (a non-molestation order) and another which deals with occupation of the family home (an occupation order). The case could be brought before the court in as little as two clear days and in emergency situations the court may, where it considers that it is just and convenient to do so, make an occupation order or a non-molestation order without notice (s. 45(1)). This would mean that Barnaby would have no notice of Amanda's application and no opportunity to reply, at this stage, with his version of events. If the court were to make an order without notice it must give Barnaby an opportunity to make representations relating to the order as soon as just and convenient at a full hearing (s. 45(3)). In determining whether to exercise its powers to make orders without notice (s. 45(2)), the court will have regard to all the circumstances including the risk of significant harm to Amanda, attributable to Barnaby's conduct, if the order is not made immediately; the likelihood that Amanda will be deterred or prevented from pursuing the application at a later date; and whether there is reason to believe that Barnaby is aware of the proceedings but is deliberately evading service and that Amanda will be seriously prejudiced by the delay involved in taking the normal steps to serve Barnaby. In the present circumstances, with Barnaby out of the house, it may be thought unnecessary to abridge the time for service.

At this stage Amanda's first priority is her own protection and occupation of the home. She may wish to consider divorce in the future or she may hope for a reconciliation (and rehabilitation of Barnaby). Such matters would be discussed with Amanda, but not here and now.

The court may make a non-molestation order where an application has been made by a person associated with the respondent, whether or not other family proceedings have been instituted (s. 42(2)(a)); or, of its own motion in any family proceedings (s. 42(2)(b)). Amanda and Barnaby are married to each other and therefore come within the definition of associated persons (s. 62(3)(a)). Although molestation is not defined in the Act, the lack of a statutory definition has not given rise to difficulty in the past. Molestation has been described as 'pestering' in *Vaughan* v *Vaughan* [1973] 3 All ER 449; and in *Horner* v *Horner* [1982] 2 All ER 495 included 'any conduct which could be regarded as such a degree of harassment as to call for the intervention of the court' (see *C* v *C* *(Non-molestation Order: Jurisdiction)* [1998] 2 WLR 599). In deciding whether to grant Amanda's application for a non-molestation order, and if so in what manner, the court must have regard to all the circumstances including the need to secure her health, safety and well-being (s. 42(5)). Barnaby's violence, resulting in severe bruising to Amanda, would—surely—seem to be sufficient to justify a non-molestation order.

It would appear that Amanda is neither a legal nor a beneficial owner of the property. However, by virtue of s. 30, Amanda has matrimonial home rights which give a spouse the right, if in occupation, not to be evicted or excluded from the house (which is, or has been, or was intended to be, the associated couple's home), by the other spouse, except with the leave of the court given under s. 33. (If not in occupation, she has the right, with the leave of the court, to enter and occupy the house.) Matrimonial home rights are a charge on the house (s. 31(2)). To bind third parties, where the land is unregistered, the charge must be protected by the registration of a Class F land charge against the name of the property owner in the register of land charges (Land Charges Act 1972), or, in the case of registered land, by the entry of a notice in the Charges Register under the Land Registration Act 1925 (s. 31(10) of the 1996 Act). Occupation orders are available under five different sections of the Act (ss. 33, 35, 36, 37, 38). Amanda is 'a person entitled', due to her matrimonial home rights, and, therefore, would make her application under s. 33. An order may enforce Amanda's entitlement to remain in occupation as against Barnaby (s. 33(3)(a)); prohibit, suspend or restrict Barnaby's right to occupy the house (s. 33(3)(d); or exclude him from a defined area in which the dwelling house is included (s. 33(3)(g)). In deciding whether to exercise its powers under s. 33(3) and, if so, in what manner, the court is to have regard to all the circumstances including the housing needs and housing resources of each of the parties and any relevant children; the financial resources of the parties; the likely effect of any order, or of any decision by the court not to exercise its powers to make regulatory orders, on the health, safety or well-being of the parties and any relevant child; and the conduct of the parties in relation to each other and otherwise (s. 33(6)). As Amanda is an entitled person the court has a duty to make an order if it appears that she is likely to suffer significant harm attributable to Barnaby's conduct, if an order is not made, which is as great or greater than the harm likely to be suffered by Barnaby (s. 33(7)). Conduct is attributable to the respondent even if it is unintentional. The important issue is the effect on the applicant not the respondent's intention (*G* v *G* *(Occupation Order: Conduct)* [1999] 1 FLR 392). Harm, in relation to Amanda, who is at least 18, means ill-treatment or impairment of health (s. 63(1)). Significant harm is likely to be inter-preted, as in the Children Act 1989 proceedings, as 'considerable, noteworthy or important' (*Humberside CC* v *B* [1993] 1 FLR 257 at 263, *per* Booth J). Amanda's need for a specially adapted home is more difficult to satisfy than Barnaby's housing needs. Although Amanda may be more affluent, Barnaby would appear to have an adequate income. The violence inflicted on Amanda is likely to be a decisive factor in the court's deliberations. On the balance of harm test, an order should be made in favour of Amanda. In contrast, in *B* v *B* [1999] 1 FLR 715, despite the respondent's violence, the harm to the husband and his child was likely to be greater if an order were made than the harm likely to be suffered by the applicant wife and the couple's child if an order were not made. If the balance is tipped in the applicant's favour under s. 33 then the court has a duty to make the order. However, if the scales do not tip in the applicant's favour, the court still has a discretion to make the order after considering s. 33(6) (*Chalmers* v *Johns* [1999] 1 FLR 392). The court should consider s. 33(7) and then if the test for significant harm is not satisfied it should move on to s. 33(6) (*G* v *G* (*Occupation Order: Conduct)* [2000] 2 FLR 36 confirming *Chalmers* (above)). The order may be made for a specified period, until the occurrence of a specified event or until further order (s. 33(10) of the 1996 Act). The court may impose on Amanda obligations as to repair and maintenance, discharge of rent, mortgage payments or any other outgoings affecting the home (s. 40(1)(a)). She could be ordered to pay rent to Barnaby (s. 40(1)(b)). Either party may be granted possession or use of the furniture or other contents of the house (s. 40(1)(c)). There is, however, no power to commit a defaulter to prison (*Nwogbe* v *Nwogbe* [2000] 2 FLR 744.) This is an omission in the statute which requires urgent attention. In deciding how to exercise these powers the court is to have regard to all the circumstances of the case including the financial needs and financial resources of the parties (s. 40(2)(a)). A payment of rent by Amanda to Barnaby should allow him to find more comfortable accommodation.

The court would attach a power of arrest to the occupation or non-molestation order, as Barnaby has used or threatened violence against Amanda, unless the court was satisfied that in all the circumstances of the case Amanda would be adequately protected without such a power of arrest (s. 47(2)). Although the Family Law Act 1996 gives the court the power to accept undertakings, where it has power to make non-molestation or occupation orders, there is no power to attach a power of arrest to an undertaking. The court cannot accept an undertaking in any case where a power of arrest would be attached to the order. In 2001, undertakings were accepted in 4,492 cases (*Judicial Statistics* 2003, Cm. 6251, Table 5.9 overleaf). Were the court to accept Barnaby's undertaking, he would not be required to admit that the allegations are true and the court would make no finding of fact regarding his conduct. If the couple hope for a reconciliation this may be sufficient to force Barnaby to take stock of the situation. However, Amanda's protection must take precedence to Barnaby's feelings.

Under the Domestic Violence, Crime and Victims Bill (DVCVB) 2003, s. 42A would be inserted into the Family Law Act 1996. This would make breach of a

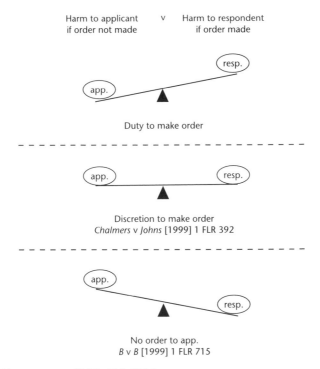

Harm to applicant v Harm to respondent
if order not made if order made

Duty to make order

Discretion to make order
Chalmers v *Johns* [1999] 1 FLR 392

No order to app.
B v *B* [1999] 1 FLR 715

Balance of harm test, s. 33(7), FLA 1996.

non-molestation order a criminal offence. A person guilty of the offence would be liable on conviction on indictment, to imprisonment for a maximum sentence of five years, or a fine, or both; or on summary conviction, to 12 months' imprisonment or a fine, or both. As the maximum penalty for the offence would be five years' imprisonment, the offence would be arrestable under s. 24(1) of the Police and Criminal Evidence Act 1984. The police would, therefore, always be able to arrest for breach of a non-molestation order, without the need for the attachment of a power of arrest to the order, or for the applicant to apply to the civil court for an arrest warrant. The respondent would only be guilty of a criminal offence if he were aware of the existence of the non-molestation order.

When the court is considering whether to make an occupation order under FLA 1996, s. 42(4A) (as amended by DVCV Bill 2004) would place a duty on the court to consider making a non-molestation order. Breach of an occupation order is not to be made a criminal offence, as past conduct of violence or molestation is not a requirement for the grant of an occupation order.

However, if Amanda did not wish to pursue criminal proceedings, she could follow the civil route. If that were to happen, and Barnaby were to be punished for contempt in the civil court, he could not be convicted of breach of a non-molestation order, and vice versa. This would not prevent a prosecution for other offences, for example, assault or grievous bodily harm.

The choice of civil or criminal proceedings, for breach of the non-molestation orders, would be Amanda's. She may have been reluctant to involve the police initially, but may take a different view on breach of a molestation order.

(b) Cohabitants are defined as a man and woman who, although not married to each other, are living together as husband and wife (s. 62(1)(a)); and former cohabitants is to be read accordingly (s. 62(1)(b)). However, under the DVCVB 2003 the definition of cohabitants would be amended to read, 'two persons who, although not married to each other, are living together as husband and wife or (if of the same sex) in an equivalent relationship' (s. 62(1)(a) FLA 1996); and 'former cohabitants is to be read accordingly' (s. 62(1)(b)) As cohabitants, or former cohabitants, Amanda and Barnaby would come within the definition of associated persons (s. 62(3)(b)) and, as such, Amanda may apply for a non-molestation order (s. 42(2)(a)) (with the same outcome as in part **(a)** of this answer).

Amanda, a cohabitant, would not be entitled to matrimonial home rights. Her occupation order application would be as one cohabitant with no existing right to occupy (s. 36). In addition to circumstances comparable to those contained in s. 33(6), the court must consider the nature of the parties' relationship; the length of time they lived together as cohabitants; any children of both parties or for whom both parties have or have had parental responsibility; the time elapsed since they lived together; and any pending proceedings relating to ownership of the house, or financial relief for a child under the Children Act 1989 (s. 36(6), FLA 1996). Also, the court must have regard to the fact that the couple have not given each other the commitment involved in marriage (s. 41). As a result of the definition of cohabitants being amended to include same sex couples (who do not have the capacity to marry, s. 11 Matrimonial Causes Act 1973), s. 41 FLA 1996 would be repealed by the enacted DVCVB 2003. Following from that, s. 36(6) would be amended to provide that, when considering the nature of the parties' relationship, the court must take into account, in particular, the level of commitment involved in that relationship.

The court has a discretion (not a duty as it does with entitled persons, spouses and former spouses) to make an occupation order, if the balance of harm test tips in a cohabitant applicant's favour (s. 36(7)). For Amanda (a non-entitled cohabitant) the order must not exceed six months, but may be extended on one occasion for a further specified period not exceeding six months (s. 36(10)). However, non-molestation orders can be made for a specified period or until further order. That may not provide much consolation for Amanda if there is no reconciliation and she is compelled to seek alternative accommodation.

Q Question 2

(a) Charles and Damian, 19-year-old twin brothers, are nephews of Edward, who is a 70-year-old widower. The twins leave home to attend the university in the town where Edward lives. During term time they live (rent-free) with Edward in his large house on the edge of town. As he likes to take an early morning run, Edward aims to be asleep by eleven o'clock at night. He has told Charles and Damian that they can come and go as they please, play music whenever they want, and as loudly as they want, provided it does not keep him awake. Charles keeps his door closed and does not disturb his uncle. However, Damian insists on leaving his door open. On a number of occasions Edward has gone along to Damian's room to complain about the noise, only to be met by verbal abuse and threats of violence. Charles went to his uncle's aid each time and was punched and kicked by Damian. Damian received some minor bruising from Charles in the last scuffle. Edward is very upset by these incidents and has become nervous and withdrawn. Damian's parents say they cannot cope with him. They confess to Edward that Damian has been a bully for years.

As a result of Damian's behaviour Charles is sleeping on the floor of the room of a fellow student who lives nearby. Edward has gone to a local bed and breakfast guest house. Damian remains in Edward's home. The family does not wish to involve the police.

Damian seeks your advice. He tells you that he likes 'having the house to myself'. He has heard that as a 'victim of domestic violence' he can go to court to get orders that will protect him and exclude Edward and Charles.

(b) How would your answer differ if Charles were not Damian's twin brother, but his homosexual partner?

Commentary

This question is here to illustrate that at some time you will be asked to advise the unpleasant, the devious and the morally reprehensible as well as the deserving and/or downtrodden. Everyone is entitled to ask for legal advice: it is not your function to pass judgment. Remember that sometimes you have to give 'bad news'; the person who has asked for your advice may have to be told that he does not stand a chance of being granted an order. You have to explain why that is so. Also you must warn your client where, as in the present circumstances, other persons are very likely to apply, and succeed, in their applications for orders against him.

The question is inviting you to discuss the remedies available to a new group of people, 'associated persons', who are now protected by domestic violence legislation contained in Part IV of the Family Law Act 1996. Previously such persons had to resort to the law of tort (nuisance or trespass) or the criminal law for protection. Now, in addition to Part IV, the

Protection from Harassment Act 1997 provides, for the tort of harassment, a parallel set of remedies which are available to anyone, whether associated or not.

Answer plan

- Identify relevant area of law—domestic violence—Part IV, Family Law Act 1996.

- Associated persons—relatives—s. 62 and s. 63.

- Orders available—non-molestation and occupation orders.

- Molestation—meaning. Factors courts take into account when deciding whether to grant order.

- Apply relevant cases and statutes to facts. Occupation order—who may apply? Appropriate section? Factors considered by court. Balance of harm test.

- Power of arrest, s. 47.

- Same sex couples. Cohabitants, s. 62(1)(a)? Associated persons, s. 62(c) living in same household.

⚬ Suggested answer

(a) As 'relatives' Damian and Edward come into the category of 'associated persons' who may apply for orders under Part IV (Family Homes and Domestic Violence) of the Family Law Act 1996 (s. 62(3)(d)). 'Relatives' are defined in s. 63(1) to include uncle and nephew. Damian and Charles are also associated persons, again relatives (s. 62(3)(d)) i.e. brothers *Chechi* v *Bashier* [1999] 2 FLR 489 (s. 63(1)). The court may make a non-molestation order where an application has been made by a person associated with the respondent, whether or not other family proceedings have been instituted (s. 42(2)(a)); or, of its own motion in any family proceedings (s. 42(2)(b)). A non-molestation order extends beyond restraining violence to forbidding the respondent from pestering (*Vaughan* v *Vaughan* [1973] 3 All ER 449) or harassing (*Horner* v *Horner* [1982] 2 All ER 495) the applicant. A non-molestation order application by Damian against Edward would be doomed to failure as there appears to be no evidence of anything which could be described as molestation by Edward directed against Damian; a similar application against Charles would also be doomed to failure (*C* v *C (Non-Molestation: Jurisdiction)* [1998] 2 WLR 599). Even though Damian received some minor bruising in the last scuffle with his twin, the court, in deciding whether to exercise its powers, must have regard to all the circumstances including the need to secure the health, safety and well-being of the applicant (s. 42(5)(a)). When set in the context of all the incidents it would be seen by the court that it is not Damian who needs a non-molestation order but Charles and Edward; it is their health, safety and well-being that needs to be secured. Charles was punched and kicked by Damian and Edward was met by verbal abuse and threats of violence and has become nervous and withdrawn. The court can go ahead and make the non-molestation orders against Damian of its own motion even though no such applications have been made by Charles and Edward (s. 42(2)(b)). In *Davis v Johnson* [1979] AC 264, at 334, Viscount Dilhorne said, 'violence is a form of molestation, but molestation may take place without the threat or use of violence and still be serious and inimical to mental or physical health'.

Although Damian and Edward are associated persons, Damian would not be entitled to apply under Part IV, FLA 1996 for an occupation order excluding Edward from the dwelling-house which is or has been their home. Damian has no estate or interest in the dwelling-house so could not make an application under s. 33. Nor does he fit into any of the other four categories of applicant, i.e. spouse (ss. 33, 37), former spouse (ss. 33, 35) cohabitant (ss. 33, 36, 38) or former cohabitant (ss. 33, 36, 38). By the same reasoning Damian could not apply for an occupation order against Charles. Furthermore, having strongly suggested to Damian that his own applications have little chance of success, you must warn him that he may face applications from the others. Edward (an entitled applicant by virtue of a beneficial estate) may apply for an occupation order requiring Damian to leave the dwelling-house which has been his and Damian's (the associated person's) home (s. 33(3)(f)). In deciding whether to exercise its powers under s. 33(3) and, if so, in what manner, the court is to have regard to all the circumstances, including the housing needs and housing resources, of each of the parties and any relevant children; the financial resources of the parties; the likely effect of any order, or of any decision by the court not to exercise its powers to make regulatory orders, on the health, safety or well-being of the parties and any relevant child; and the conduct of the parties in relation to each other and otherwise (s. 33(6)). As Edward is an entitled person the court has a duty to make an order if it appears that he is likely to suffer significant harm attributable to Damian's conduct, if an order is not made, which is as great or greater than the harm likely to be suffered by Damian (s. 33(7)). Harm, in relation to Edward, who is at least 18, means ill-treatment or impairment of health (s. 63(1)). Significant harm is likely to be interpreted, as in the Children Act 1989 proceedings, as 'considerable, noteworthy or important' (*Humberside CC v B* [1993] 1 FLR 257 at 263, *per* Booth J). It is highly likely that Damian, threatened with exclusion on account of his behaviour, would be able to establish a degree of hardship in terms of the difficulty in finding similarly comfortable, congenial and convenient accommodation. However, he is unlikely to suffer significant harm, whereas Edward who is being subjected to abuse and threats of violence may very easily suffer harm if Damian remains in the house, as it seems likely that the incidents would be repeated. The Law Commission (*Domestic Violence and Occupation of the Family Home* (1992 Law Com. No. 207, para. 4.34)) thought that the law would treat violence or other forms of abuse as deserving immediate relief. If it were thought to be appropriate, the occupation order could also include a term excluding Damian from a defined area in which the dwelling-house is included (s. 33(3)(g)). An order under s. 33 may, in so far as it has a continuing effect, be made for a specified period, until the occurrence of a specified event or until further order (s. 33(10)). There is a presumption that the court will attach a power of arrest to one or more provisions of each of the occupation and non-molestation orders, as Damian has used violence against Charles and threatened violence against Edward, unless the court was satisfied that in all the circumstances of the case Edward and Charles would be adequately protected without such a power of arrest (s. 47(2)). Where a court decides not to attach a power of arrest to an order it may accept an undertaking, e.g. by the respondent not to molest the applicant (s. 46(1)). The undertaking is enforceable as if it were an order of the court.

Under the Domestic Violence, Crime and Victims Bill (DVCVB) 2003, s. 42A would be inserted into the Family Law Act 1996. This would make breach of a non-molestation order a criminal offence. A person guilty of the offence would be liable on conviction on indictment, to imprisonment for a maximum sentence of five years, or a fine, or both; or on summary conviction, to 12 months' imprisonment or a fine, or both. As the maximum penalty for the offence would be five years' imprisonment, the offence would be arrestable under s. 24(1) of the Police and Criminal Evidence Act 1984. The police would, therefore, always be able to arrest for breach of a non-molestation order, without the need for the attachment of a power of arrest to the order, or for the applicant to apply to the civil court for an arrest warrant. The respondent would only be guilty of a criminal offence if he were aware of the existence of the non-molestation order.

However, if either Charles or Edward did not wish to pursue criminal proceedings, they could follow the civil route. If that were to happen, and Damian were to be punished for contempt in the civil court, he could not be convicted of breach of a non-molestation order, and vice versa. This would not prevent a prosecution for other offences, for example, assault or grievous bodily harm.

The choice of civil or criminal proceedings, for breach of the non-molestation orders, would be for Charles and Edward to decide. Although they may have been reluctant to involve the police initially, they may take a different view on breach of a molestation order.

(b) Prior to the amendments introduced by the DVCVB 2003, as homosexual partners, Damian and Charles are neither cohabitants nor former cohabitants within the FLA 1996. Cohabitants must be a man and a woman who, although not married to each other, are living together as husband and wife (s. 62(1)(a)). However, Damian and Charles (and Damian and Edward) would be associated persons as they live or have lived in the same household, otherwise than merely by reason of one of them being the other's employee, tenant, lodger or boarder (s. 62(c)). Otherwise, all the advice in part **(a)** above would remain the same.

Once enacted, the DVCVB 2003 would amend the definition of cohabitants to include same-sex couples living in an equivalent relationship to husband and wife. This would allow either Charles or Damian to apply for an occupation order under s. 38 (neither cohabitant nor former cohabitant entitled to occupy, i.e. they have no beneficial estate, interest or contract or statutory right to remain). Taking into account the balance of harm test in s. 38(5) and Damian's conduct (s. 36 (4)(d)), it is unlikely that Damian would be successful in his application. However, Charles would have a much greater chance of a positive outcome.

Also, Charles would be able to apply for a non-molestation order as a cohabitant, rather than being part of the same household as Damian. Otherwise, all the advice in part **(a)** above would remain the same.

Q Question 3

Three years ago a group of friends (Fiona, George and Ian) who had been medical students at the same hospital, bought and became joint owners of a large house with the intention of living there together.

(a) Fiona and George were engaged at the time of the purchase and intended to marry after a five-year engagement (the lengthy engagement was Fiona's idea). Fiona has never lived in the intended matrimonial home. George moved in at the time of the purchase and suggested that Fiona should join him. Fiona thinks that George has consistently failed to show sufficient respect for her. A year ago, on George's suggestion that they should bring forward the date of the wedding, Fiona terminated the engagement. George has bombarded Fiona with flowers and begged her to reinstate the engagement. Fiona has decided that George is an unsuitable partner.

Advise Fiona. She wishes to remove George from the house and live there herself as it is nearer to the hospital than her present accommodation. Fiona wants George to refrain from sending pleading letters and flowers. [50 marks]

(b) Harriet and Ian had been living together for two years before they moved into the house three years ago. Although Harriet made a contribution to the purchase price Ian told her that there was a limit to the number of names that could appear on the deeds to the property. Harriet worked as a nurse until she gave birth two years ago. The baby died a few days after he was born. Harriet has suffered two miscarriages since then. Ian has been very unsympathetic and said to Harriet that it is just as well that he had not bothered to marry her. Eight months ago he left to live with June. That relationship has now ended. During the last month he has called on Harriet every day. He told her to get out of his house. He has told her that she 'looks a mess' and has 'let herself go'. He has threatened to display, on the railings outside the house, photographs of Harriet in the nude, so that, he says, everyone can compare her present appearance with that of four years ago. Yesterday he bundled her out of the house and threw her clothes after her.

Harriet has no family and her close friends live near to the house. She is at a women's refuge. However, the close proximity of so many young children and babies is making her very tearful. Advise Harriet. [50 marks]

Commentary

This is a demanding question which requires a detailed answer. It is the type of question which may be set for coursework or as a 'pre-seen' exam question or in an open book exam.

Part **(a)** concentrates on an engaged couple and the conditions they must fulfil to be eligible to make an application for remedies under Part IV, FLA 1996. There also appears to be some doubt about whether George's behaviour is sufficient to warrant any orders under the Act.

Part **(b)** raises little doubt about behaviour and worthiness. However, what is required is a discussion about the choice of the appropriate section under which to make an application.

Answer plan

- Identify relevant area of law—domestic violence—Part IV, Family Law Act 1996.

- Associated persons. Engaged couples. Evidence of engagement.

- Orders available. Non-molestation and occupation orders.

- Molestation—meaning. Factors court take into account when deciding whether to make an order.

- Power of arrest, s. 47/undertakings, s. 46.

- Apply relevant cases and statutes to facts. Occupation order—entitled applicant, s. 33. Factors. Balance of harm test.

- Cohabitants. Occupation order, s. 36. Factors. Balance of harm test. Contrast with entitled applicant.

:Q: Suggested answer

(a) Part IV of the Family Law Act 1996 enlarges the class of persons who can use civil domestic violence legislation. A wide group of 'associated persons' may apply for non-molestation orders and a narrower group may apply for occupation orders. Fiona and George agreed to marry one another, therefore they are associated persons (even though the engagement is over) (s. 62(3)(e)). As Fiona ended the engagement only a year ago, her application will be within the three-year limit (s. 42(4)). The court can neither make a non-molestation order under s. 42 nor an occupation order under s. 33 (entitled applicants) unless there is evidence in writing (s. 44(1)) of the agreement;

however s. 44(1) does not apply if the court is satisfied that the agreement to marry was evidenced by the gift of an engagement ring in contemplation of marriage (s. 44(2)(a)), or a ceremony entered into by the couple in the presence of one or more witnesses (s. 44(2)(b)). The most common way to provide evidence of an engagement is likely to be an engagement ring (see John Murphy, 'Domestic Violence: The New Law' [1996] *MLR* 845). Problems may arise if: (a) the ring was returned on the termination of the engagement; (b) the man is making the application (they seldom wear engagement rings); (c) the couple could not afford a ring; or (d) they simply chose not to have a ring. However, provided that Fiona can prove the engagement by one of the means stipulated in s. 44, she and George will be associated persons.

If Fiona could not prove the existence of an engagement, or she was outside the three-year limit, she may be assisted by the proposed amendments to the FLA 1996 made by the Domestic Violence, Crime and Victims Bill (DVCVB) 2003. Section 62(3)(ea) would include in the definition of associated persons, those who have had an intimate personal relationship with each other, which is or was of a significant duration. This will cover a long-standing relationship which may, or may not, be a sexual relationship. However, it must be an intimate and personal relationship. This will not include long-term platonic friends or 'one-night stands'.

In deciding whether to exercise its powers to grant a non-molestation order and, if so, in what manner, the court must have regard to all the circumstances including the need to secure the health, safety and well-being of Fiona (s. 42(5)(a)). 'Molestation may take place without the threat or use of violence and still be serious and inimical to mental or physical health' (*Davis* v *Johnson* [1979] AC 264). A non-molestation order has been held to extend beyond restraining violence to forbidding the respondent from pestering (*Vaughan* v *Vaughan* [1973] 3 All ER 449) or harassing (*Horner* v *Horner* [1982] 2 All ER 495) the applicant, and includes the forcing by the other party of his society on the unwilling suffering party for the purpose of seeking to resume affectionate relations (*F* v *F* [1989] 2 FLR 451). (For a more limited interpret-ation of the term 'molestation' see *C* v *C* (*Non-Molestation Order: Jurisdiction*) [1998] 2 WLR 599.) The court would consider the number and frequency of the letters and bouquets along with their effect on Fiona. It may be thought appropriate in the circumstances for George to give an undertaking not to molest Fiona (s. 46(1)). An undertaking would be permissible here because the presumption of a power of arrest would not apply, as George has neither used nor threatened violence against Fiona (s. 47(2)). George, in giving an undertaking to the court, would not have to admit the truth of Fiona's allegations and the court would make no finding of fact regarding his conduct. A breach of the undertaking would be contempt of court (s. 46(4)).

Fiona's application for an occupation order would be under s. 33 as an entitled person. Fiona is one of the legal owners of the property. She is entitled to occupy the dwelling-house by virtue of a beneficial estate or interest giving her the right to remain in occupation (s. 33(1)(a)(i)). Although the dwelling-house has never been

Fiona's home (s. 33(1)(b)(i)) the couple intended it to be their home (s. 33(1)(b)(ii)). As with the non-molestation order, the occupation order application must be within three years of the termination of the engagement (s. 33(2)). On the enactment of the DVCVB 2003, even if there were no evidence of the engagement, she may claim to be an associated person because of their 'intimate personal relationship'(s. 62(3)(ea)) and as an entitled person she would be able to apply under s. 33(1)(b)(ii). Fiona would wish the order to contain a term requiring George to leave the house (s. 33(f)). In deciding whether to grant such an order and (if so) in what manner, the court is to have regard to all the circumstances including the housing needs and housing resources of Fiona and George; their financial resources; the likely effect of any order, or of any decision by the court not to make an order, on the health, safety and well-being of Fiona and George; and the conduct of the parties in relation to each other (s. 33(6)). As Fiona is an entitled person, the court has a duty to make an order if it appears that she is likely to suffer significant harm attributable to George's conduct, if an order is not made, which is as great or greater than the harm likely to be suffered by George (s. 33(7)). Harm, in relation to Fiona, who is at least 18, means ill-treatment or impairment of health (s. 63(1)). Significant harm is likely to be interpreted, as in the Children Act 1989 proceedings, as 'considerable, noteworthy or important' (*Humberside CC* v *B* [1993] 1 FLR 257 at 263, *per* Booth J). It is difficult to conclude on the facts given that, without an order, Fiona would suffer significant harm due to George's conduct. As in *Wiseman* v *Simpson* [1988] 1 All ER 245 it appears that Fiona has 'simply ceased to be in love' with George (if she ever were). However, in *Scott* v *Scott* [1992] 1 FLR 529 the Court of Appeal upheld an order prohibiting the husband from exercising his right to occupy the matrimonial home where there was no violence, because the husband, who would not accept the marriage was over, had repeatedly tried to persuade his wife to effect a reconciliation and had also broken an earlier undertaking.

Were an occupation order to be made in Fiona's favour either party could be granted possession or use of the furniture or other contents (s. 40(1)(c)–(e)). Obligations as to repair, maintenance and the discharge of outgoings in respect of the house could be imposed by the court (s. 40(1)(a)). Additionally, Fiona could be ordered to pay 'rent' to George (s. 40(1)(b)) (the guidelines to be followed by the court when exercising its discretion to make such orders are contained in s. 40(2)). (Note—there is no power of enforcement in s. 40 *Nwogbe* v *Nwogbe* [2000] 2 FLR 744.)

Our advice to Fiona is that she and her erstwhile fiancé need to decide what to do with their property, e.g. sell it, or one buy the other out (of course, any such arrangement would need both the consent and formal participation of Ian). Part IV orders should be unnecessary here.

(b) Harriet and Ian are former cohabitants, a man and woman who, although not married to each other, were living together as husband and wife (s. 62(1)(b)) and therefore they are associated persons (s. 62(3)(b)). Harriet could apply for an occupation order giving her the right to enter and occupy and requiring Ian to leave the dwelling house which has been their home. The application may be either as a former cohabitant with no existing right to occupy (s. 36), or as an entitled person, by virtue of a beneficial estate or interest, under s. 33. Although Harriet is not a legal owner of the property, she should be able to establish a beneficial interest by way of a resulting trust as she made a financial contribution to the purchase price of the property (*Sekhon* v *Alissa* [1989] 2 FLR 94). As a s. 36 applicant, Harriet is only entitled to an order for a specified period not exceeding six months and to one extension for a further specified period not exceeding six months. However, a s. 33 order may be granted for an unlimited period. Also, under s. 36, the order must contain a provision giving Harriet the right to enter and occupy the dwelling house for the period specified and requiring Ian to permit the exercise of that right (s. 36(4)). This provision is necessary, as an applicant under s. 36 is, by definition, non-entitled.

In deciding whether to make an order, if she is 'entitled', the court would look to s. 33(6) (see above in part **(a)**) but if she is not entitled, s. 36(6) would be applied, which requires the court, additionally, to consider the nature of the parties' relationship; the length of time they lived together as husband and wife and the length of time that has elapsed since they lived together. When the nature of the couple's relationship is being considered, the court must have regard to the fact that the parties have not given each other the commitment involved in marriage (s. 41(2)).

As a result of the definition of cohabitants being amended to include same sex couples, who cannot give each other the commitment involved in marriage, s. 41 will be repealed by the DVCVB 2003. Section 36(6) will be amended to provide that, when considering the nature of the parties' relationship, the court must take into account, in particular, the level of commitment involved in that relationship.

When, on the balance of harm test, the scales tip in favour of an entitled applicant (s. 33(7)) the court is under a duty to grant an order. However, for a s. 36 applicant, the court has a discretion to grant an order (s. 36(7)). Considering the heart-rending circumstances, coupled with Ian's dastardly behaviour, it is almost certain that the court would grant an occupation order whether it be as a result of a duty (s. 33) or merely a discretion (s. 36).

The dilemma then is, under which section should Harriet make her application? If she makes the wrong choice, will it jeopardise her chance of an order? If an application is made under one section and the court considers that it has no power to make an order under that section, but that it has power to make an order under another section, then the court may make an order under that other section (s. 39(3)). Were Harriet to be granted an order under s. 36, could Ian claim that there has been a finding of fact that an order had been granted to Harriet as a cohabitant with no rights in the property (Conway, 'Abused Cohabitees, Property Disputes and the Family Law Act 1996' [1996] *Fam Law* 499)? That danger appears to have been defused by s. 39(4) which states that the fact that a person has applied for an occupation order under sections 35 to 38, or that an occupation order has been made, does not affect the right of any person to claim a legal or equitable interest in any property in any subsequent proceedings (including Part IV). This allows the more urgent Part IV applications to proceed without the need to get bogged down in a property dispute at this stage.

Molestation covers a wide range of behaviour (see part **(a)**). In *Johnson* v *Walton* [1990] 1 FLR 350, sending photographs of the partially nude applicant to a national newspaper with the intention of causing her distress was held to constitute molestation. A non-molestation order may include terms which prohibit threats, harassment or pestering. Harriet seems eminently deserving of an order which will secure her health, safety and well-being (s. 42(5)(a)).

Q Question 4

Does Part IV of the Family Law Act 1996 provide 'equality of opportunity' for spouses, cohabitants and homosexual couples?

Commentary

An answer which displays not only that you are aware that there is inequality among the groups but also that you know why and how that inequality came about, together with your opinion(s) on the matter will bring high marks.

Answer plan

- Associated persons—spouse—cohabitant—living in same household—same sex partner, s. 62, Part IV Family Law Act 1996.

- Definition of cohabitant. Reform?

- Availability of occupation orders. Relevant sections. Compare and contrast— factors considered by court—balance of harm test—duration.

- Background—passage of Bill through Parliament. Comments.

- Commitment involved in marriage, s. 41. Comments.

- Spouses—property interests—entitled applicants. Comments.

☼ Suggested answer

Before the implementation of Part IV of the Family Law Act 1996 only spouses and cohabitants were protected by civil domestic violence legislation. Part IV enlarged the class of persons who can use such legislation. A wide group of 'associated persons' may apply for non-molestation orders and a narrower group may apply for occupation orders. Those who are or who have been married to each other

(s. 62(3)(a)) and cohabitants and former cohabitants (s. 62(3)(b)) were specifically identified as associated persons. Cohabitants were defined as a man and woman who, although not married to each other, are living together as husband and wife (s. 62(1)(a)). Homosexual couples, therefore, were not recognised within that definition of cohabitants. However, although not specifically identified elsewhere, they were able to bring themselves into the category of associated persons if they live or have lived in the same household, otherwise than merely by reason of one of them being the other's employee, tenant, lodger or boarder (s. 62(3)(c)). Susan Edwards and Ann Halpern ('The progress towards protection' [1992] *NLJ* 798) commenting on the Law Commission report, *Domestic Violence and Occupation of the Family Home* (1992 Law Com. No. 207) stated that to put beyond doubt the intention to include homosexuals it would have been better to include them as a specific category. The Domestic Violence, Crime and Victims Bill (DVCVB) 2003 does precisely that; it amends the definition of cohabitants to 'two persons who, although not married to each other, are living together as husband and wife or (if of the same sex) in an equivalent relationship (s. 62(1)(a) FLA 1996 as it would be amended by DVCVB 2003); and former cohabitants is to be read accordingly (s. 62(1)(b)).

All the groups referred to in the question are protected to some extent by Part IV FLA 1996. However, the Act does not afford them equal protection. Although they may each apply, as associated persons, for a non-molestation order (s. 42) it is with occupation orders that the discrimination emerges. Even if a spouse has no estate in the dwelling house which is, has been or was intended to be the associated couple's home (s. 33(1)(b), nevertheless she will have matrimonial home rights of occupation (s. 30(2)). Such matrimonial home rights give her a right to make an application for an occupation order, as an entitled person (s. 33(1)(a)). Entitled persons (which as we have seen includes spouses (s. 33), former spouse, cohabitants and former cohabitants are all specifically identified as being able to make applications for occupation orders (s. 35 to s. 38)). Persons involved in a homosexual relationship (together with other associated persons e.g. relatives and engaged couples) were only qualified to make an application for an occupation order if they had occupation rights in the dwelling house and therefore could make their applications under s. 33. If a person (the person entitled) is entitled to occupy a dwelling house by virtue of a beneficial estate or interest or contract or by virtue of any enactment giving him the rights to remain in occupation then he may apply to court for an occupation order (s. 33(1)).

Under s. 33 (entitled applicants) the court is directed to make the occupation order for a specified period, however, no time limit is imposed. By contrast, where the applicant has no such right of occupation the order cannot exceed six months. The FLA 1996, introduced a further distinction between applicants who are cohabitants (or former cohabitants) and those who are former spouses. In the case of former spouses, there is no limit to the number of times an occupation order can be renewed

(s. 35(10) and s. 37(5)). However, where the applicant is a cohabitant or former cohabitant the occupation order can be renewed only once (s. 36(10) and s. 38(6)). John Murphy ('Domestic Violence: The New Law' [1996] *MLR* 845) said, 'The avowed intention was to make plain the distinction between marriage and cohabitation as a concession to those who, on the heels of what the *Daily Mail* had uninformedly claimed about the 1995 Bill, had believed the institution of marriage to be under threat. In the overwhelming majority of cases this will be of only symbolic effect'.

In deciding whether to make an order, for an entitled applicant, the court considers s. 33(6). At the moment, for a non-entitled cohabitant or former cohabitant applicant under s. 36, the court is required, additionally to circumstances identical to those in s 33(6), to consider the nature of the parties' relationship; the length of time they lived together as husband and wife and the length of time that has elapsed since they lived together. When the nature of the couple's relationship is being considered, the court must have regard to the fact that the parties have not given each other the commitment involved in marriage (s. 41(2)) (was this another 'symbolic' amendment?). At the Committee stage of the Family Law Bill, Earl Russell said 'However deep an attachment people may have to the principle of lawful matrimony it is the first duty of the state to ensure the preservation of the Queen's peace. I feel a certain anxiety about the idea that anybody's morals, however bad, should make them less entitled to protection' (HL, 30 January 1996, vol. 573 col. 1384). Earl Russell noted that on the previous day, when discussing jobseekers' regulations, the House of Lords had approved a reference to benefits going to a married or unmarried couple. He went on to say that cohabitation is 'a public status, recognised through shared finances, shared bank account, joint responsibility for the housekeeping ... and all the things that married people do together'. He concluded that cohabitation is now a recognised status. Lord Simon took the view that, nevertheless, it was a separate status which is not the same as marriage. 'It is because [the changes] differentiate the status of marriage from the status of concubinage that I believe they are to be supported', he said. The Lord Chancellor said that the amendment did not say anything that had not already been approved by Parliament. The introduction of this general 'lack of commitment' factor was dubbed by Michael Horton ('The Family Law Bill—Domestic Violence', [1996] *Fam Law* 49) as 'political posturing at its most blatant'.

The good news is that, as a result of the definition of cohabitants being amended by DVCVB 2003 to include same sex couples, who cannot give each other the commitment involved in marriage, s. 41 will be repealed. Following from that, s. 36(6) will be amended to provide that, when considering the nature of the parties' relationship the court must take into account, in particular, the level of commitment involved in that relationship.

When, on the balance of harm test, the scales tip in favour of an entitled applicant (s. 33(7)) or a former spouse (s. 35(8)), the court is under a duty to grant an order.

However, for a non-entitled cohabitant or former cohabitant the court has no duty, merely a discretion, to grant an order (s. 36(7) and s. 38(5)).

These days, many young married couples are co-owners of their home, as are many young cohabitants. They, therefore, are categorised as entitled applicants. A non-owning spouse (where the other is entitled) is drawn into the entitled category by virtue of matrimonial home rights (s. 30). Non-owning cohabitants and non-owning former cohabitants, although they cannot acquire matrimonial home rights, are at least given some recognition and benefits as a result of their status, as are non-owning former spouses. No such specific recognition was given to homosexual couples, who do not have the option of marrying each other, and no matter how stable their relationship a non-owning same sex partner could not apply for an occupation order against his property-owning partner. John Murphy ('Domestic Violence: The New Law' [1996] *MLR* 845) viewed this as a 'cruel distinction', affording appreciably less protection to homosexuals than it did to former spouses and cohabitants. He pointed out that all that was needed was a slight amendment to the definition of cohabitants. With the prevailing climate in the press and in Parliament at the time, such a redefinition was unlikely. Those who objected to the inclusion of 'live-in girlfriends', and who must have failed to appreciate that non-molestation protection was being offered to homosexuals as associated persons, would almost certainly have demanded a removal of even that minimal protection. However, once the DVCVB 2003 is enacted, same sex partners will be cohabitants and, therefore, as with opposite sex partners, even the non-entitled partner will be able to apply for an occupation order under either s. 36 or s. 38.

The Draconian nature of an order excluding a property owner from his home was the subject of comment in many cases prior to the introduction of Part IV FLA 1996, e.g. *Summers* v *Summers* [1986] 1 FLR 343; *Wiseman* v *Simpson* [1988] 1 All ER 245; *Shipp* v *Shipp* [1988] 1 FLR 345; and *Blackstock* v *Blackstock* [1991] 2 FLR 308. Recognising that an occupation order is a severe order whose potential consequences are more serious than a non-molestation order, the Law Commission thought it necessary to distinguish between entitled and non-entitled applicants (Domestic Violence and Occupation of the Family Home (1992 Law Com. No. 207)).

The result is that property owners and spouses are placed together in a special category and only they are on an equal footing with each other. Therefore, although the Act recognises that some family relationships are special, nevertheless, as Roger Holmes ('Inequality and family values', [1997] *NLJ* 608) notes, 'Even given Parliament's determination to downgrade cohabitants, property rights come first'.

Further reading

Bird, R., *Domestic Violence Law and Practice*, 4th edn., (Family Law, 2003).

Burton, M., 'Domestic Violence—From Consultation to Bill' [2004] Fam Law 128.

Conway, H. L., 'The Domestic Violence, Crime and Victims Bill' [2004] Fam Law 132.

Ellison, L., 'Prosecuting Domestic Violence without Victim Participation' [2002] MLR 834.

Hanson, N., 'Domestic Conflict' (2004) 101(12) *LSG* 20.

Humphreys, C., Harrison, C., 'Focusing on safety—domestic violence and the role of child contact centres' [2003] CFLQ 237.

Law Commission, *Domestic Violence and Occupation of the Family Home*, 1992, LC Report 207, HMSO.

Mullender, A., *Rethinking Domestic Violence* (Routledge, 1996).

Mullender, A. and Morley, R., *Children Living with Domestic Violence* (Whiting and Birch, 1994).

Pizzey, E., *Scream Quietly or the Neighbours Will Hear* (Harmondsworth: Penguin Books, 1974).

Websites

Domestic violence data source (DVDS) www.domesticviolencedata.org/
Home Office Domestic Violence Website
www.homeoffice.gov.uk/domesticviolence/index.htm
London Domestic Violence Strategy
www.london.gov.uk/mayor/strategies/dom-violence/index
Women's Aid Federation www.womensaid.org.uk

Children: general principles, status and wardship

Introduction

Family law in recent decades has become increasingly child-centred (see e.g. the Matrimonial Causes Act 1973, s. 25 (as amended by the Matrimonial and Family Proceedings Act 1984) where the welfare of minor children is the first consideration when the court is assessing financial relief for spouses). The United Nations Convention on the Rights of the Child (1989) reflects the views that children and family relationships should have special protection and that their rights as individuals should be guaranteed with regard to such matters as nationality and freedom of expression. More recently still, the Child Support Acts 1991–2000 have galvanised the financial duties of absent parents. Now, the Adoption and Children Act 2002 applies to adoption the 'welfare principle' applied in many other areas of child law—i.e. that the child's welfare shall be the *paramount* consideration of the court.

Two pieces of legislation in particular have had a significant impact on children, i.e. the Family Law Reform Act 1987 which, without abolishing illegitimacy, made significant changes to the position of the ever increasing number of children born outside wedlock and their parents, and, of course, the Children Act 1989. Described by the then Lord Chancellor, Lord Mackay LC, as 'the most comprehensive piece of legislation which Parliament has ever enacted about children', the Act made it necessary for all involved with children to 'unlearn' all the provisions they were so familiar with and to adopt an entirely new approach. (A decade and a half on, the present day family law student, immersing herself in 'residence' and 'contact', may well be wondering what the newspapers and others mean by 'custody' and 'access'.) Few areas of child law were unaffected by the legislation.

It would be difficult to overestimate the importance of the 1989 Act. All students need to have a sound knowledge of the general principles of welfare and non-intervention and the concept of parental responsibility: they permeate child law. You should also appreciate the underlying policies and aims of the legislation as it is quite likely that the examiner will wish to include a general question on such areas. Most courses concentrate on the first five 'Parts' of the Act: Introductory (the welfare principle and parental responsibility); Orders with Respect to Children in Family Proceedings; Local Authority Support for Children and Families; Care and Supervision; Protection of Children. The sequence segues from the private through to the public law, ranging from the status quo, through disputes within the family, to state intervention. Now, the Children Bill 2004 aims to create clear accountability for children's services, better joint working and a better focus on safeguarding children. It concentrates on outcomes that children themselves have said are important.

This chapter contains a hotchpotch of questions on, as the title suggests, general principles and concepts of child law (particularly the welfare principle and parental responsibility), the status of children (recognising the huge rise of the recorded non-marital birth rate in recent years) and, importantly, wardship, whose role has been significantly affected by the 1989 Act. Such topics lend themselves to essay type questions and three of the questions take this form, but there is one problem question too.

Q Question 1

'The unmarried father is . . . a person with a potentially significant status in relation to his children, and with the increasing numbers of children born outside marriage, this must be right' (Christina Sachs, 1991).

Do you agree?

Commentary

It may be that if the examiner uses a quotation from an article as an essay title you will have been referred to the article during the course. It is always helpful to have read the article and thus be able to place the title quote in context. However, in this case even if you have not read Christina Sachs's article ('The Unmarried Father' [1991] *Fam Law* 583), you will easily recognise that you are concerned here with the unmarried father. (Cretney (*Family Law*, 4th edn, 2000 at p. 218) considered it unacceptable to refer to the father of an illegitimate child as the 'unmarried father', as the issue is not simply whether he is married, but whether he is married to the child's mother. The expression 'unmarried father' is therefore somewhat misleading, but will nevertheless be used in the following answer, not least because it is used in the title quote.) Note, however, that so far as the 'i' word is concerned, the current, 5th, 2003, edn. of *Family Law* '(pp. 212–3) 'eschews the terminology of legitimacy wherever possible' because Hale LJ in *Re R (Surname: Using Both Parents)* [2001] EWCA 1344 regretted that a case had been reported using the term 'illegitimate' in the title.

In your answer you will need to examine the statement in detail before deciding whether you agree with it or not. 'Is *now* a person with a *potentially* significant status' implies first that this has not always been the case and secondly, that he has no automatic status. What changes have been introduced? Discussion is invited of the relevant provisions found in the Children Act 1989, as now amended by the Adoption and Children Act 2002. How prescient was Sachs? Remember that she was writing in the year that the 1989 Act was first activated.

The weaker answer will do little more than list the various ways in which an unmarried father can acquire a relationship with his children. The better answer will not only do this, but will also critically analyse each course of action. In addition you are required by the latter part of the statement to put it into context; if you can give some statistics, do so. You should also show that you are aware of the many different variations on a theme here. Finally, as you are asked whether you agree with the statement made, there is scope for your own opinions on the matter, preferably backed with some authority.

* Numbers

* Sorts of 'unmarried fathers'

* Meaning of parental responsibility

* s. 4, CA 1989—'agreements' and 'orders'

* ACA 2002—joint registration

* s. 8, CA Orders

☀ Suggested answer

Statistics show that the number of children born out of wedlock is increasing and that some 40 per cent (and growing) of the 600,000 or so children born annually in England and Wales are non-marital. Yet by 2001 over 80 per cent of them were jointly registered, the bulk to co-resident parents, which would seem to indicate that a significant number of children are born into stable extra-marital relationships with two actively involved parents.

The question invites us to look at the status of the unmarried father. At the outset, it is important to appreciate the many different situations which may exist in this context, and hence the many different types or categories of unmarried fathers. Over the last twenty years or so, as extra-marital cohabitation has become more socially acceptable, many children have been born into stable relationships where the unmarried father plays a full part in the child's life. At the other end of the spectrum a man may father a child as the result of a one night stand, or even by rape; this unmarried father is not likely to play any part in the child's life.

The quotation in the question says that the unmarried father has a potentially significant status, implying that this has not always been the case. Historically, the law tended to stereotype the unmarried father as either being 'in denial' or as some sort of social deviant who existed to pressurise, harass and blackmail the mother of his child. No legal procedures existed whereby an actively involved father, living with the mother, could acquire legal recognition of this fact, and there was no way in which he could legally share parental responsibility with the mother.

The Law Commission decided in its 'Report on Illegitimacy' (1982), not to abolish illegitimacy altogether, as to do so would mean not only that all children would be the same, but that all parents would also be the same and have equal parental rights and duties in relation to their children. To give indiscriminately all unmarried fathers equal rights fails—the argument ran—to distinguish between the many different types and situations and could lead to harassment, blackmail and disruption of new family units. It was decided to not automatically equate the legal position of the unmarried father with that of the mother (1982 Law Com. No. 118).

For the 'unmarried' father, therefore, the starting point is that he has no automatic 'parental responsibility' (PR) for his children: the mother of a non-marital child has sole PR (s. 2(2), Children Act 1989). The father can, however, acquire it; he just has to take positive steps to do so and he thus has a potentially significant status.

PR ('all the rights, duties, powers, responsibilities and authority which by law a parent of a child has in relation to the child and his property' (s. 3, Children Act (CA) 1989)) is a key concept of the 1989 Act and its importance is emphasised by the fact that the Act makes it easier for unmarried fathers to acquire parental responsibility. However, the amount of parental involvement allowed him will ultimately be left to the discretion of the court, applying the welfare principle (s. 1, CA 1989). Also, acquisition of any legal status is, of course, dependent on paternity being established if there is a dispute: there is no rebuttable presumption of parentage from cohabitation (in marked contrast to the marital position).

So what are the options available to the unmarried father? If he is living with the mother and child (or not living with them but able to reach agreement), he could suggest a parental responsibility agreement, whereby the father and mother can, by agreement, provide for the father to have parental responsibility (s. 4(1)(b)). The agreement is only effective if in the form prescribed by regulations and filed in the Principal Registry of the Family Division. The court's role here is administrative only, i.e. there is no investigation of the child's welfare, but the agreement can be terminated by court order, when the welfare principle does apply. In the early years it seems that many agreements were forged and that, after witnessing by a court official or JP was introduced in 1994, numbers fell. Even now, only a few thousand are registered annually, although in *Re X (Parental Responsibility Agreement)* [2000] 1 FLR 517, they were held to be an important example of the right to respect for family life under Art. 8, ECHR 1957. It was also there held that the right to enter such agreements continues whilst the child is in care. It should be noted that (as with parental responsibility *orders* below) the court can subsequently excise his status on the application of anyone with parental responsibility, or the child with leave of the court. Such an order was made in *Re P (Terminating Parental Responsibility)* [1995] 1 FLR 1048 on the basis that the father had been imprisoned for assaulting the nine-week-old daughter in question.

If the relationship with the mother has broken down then a parental responsibility agreement is unlikely to be a realistic option and the unmarried father may instead apply to the court for a parental responsibility order (PRO) for the child (s. 4(1)(a), CA 1989). On an application by the father for a PRO the welfare of the child is the paramount consideration (s. 1, CA 1989). The non-intervention principle (s. 1(5)) also applies and the court will only make an order if it is in the child's best interests to do so.

The 1989 Act is silent as to the factors which the court should consider, but there is now judicial guidance: *Re H (Illegitimate Children: Father: Parental Rights) (No. 2)* [1991] 1 FLR 214 *per* Balcombe LJ. Relevant factors would appear to include: how the PRO is likely to benefit the child, the relationship the father has with the child, the reasons for the application, his level of commitment to and involvement with the child, and whether making the order is likely to destabilise the child's new family unit. But in *Re H (Parental Responsibility)* [1998] 1 FLR 855, the Court of Appeal held that the Balcombe list is neither exhaustive nor determinative and that the welfare principle is the over-riding criterion.

PROs made have risen to nearly 10,000 p.a. in recent years and it seems that only rarely will an application be refused (267 in 2003) as the actual powers involved can be controlled (if necessary) by the court's powers under the 1989 Act. But there is no presumption that the order be made: injuring both the child concerned, and another child by a former partner (*Re H (Parental Responsibility)* [1998] 1 FLR 855); possession of pederastic *material* (*Re P (Parental Responsibility)* [1998] 2 FLR 96), and being brain-damaged in a road accident (*M v M (Parental Responsibility)* [1999] 2 FLR 737, have all led to refusals, yet in *Re J-S (Contact: Parental Responsibility)* [2003] 1 FLR 399 (CA) a finding of violence against the father did not preclude a PRO–he had shown commitment, attachment and reasons (CAR).

If the unmarried father is successful in getting a PRO, then it means, *inter alia*, that he acquires a status as a parent for adoption proceedings and his consent must be obtained or dispensed with; he acquires the right to appoint a guardian for the child (s. 5(3), CA 1989), the right to consent to the child's marriage (s. 3, Marriage Act 1949 as amended) and the right to object to the provision of and removal from local authority accommodation (s. 20, CA 1989). It has important implications for Hague Convention (abduction) proceedings.

Applications for a PRO are 'family proceedings' and the court may make any s. 8, CA 1989 order (e.g. a contact order) instead of a PRO if it considers that the best way of promoting the child's welfare. The unmarried father may also apply as of right (*M v C and Calderdale MBC* [1992] Fam Law 571) for a s. 8 order. Hence he may apply for a residence order. If successful, the court must make a s. 4, PRO to confer on him the powers and responsibilities of a parent (s. 12(1)) otherwise his parental responsibility would be limited (e.g. no right to appoint a guardian) and would end if the residence order ended.

The unmarried father is likely to apply for a s. 8 contact order with a PRO but it is possible to apply for contact on its own. Although a father's claims are not usually ignored it may well be that the child's welfare would best be served by no order being made, as any order is likely to prove unworkable in such circumstances (see *Re SM (A Minor) (Natural Father: Access)* [1991] 2 FLR 333 where contact by the unmarried father was ended when the mother remarried, as continued contact was of no benefit to the child and was likely to destabilise the new family unit).

A decade and more has passed since both the coming into force of Children Act and Sach's remark (both 1991), and the passing of time has given her viewpoint some prescience. The growth in numbers, both of non-marital children and non-marital cohabitation—together with much evidence that such parents are unaware of the father's lack of equal standing, see R. Pickford, 'Unmarried Fathers and the Law', in *What is a Parent?* ed A. Bainham et al (1999) at p. 143—have challenged the view that there should be no automatic recognition of unmarried fathers. On the other hand, discrimination on the grounds of sex/marital status (art. 14 ECHR) and respect for family life (art. 8) have yet to win a court case for such men, and the spectres of the rapist, mis-using, or inactive father are still raised today.

Yet why should an increasing number of children be condemned to having only one parent with parental responsibility (problematic on death), and why should a similar number of men be lumbered with financial obligation but no concomitant recognition? In 1998, a Lord Chancellor's Department Paper, *Court Procedures for the Determination of Paternity* stated that 'all' parents should be encouraged to exercise responsibility, and art. 18 of the 1989 UNCRC has long recognised the principle of joint parental responsibility. Accordingly, the Adoption and Children Act 2002 by inserting s. 4(1)(a) into the 1989 Act will give the 'unmarried' father parental responsibility if he becomes registered as the child's father (still losing it in the same ways as if gained by order or agreement, see above). On current practice, this would hugely expand the numbers who qualify—nearly 200,000 men p.a. on current figures—and presumably satisfy, on the basis that such men are presumably acting as social parents, those critics who would otherwise deny them (and their children) full recognition. Yet even this reform is probably just a staging post to complete parity: why should the Children Act 1989 allow non-resident divorced fathers—and mothers—to retain their parental responsibility whilst denying their non-marital counterparts from the start?

Q Question 2

Last year, Rose (a single woman) had a brief affair with Fred, a wealthy married man 20 years older than herself. After Rose had ended the relationship, she discovered that she was pregnant. Fred offered to leave his wife and to marry Rose but Rose did not want anything more to do with him. The baby, John, was born six months ago. Fred and his wife never had any children and he is delighted that he now has a son. He continually asks to see John and says that he wants to be actively involved in the child's upbringing. Rose is now living with Simon who is willing and able to support both of them. They plan to marry and wish to bring John up as their own child without interference from Fred.

Last week Fred told Rose that John would be at a real disadvantage if they (Fred and Rose) did not get married and make him legitimate. During the heated argument which followed, and in an attempt to make Fred leave them alone, Rose told Fred that he might not be John's father anyway.

Rose has no intention of claiming anything from Fred. She has, however, discovered that Fred's father has just died leaving his estate to be divided equally between all his grandchildren, and wonders whether John would have a claim.

Advise Rose.

Commentary

Here you are asked to advise the mother of an 'illegitimate' child, who is being (she will argue) pestered by the child's father. The facts raise a number of issues which require discussion and you should try to use all the information you are given.

With any problem involving children you can expect to have to weave into your answer the pervasive principles and concepts, i.e. parental responsibility, welfare and non-intervention are all going to be relevant. You can begin by reassuring a mother in such circumstances on the issue of *prima facie* parental responsibility and then go on to deal with the specific areas of concern. The main one is obviously what the father's rights are and what action he could take in relation to the child. Look at the facts here: they have never cohabited, the affair was brief and the mother is now living with someone else whom she intends to marry. All this may well influence the outcome of any application by the natural father.

Proof of paternity is the key to the father's application for parental responsibility or for a s. 8 order without leave and indeed the relationship will also have to be proved before any claim can be made on the grandfather's estate. Therefore, at some point in your answer you will need to include a discussion of how paternity can be proved.

You are told that 'Rose has no intention of claiming anything from Fred', indicating that you are not expected to discuss child support (see chapter 14). It is often difficult to avoid overlaps completely between different chapters and occasionally, in an effort to do so, the facts of the problem might appear rather unrealistic, as they do here. In reality, of course, despite what Rose says, the issue of child support would be discussed, to ensure that Rose is properly advised.

Finally, is there anything in what Fred has said about the baby being at a disadvantage if his parents do not marry? Rose is likely to be concerned about this and you will need to look at the status of the illegitimate child in succession law (which this examiner—unlike some family law teachers—has presumably covered during the course).

Plan and structure your answer and do not forget that, by the end of it, Rose should know exactly where she stands—which may, of course, include a degree of uncertainty!

- 'Unmarried' father's legal position

- Proof of paternity

- CA 1989, s. 8 Orders

- Disadvantages of 'illegitimacy'

- Succession rights

:̣Q̣: **Suggested answer**

Here we are asked to advise Rose, the mother of six-month-old John, born as the result of a brief affair with Fred.

First, Rose's mind can be put at rest to some extent by telling her that as the mother of an 'illegitimate' child all parental responsibility currently vests in her alone (s. 2, Children Act (CA) 1989). Fred, however, obviously wants to be recognised as John's father: we are told that he keeps asking to see him and that he wants to be actively involved in the child's upbringing. Rose, on the other hand, is now planning to marry Simon and wishes to forget about Fred (at least so far as active-fatherhood ambitions are concerned). But can she do this? What, if anything, can Fred, as an 'unmarried' father, do? There are a number of options open to him, though whether he would be successful in any application remains to be seen. The paramount objective is the welfare of John (s. 1(1)) and any order made must be in his best interests. The non-intervention principle (s. 1(5)) will also apply so the court will only make an order if it thinks that to do so is better for the child than making no order at all.

Before Fred can acquire any legal status in relation to John, the relationship has to be established and paternity will have to be proved, particularly as Rose has told Fred that he might not be John's father anyway (though this was said, we are told, in the heat of the moment and to try to make Fred go away). The Family Law Reform Act 1969, s. 20(1), empowers a court to require the use of genetic tests in any civil proceedings involving an issue of paternity. Each individual's DNA is unique and provides a sort of genetic fingerprint of identity. It is inherited from one's parents and by elimination it is possible to determine precisely which characteristic must be inherited from the disputed parent. DNA testing could here determine beyond any reasonable doubt whether Fred is John's father, i.e. a *positive* test (*Re A (A Minor) (Paternity: Refusal of Blood Test)* [1994] 2 FLR 463), not mere probability. The Family Law Reform Act (FLRA) 1987 now gives courts a general power to direct the use of scientific tests to ascertain parentage, as DNA testing can be carried out not just on blood but on other bodily fluids and tissue.

Once Fred has proved that he is John's father then he can apply to the court for a number of orders. However, it should be noted here that if Rose opposed his application for blood or DNA tests, Fred may be stopped in his tracks at this point, like the natural father in *Re F (A Minor: Paternity Tests)* [1993] Fam Law 163. The court may decide as it did in that case, that there is no realistic prospect of Fred succeeding in his application for parental responsibility or contact, as it would not be for John's benefit, and that consequently to establish who John's natural father is would make no real difference. An order for blood tests might disturb the stability of the family unit and should therefore be refused. However, it will in fact be in Rose's interests for paternity to be established if a claim is to be made on Fred's father's estate, or should child support become an issue. Moreover she should be advised that the court generally prefers the truth to come out (*Re H (Paternity: Blood Test)* [1996] 2 FLR 65) where Ward LJ said that 'every child has the right to know the truth unless his welfare clearly justifies the cover up', citing art. 7 of UNCRC 1989 which refers to the 'right to know' one's parents. Now, in *Re H and A (Children)* [2002] EWCA Civ 383, a test was ordered despite the husband's statement that he would leave the wife and children were it to show that he had not fathered them. If the court is not impressed by Rose's argument that DNA testing might destabilise her family unit with Simon, it would not be in her advantage to refuse to supply her and John's samples, as that would allow the court to presume Fred's paternity under s. 23(1) of the FLRA 1969.

Assuming that paternity is proved, what is available to Fred? Two options can be quickly dismissed as unrealistic: a s. 4 parental responsibility agreement (as Rose will obviously not agree to Fred acquiring equal parental responsibility) and a s. 8 residence order (as on the facts, the welfare of the child would dictate that John should remain with Rose). Fred could, however, apply for a s. 4 parental responsiblity order (PRO) and/or a s. 8 contact order. The effect of the PRO—although it can be rescinded—would be to equate Fred's legal position, at least during its tenure, with that of a married father. The court, applying the welfare principle (s. 1, CA 1989) must be satisfied that it is appropriate so to do. The court will look at how the PRO is likely to benefit John; what relationship Fred has with John and why he is applying for parental responsibility; how committed he is and whether the PRO would be likely to destabilise John's family unit (*Re H (Illegitimate Children: Father: Parental Rights) (No. 2)* [1991] 1 FLR 214). Fred would obviously be applying for a PRO because he genuinely wants to be actively involved with the child's upbringing and Rose should be advised that he could well succeed. In *Re C (Minors) (Parental Rights)* [1992] 2 All ER 86, it was held that a PRO may be granted even though there may be a problem enforcing the rights which arise—that can be resolved by a s. 8 order. Even acrimony between the parties need not be fatal (*Re P (A Minor) (Parental Responsibility Order)* [1994] 1 FLR 578) nor even violence (*Re J-S (Contact: Parental Responsibility)* [2003] 1 FLR 399 (CA)).

In any event, Fred as father could apply for a contact order (s. 8, CA 1989). However, despite Baker P's statement in *S v O* [1977] 3 FLR 15 that 'children, whether born in wedlock or not, need fathers' it is doubtful whether John's welfare would be served by having contact with Fred whose only real claim here is that he is the natural father. There is no meaningful father/son relationship here, and Rose does not want to be reminded of their brief affair, particularly now that she intends to marry Simon. On the other hand, Rose should be cautioned that maternal intransigence is not self-fulfilling in law: in *Re H (A Minor) (Contact)* [1994] 2 FLR 776, Butler Sloss LJ said that there should not be 'a selfish parents' charter'. Here, indirect contact—in *Re O (Contact: Imposition of Conditions)* [1995] 2 FLR 124, the mother was required to supply the father with updates on the boy's progress—might be the answer. Rose must be advised that imprisonment for contempt may await those who defy court orders (see *Re M (Intractable Contact Dispute: Interim Care Order)* [2003] 2 FLR 636) and that in *Re H (A Minor) (Parental Responsiblity)* [1993] 1 FLR 484, the Court of Appeal held that although the mother's new relationship might preclude a contact order, a PRO would not be ruled out. Another possibility, also with reference to reluctant resident parents, might be 'supervised' contact as in *F v F (Contempt: Committal)* [1998] 2 FLR 237 where the mother was ordered to hand over the children to the person in charge of a Contact Centre—and was made subject to a committal order, actionable if she did not comply. If the court is minded to order contact, it must first consider the nature of the resident parent's hostility (the term 'parental alienation syndrome' has had a mixed reception in this context) and, second, address the enforcement problem.

Two further issues need to be discussed. First, is what Fred says true, i.e. John will be disadvantaged if Fred and Rose do not marry and make John legitimate? The general principle, now embodied in the Family Law Reform Act 1987, is that there should be equality for all children at law, regardless of whether they are born in wedlock or not. Section 1 of the 1987 Act introduces a new rule of construction that references to relationship are to be construed without regard to whether or not the mother and father were married to each other at any particular time. Discrimination cannot be justified and is inconsistent with UK international obligations under the European Convention on Human Rights (1950) and the European Convention on the Legal Status of Children Born out of Wedlock (1981). The position of the illegitimate child in relation to maintenance and inheritance was largely assimilated with that of the legitimate child by the 1987 Act. The one remaining difference which affects John is that he falls into the category of children who do not have a normal relationship with both parents. But there is no longer any label attaching to him, and he is rarely, if ever, likely to be conscious of any distinction between himself and a legitimate child. Section 9 of the Nationality, Asylum and Immigration Act 2002 now enables British citizenship to be bestowed by a proven parental link. John could not, however, inherit his father's title or succeed to the throne (the Act of Settlement 1701 restricts rights of succession to legitimate offspring, and hereditary peerages granted before FLRA 1987 are limited to heirs 'lawfully begotten' as confirmed by the House of Lords in *Re Moynihan* [2000] 1 FLR 113). It seems unlikely that these provisions will affect John.

The last issue needing to be discussed is that Fred's father has died leaving his estate to be divided equally between all his grandchildren. One assumes from this that there is a will, in which case by s. 19, FLRA 1987, all words such as children, or as here grandchildren, are to be construed as including illegitimate children unless a contrary intention appears. In the absence of such a contrary intention, John will in fact have a claim on Fred's father's estate, provided of course that the relationship can be proved.

Q Question 3

The Children Act 1989 adopts the policy of incorporating the best features of wardship into the statutory framework, thereby obviating the need to resort to wardship in many cases. The inevitable result is a greatly reduced role for wardship.

Discuss.

Commentary

Most family law courses cover wardship at some point. It is a long-established and extremely flexible jurisdiction. As Andrew Bainham points out (*Children—the New Law*, Jordan & Sons Ltd, 1990) and as all Gilbert and Sullivan fans will undoubtedly be aware, the concept was incorporated into 'The Pirates of Penzance' which provides an illustration of one of wardship's original uses, i.e. to prevent a minor taking 'a first rate opportunity to be married with impunity'!

Wardship had proved to be very popular and much used. In 1991, 4,961 originating summonses were issued, 2,752 by local authorities and 2,209 by others (Judicial Statistics 1991). The Children Act 1989 has had a significant effect on the role of wardship, and highlights the difference between wardship and other inherent jurisdiction of the High Court over children. In 1992, the year after the Children Act 1989 came into force, the number of originating summonses issued had fallen to 492 (Children Act Advisory Committee Annual Report 1992/3, p. 25). In 1993, there were only 269 wardship applications (White, Carr and Lowe, *The Children Act in Practice*, 2nd edn, 1995). The *Judicial Statistics Annual Reports* ceased to give statistics about wardship in 1992.

This question is asking you to consider the role of wardship today in the light of the Children Act 1989. You must address the issues raised in the title quotation and avoid writing 'all you know' about wardship. You will need to define wardship and to discuss its 'best features'. To assess whether it now has a reduced role you will need to look at its role prior to the 1989 Act in both public and private law cases. Use examples from case law here. The better student will remember that wardship was specifically referred to by Butler Sloss LJ in the Cleveland Report in 1988 and that there has been a Law Commission Working Paper on the subject (*Wards of Court* (1987 Law Com. No. 101)). You should then consider how the Act incorporates wardship's best features and whether this, together with the further statutory restrictions imposed on its use, will in fact mean a much reduced role for wardship.

It is unlikely that many students will have read the leading work on wardship, i.e. Lowe and White, *Wards of Court*, but you should provide evidence of some wider reading. Further reading may include: N. V. Lowe, 'The Role of Wardship in Child Care Cases' [1989] *Fam Law* 38; Andrew Bainham, 'The Children Act 1989: The Future of Wardship' [1990] *Fam Law* 270.

Answer plan

- Wardship—one use of High Court's inherent jurisdiction.

- Applicant? Anyone with sufficient and proper interest.

- Advantages of wardship.

- Wardship before the Children Act 1989. Private and public law cases.

- Wardship after the Children Act 1989. Private law—'open door' policy of Children Act 1989. Flexible orders—s. 8, Children Act 1989. Residual role—child abduction—where continuing judicial control desirable.

- Local authorities and wardship. Restrictions imposed by Children Act 1989.

- Inherent jurisdiction of the High Court.

:Q: Suggested answer

Wardship is just one use of the High Court's inherent jurisdiction over children and provides what many see as an essential residual protection for children. Anyone with a sufficient and proper interest in a child may, without leave, seek to make the child a ward of court. The child becomes a ward immediately on the issuing of the originating summons (s. 41(2), Supreme Court Act 1981) and becomes subject to wardship's 'all-embracing parental nature, implying automatic, comprehensive and enduring protection' (Andrew Bainham, *Children—The New Law*).

Wardship is flexible. No ground needs to be established to invoke the jurisdiction, which is characterised by the 'golden thread' which runs through it, namely that the welfare of the child is considered 'first, last and all the time' (*per* Dunn J in *Re D (A Minor) (Justices' Decision: Review)* [1977] 3 All ER 481).

The advantages of wardship stem from the fact that cases are heard in the High Court (which is suited to hearing long and complex cases, with one continuous hearing by an experienced judge), under a largely non-statutory jurisdiction in which there are the widest possible powers to protect a child, and which can easily adapt to changing conditions. The unique feature of wardship, however, is that legal control over the child vests in the court, which takes over ultimate responsibility for the child and 'no important step in the child's life can be taken without the court's consent' (*per* Cross J in *Re S (Infants)* [1967] 1 All ER 202) without committing contempt of court. The prior sanction of the court is therefore required if, for example, a ward wishes to marry or to leave the jurisdiction. This obviously places a considerable burden on judicial resources and is seen by some as a disadvantage of the jurisdiction, others being delay and cost.

So what role did wardship play before the Children Act 1989? First, it was used in private law disputes by individuals, e.g. parents, relatives, friends, in situations where immediate freezing of the position was required. Examples include preventing child abduction or irrevocable surgery such as abortion (*Re G-U (A Minor) (Wardship)* [1984] FLR 811), or solving novel cases where the court's expertise and wide powers were advantageous (*Re F (In Utero)* [1988] 2 All ER 193). Wardship additionally had a role in public law cases. Any child can be made a ward and, until the 1989 Act, this included a child in care. Consequently wardship was often used to question local authority decisions about children in care. However, in *A* v *Liverpool City Council* [1981] 2 FLR 222, where a mother in effect wished to challenge the access arrangements to her child, the House of Lords decided that there is no general reviewing power in the court over local authority decisions and wardship cannot be used to this end. The judicially imposed restrictions on the use of wardship meant that it was really only an option in such circumstances if a local authority was willing to waive the jurisdictional point and was happy for the case to be looked at on its merits (*A* v *B and Hereford and Worcestershire County Council* [1986] 1 FLR 289). Wardship might also be invoked if a lacuna could be found in the statutory scheme, but only one left inadvertently and not as a matter of deliberate policy. Such gaps were increasingly difficult to find.

By comparison, local authorities were encouraged to use wardship as providing another route into care. Wardship in this context was invoked to commit a child into care or to keep a child in care where, for example, a ground for an order under the Children and Young Persons Act 1969 could not be established. Wardship was the only option if the authority wanted to protect a child at risk of harm, as the 1969 Act did not provide for predicted harm. Similarly, where a court refused an order and the authority had no right of appeal, wardship would be used (*Re C (A Minor) (Justices' Decision: Review)* [1981] 2 FLR 62). It could also be used to supplement local authority powers in relation to children in care, e.g. to solve medical problems, to prevent publicity, to obtain injunctions. Gradually local authorities started to use wardship not just in situations where the statutory scheme proved to be lacking, but increasingly in preference to an existing and available statutory alternative; a use disapproved of by Dillon LJ *obiter* in *D (A Minor)* v *Berkshire County Council* [1987] 1 All ER 20.

It can be seen from the above that in both private and public law disputes wardship was regarded as a valuable and useful jurisdiction with a significant role to play.

Indeed in 1988 Butler Sloss LJ said that wardship had proved invaluable in Cleveland to enable issues to be fully considered and that it should continue to play a role in care proceedings (Report of the Inquiry into Child Abuse in Cleveland 1987).

In 1987 the Law Commission put forward three options for redefining the role of wardship (*Wards of Court* (1987 Law Com. Working Paper No. 101)). The first option was to retain wardship in its existing form as an independent jurisdiction alongside the new statutory scheme; the second, to retain it as a residuary jurisdiction; the third, to abolish wardship as a separate jurisdiction and to incorporate its most satisfactory features into the statutory code. The Children Act 1989 seems to have settled for a combination of the second and third of the Law Commission's options. Wardship is not abolished: the jurisdiction remains intact and retains a residual role, to support but not supplant the new statutory framework.

As the title of the question suggests, one of the underlying policies of the Act is to vest in the courts, powers and procedures formerly unique to wardship. This is achieved in a number of ways. An 'open door' policy of access to the courts is introduced together with easier access to the High Court. In all 'family proceedings' (which includes wardship), hearsay evidence is admissible and the whole range of s. 8 orders can be made. In addition, the need to invoke wardship is reduced in that wardship powers are narrowed and the powers of the courts under other jurisdictions are expanded.

Private law cases are probably the least affected by the 1989 Act in that here wardship remains as an alternative to the new statutory orders, whether or not it would be possible to achieve the same result under the statutory scheme. Even in the rare cases where private individuals resort to wardship, it may be declined by the court. Wardship is expensive and the prohibited steps and specific issue orders (s. 8) provide flexible orders similar to those that were once only obtainable in wardship. For many people wardship was the only means of access to the courts. However, the 1989 Act opened that door—to parents as of right and to third parties with leave. Nevertheless, wardship in this context still has unique features which make it attractive, e.g. no leave is required; there is immediate access as of right to the High Court and immediate freezing of the *status quo*. Consequently it is likely to continue to be of particular use in child abduction cases (*Re S (Leave to Remove from Jurisdiction Securing Return from Holiday)* [2001] 2 FLR 498) and others where continuing judicial control is considered desirable (*Re T (A Minor) (Child: Representation)* [1993] 4 All ER 518).

The Act is silent on the use of wardship by individuals against a local authority and it is assumed that the judicial restrictions imposed by *A* v *Liverpool City Council* [1981] 2 FLR 222 are preserved. The provisions of the Children Act, particularly the presumption of reasonable contact (s. 34) and the new rights of appeal, mean that many of the old grievances about decisions relating to children in care should disappear. Presumably if any inadvertently left lacunae are discovered, the court could use wardship in its role as a safety net.

It is in the context of use of wardship by a local authority that the Children Act has had the greatest impact. Previously the main function of wardship here was to underpin the statutory scheme and to remedy any deficiencies. It follows, therefore, that if the scheme is modernised and the defects remedied, then wardship could lose its *raison d'etre* and become redundant. Certainly the need for local authority use of wardship is reduced in that orders are available on prospective grounds, there are full rights of appeal and the county and High Courts have concurrent jurisdiction to hear care proceedings. The Act, however, goes further: wardship and care become incompatible and wardship is made no longer available to a local authority (s. 100). The effect is that a local authority is precluded from acquiring rights over children which it cannot get under the statute, which in turn aims to provide improved machinery for protecting children. Section 31 now provides the sole ground for compulsory action and a local authority cannot ever use wardship to take a child into care, to keep a child in local authority accommodation or to acquire any aspect of parental responsibility (s. 100(2)). These provisions remove wardship as a safety net completely in such cases. Nigel Lowe ('Caring for Children' (1989) 139 *NLJ* 87) feels that the Act has gone too far here and that the role of wardship of underpinning the statutory grounds for care should be preserved to ensure that no child is ever left without protection.

If a local authority wishes to resolve a specific question about a child being looked after, then it may now with leave invoke the inherent jurisdiction of the High Court (s. 100), a jurisdiction quite separate from wardship and use of which does not place the child under the ultimate responsibility of the court. Leave under s. 100(3) will be granted if the court is satisfied that first, the result sought cannot be achieved under any statutory jurisdiction and secondly, that there is reasonable cause to believe that if the jurisdiction is not exercised the child is likely to suffer significant harm. In relation to a child in care, the first condition should cause no problems, as none of the s. 8 orders is available to the local authority (s. 9(1) and (2)) and use of the inherent jurisdiction is now the only option. The second condition has been criticised by Nigel Lowe for being too narrow. He argues ((1989) 139 *NLJ* 87) that a test based on the child's welfare would suffice when a local authority is concerned about a single aspect of its upbringing. If leave is granted, the authority will be able to seek High Court assistance on difficult or sensitive issues (a sort of specific issues jurisdiction for children in care) (see *Re W (A Minor) (Medical Treatment: Court's Jurisdiction)* [1992] 4 All ER 627; *Re O (A Minor) (Medical Treatment)* [1993] 2 FLR 149 and *Re M (Care: Leave to Interview Child)* [1995] 1 FLR 825). However, the court will not assume overall control as with wardship.

In *Re M and J (Wardship: Supervision and Residence Orders)* [2003] 2 FLR 541, the local authority applied for care orders in respect of two children. It was held that, in the exceptional circumstances of the case it was appropriate to take the exceptional course of continuing wardship and also making both supervision and residence orders. Under the wardship jurisdiction, the various adults involved would be allowed to return to court and ask a third party to assist with decision-making about the children. In another case (*Re W and X (Wardship: Relatives Rejected as Foster Carers)* [2004] 1 FLR 415) a care order would not have achieved what the local authority wanted for children who were with maternal grandparents as an emergency placement. Even though there were some serious concerns about aspects of the grandparents' parenting skills, the local authority considered that the children should remain with the grandparents on the basis that the authority and the grandparents shared parental responsibility. However, the grandparents were then rejected as foster carers. The problem then was that under Fostering Services Regulations 2002 (SI 2002/57) (2002 Regulations), the local authority could not place children in their care with a person not approved as a foster carer. However, the best interests of the children required that they remain in the care of the grandparents. Yet, outstanding concerns meant that the placement should be subject to long-term external scrutiny. Here, it was decided that the wardship jurisdiction could justifiably be used to fill this significant lacuna. Wardship, together with a supervision order and a raft of orders under the Children Act 1989, s. 8, provided the best available solution for the needs of these children.

As Andrew Bainham points out ('*Children—The New Law*') the restrictions on wardship imposed by the Children Act 1989 create an imbalance between public and private law. Where the state is involved wardship may well become a thing of the past, whereas in private disputes it does have a continuing role. As a means of resolving all kinds of disputes over children wardship cannot really be matched, even by the statutory framework of the 1989 Act. As has been illustrated wardship still has a role to play, but one has to agree that the restrictions imposed on its use, and the greater flexibility in other family proceedings mean that the role has indeed been greatly reduced.

Q Question 4

One of the principal aims of the Children Act 1989 was to ensure that more attention was paid to the child's voice. Consider the extent to which this aim has been achieved.

Commentary

A general question on such a significant piece of legislation as the Children Act will quite commonly be included on an exam paper. You may be asked to assess the Act from any one of a number of different viewpoints; here it is in terms of the child's voice. This requires a sound knowledge and appreciation of the statute's provisions and its underlying philosophy, so that you can scan the Act and pick out provisions which appear to give more attention to the child's voice and, therefore, lend support to the title statement.

Such a question will not take the well-prepared student by surprise. If you have read even the basic texts on the Act, comments about the child's views, wishes and perspective are legion.

You will need to take specific substantive examples from the statute which give the child a voice, and there are quite a few to choose from. You could quite legitimately, by way of introduction, refer briefly to the previous position, including common law and the *Gillick* decision, as the phrase 'more attention' begs the question how much was paid before, but emphasis must be on the Children Act provisions and their subsequent development. You will need to consider the general principles and then to review both the private and public law provisions from the perspective required by the title.

This is not one of the harder questions, either in content or instruction. Your revision programme should have included spending time not just learning a list of provisions but looking at those provisions from different perspectives. It is a good idea to assess the Act from the point of view of all the main players, i.e. the child, the parents, the local authority, the court, and even to make lists of the good and bad features from each standpoint. Then you will be more than ready for this question or others on the 1989 Act.

- *Gillick*-competence

- The welfare principle

- s. 1(3)(a)—child's 'wishes and feelings'

- s. 8, Applications by child

- Public law and children's guardians

:Ọ́: **Suggested answer**

Prior to the implementation of the Children Act 1989, in both public and private law, although mature children had the ear of the court in some proceedings, in many cases lip-service only was paid to the child's wishes and views. At common law, before the decision in *Gillick v West Norfolk and Wisbech Area Health Authority* [1986] 1 FLR 224, the child's views were largely irrelevant. Although the law did recognise that it was usually futile for a parent to try to force his views on a mature child, the child's level of intellectual or emotional development was not relevant in deciding the extent of parental authority. However, the House of Lords in *Gillick* changed this by deciding that parents' rights to take decisions 'yield to the child's right to make his own decisions when he reaches a sufficient understanding and intelligence to be capable of making up his own mind on the matter requiring decision' (*per* Lord Scarman). Whether a child is *Gillick*-competent depends on his emotional and intellectual maturity. The decision means that the mature minor can decide whether to do or not to do something provided that he understands fully the complexity of the issues involved. This includes the right to consent to, and also one would assume the right to refuse, medical treatment, though Lord Donaldson has said that a parent can still give valid consent even if a mature minor refuses treatment (*Re R (A Minor) (Wardship: Medical Treatment)* [1991] 4 All ER 177), and the court can override the mature minor's refusal or consent in the interests of the child's welfare (*Re S (A Minor) (Consent to Medical Treatment)* [1994] 2 FLR 1065). Whether such child will be mollified or frustrated by having first been heard is, of course, a moot point.

A number of provisions in the Children Act 1989 now give statutory recognition to the claims of older children to have an independent say on issues affecting them, and a greater degree of involvement in decision making. The Act embodies the principle of respect for the child who is to be seen as an individual and not as an object of concern and recognises in both public and private law cases the importance of taking the child's wishes into account commensurate with his age and understanding.

To assess the extent to which the Act ensures that more attention is paid to the child's voice, it is necessary to examine a number of specific provisions which appear to support the statement.

Section 1 of the Act provides that when a court determines any question with respect to the upbringing of a child or the administration of a child's property, the child's welfare is to be the court's paramount consideration. This could be described as the main message of the Act and ensures that any decision taken in either a public or private law case, where the child's upbringing is central, is the one which best promotes the child's welfare. Section 1(3) contains a checklist of factors to which the court must normally have regard when considering whether to make an order. No weight is ascribed to any particular factor but the list focuses on the needs of the child and his views. The first factor on the list (s. 1(3)(a)) is the 'ascertainable wishes and feelings of the child' (considered in the light of his age and understanding). This obviously gives the child a voice. More regard is to be paid to the child's perspective, though being first on the list does not give the child's wishes priority over other items (*Re J (A Minor)* [1992] 2 FCR 785). To ascertain the child's wishes the court will normally rely on the investigations made by a CAFCASS officer or children's guardian.

Clearly the age of the child is likely to be crucial in determining how much weight should be given to his wishes. In *Re P (A Minor) (Education: Child's Wishes)* [1992] 1 FCR 145 the Court of Appeal listened to and paid respect to the views of a 14-year-old boy with regards to his choice of school. Butler Sloss LJ indicated that had the boy been 11 his views would not have carried so much weight. Other factors considered by the court when assessing the weight to be attached to the child's views include the dangers of coaching, the relative importance of the issue, the factual basis of her views, and the danger to the child of being asked to choose between parents. *Re S (Contact: Children's Views)* [2002] EWHC 540 may serve as a warning to parents who do not listen to their children. A father who sought contact with his three children aged 16, 14 and 12 was found to have hectored them, failing to learn that his attitude was counter-productive. It was held that there was no point in making an order with regard to the eldest who was opposed to it, the middle boy was required merely to make himself available for contact by common agreement, and the youngest, who had maintained contact, was allowed some choice about the form it should take in future. The court doubted the quality of contact achievable only by court order.

The other two general principles in s. 1 of the Children Act, i.e. non-intervention (s. 1(5)) and the disapproval of delay (s. 1(2)) can also be viewed in terms of listening to a child's voice. The non-intervention principle ensures that no order is made unless it is shown to be the best for the child and tends to prioritise adults' views. Thus there is a certain amount of tension between the two in that the court may fail to consider the child's wishes (to listen to his voice) if, for example, on divorce, parents agree and no order is made; yet the 'delay is harmful' principle recognises that a child's sense of time is more acute than that of an adult.

The Children Act allows a child to apply, with leave, for one of the s. 8 orders, i.e. residence, contact, prohibited steps, specific issues. A child can now initiate action: he can instruct a solicitor and obtain legal aid, as since 1990 children have been assessed on their own means making it easier to secure legal aid, so long as the 'merits test' is met. Children may therefore apply with leave for orders allowing them to live with whom they want (*Re T (A Minor) (Child Representation)* [1994] Fam 49) and to have contact (*Re F (Contact: Child in Care)* [1995] 1 FLR 510) with those people they want to see. Leave will be granted if the court is satisfied that the child has sufficient understanding to make the application (s. 10(8)). The judge must be convinced that the child can understand the consequences of his action. However, there are a number of unreported cases where children as young as 11 have successfully brought proceedings for full or interim residence orders and prohibited steps orders, where there has been a severe breakdown in their relationship with their parents. Sir Stephen Brown P has said that the children cannot start proceedings just because they do not get their own way at home, but the Act does give them the right to be heard and the court will assess their best interests. Such applications should go to the High Court (*Re AD (A Minor)* [1993] Fam Law 405 and *Practice Direction (Family Proceedings Orders: Applications by Children)* [1993] 1 All ER 820). So although there is some compliance with art. 12 UNCRC—the opportunity to be heard in judicial proceedings affecting him—the child's voiced opinion may not prove determinative.

In addition to the above there are other examples of situations where a child has access to the court. The child is a party in all public law cases. Under s. 34, a child in care can apply for contact to be refused where the presumption of contact operates and may question decisions relating to contact in court. He may also apply for a residence order to discharge the care order. A child may also challenge an emergency protection order on its merits by applying 72 hours after the order was made for its discharge (s. 44).

The new provisions relating to children's guardians also ensure that the child's voice is better heard. By s. 41 the court must appoint a children's guardian for a child unless it is not necessary to safeguard his interests. Children's guardians are now appointed at an earlier stage in a wider range of proceedings under the Children Act. The children's guardian's role includes investigating the case, explaining matters to the child and advising the court on the child's best interests and wishes. The child's enhanced right to apply for orders has implications for the guardian who must fully advise him on his rights, and help him to make informed decisions, appointing a solicitor for him where necessary. If no children's guardian is appointed and the child has sufficient understanding to instruct and wants to, then the court may appoint a solicitor to represent the child if it decides it is in the child's interests to be represented.

A number of other public law provisions embody the *Gillick* principle that a mature minor has the right to decide. Where a child assessment order (s. 43), an emergency protection order (s. 44) or an interim care or supervision order (s. 38) is made with a direction relating to examination or assessment, the mature minor has the right to refuse to submit to the assessment. The orders do not authorise medical or psychiatric examination or other assessment which a child of sufficient age and understanding refuses to undergo. Here, unlike other provisions of the Act, it seems that it is not just a case of ascertaining and giving consideration to the child's wishes but that if the child is capable of making an informed decision then his wishes are conclusive. The right to refuse under these provisions has been held at first instance to be limited to the stage of assessment, and not to actual treatment, when the court could override the child's decision (*per* Thorpe J in *Re J (A Minor)* [1992] 2 FCR 785).

A final example of attention being paid to the child's voice is s. 22 of the Act which requires a local authority to ascertain the wishes and feelings of a child being looked after and to give due consideration to them, depending on his age and understanding, before taking a decision which affects him. In addition, the child's religious persuasion, origin, cultural and linguistic background must also be considered. Local authorities must give the child information and explanations so that he can make an informed choice. The child must know his rights and what is available and feel that what he says is not being ignored. Each local authority has to establish a procedure for considering complaints and representations which must be publicised and should be 'user friendly' (s. 26). A child has the right to complain under this provision and must be told of the panel's findings and what changes should result.

The Children Act 1989, as seen from the provisions examined above, certainly pays more than lip-service to the child's wishes. The child is to be treated as an individual with a right to be consulted, kept fully informed and treated with respect commensurate with his age and understanding. Generally, with the exception of refusal to undergo medical examination or assessment, the child's wishes are not conclusive as it is recognised that a child can be influenced by all sorts of factors when expressing his wishes. It is essential that it is the child's welfare which is paramount, not his wishes, and that the ultimate decision should not be his. It is also recognised that a child wants a say in matters affecting him and to feel that he is being listened to. The Children Act 1989 has gone a long way towards ensuring that more attention is paid to the voice of the child and thus appears to have achieved one of its principal aims. Yet the tensions amongst parental power, the child's view and the welfare principle are likely to remain unresolved for the foreseeable future—and perhaps for as long as there are families. Would Part 1 of the Children Bill 2004 improve matters by establishing a new Children's Commissioner to ensure a voice for children and young people? S/he would seek and represent the views of children and young people on how far the issues they have identified as being important (being healthy, staying safe, enjoying and achieving, making a positive contribution and economic well-being) are being achieved.

Further reading

Bainham, A., *et al*, (eds), *Children and Their Families: Contact, Rights and Welfare* (Hart, 2003).

Bridgeman, J., and Monk, D. (eds), *Feminist Perspectives on Child Law* (Cavendish, 2000).

Fionda, J., (ed.), *Legal Concepts of Childhood* (Hart, 2001).

Fortin, J., *Children's Rights and the Developing Law*, 2nd edn (London: Butterworths, 2003).

Herring, J., 'Parents and Children' in J. Herring (ed.), *Family Law: Issues, Debates, Policy* (Willan, 2001).

Kay, E., Tisdale, E., *et al*, 'Children's Participation in Family Law Proceedings: A Step too Far or a Step too Small?' (2004) 21 *The Journal of Social Welfare and Family Law* 17.

Masson, J., 'The Impact of the Adoption and Children Act 2002: Part I—Parental Responsibility' [2003] Fam Law 580.

Munby, Mr Justice, 'Making Sure the Child is Heard' [2004] Fam Law 338, 427.

Assisted reproduction

Introduction

As reproductive technology becomes more successful in assisting infertile couples to produce a child 'of their own', so the technology will become a matter not merely of academic interest to family lawyers, but also of practical importance to family practitioners. This is a fascinating area of family law which raises moral, ethical and legal dilemmas and yet is of practical interest due to the increasing numbers of people who are involved, either as commissioning parents, genetic parents or carrying parents, and not forgetting the resulting children. The Human Fertilisation and Embryology Authority's annual figures, from licensed clinics, for 1 April 2000 to 31 March 2001, show that there were over 8,000 births as a result of *in vitro* fertilisation (IVF) treatment (approximately 22 per cent success (live birth) rate) and 800 births as a result of donor insemination (approximately 11 per cent success (live birth) rate). It can be seen from the figures that a considerable number of people are affected by these treatments. Since the first IVF baby was born in 1978, more than 68,000 children have been born through IVF. IVF births in the UK account for 1 per cent of all births.

A basic awareness of the available technology is necessary, to be able to find your way around the Human Fertilisation and Embryology Act 1990 and any regulations.

Q Question 1

Alma, who is two months pregnant, is married to Boris; they have four children. As Cathy, Alma's sister, is able to conceive a child but unable to carry a child to full term, Alma agreed to a full surrogacy arrangement. Cathy and her husband, Damian, are the genetic parents of the child Alma is carrying. The *in vitro* fertilisation treatment was carried out at a licensed clinic. Boris disapproves of the arrangement.

Alma has received results of tests which show that the child will be born disabled. Damian did not reveal, but was aware at the time of the donation, that there was a history of such a disability in his family.

Boris wants Alma to give birth then hand the child over to Cathy and Damian.

Cathy wants Alma to have an abortion. Damian wants Alma to give birth but he does not wish to raise or acknowledge the child as his own.

Alma seeks your legal advice for herself and for the 'poor motherless and fatherless child' she is carrying.

Commentary

Poor Alma, the reward for her generous act seems to be rejection by all the other parties. You are told what everyone else wants but not given Alma's view. It is for Alma to make a decision and for you to help her by setting out all the options that are open to her. Discuss the legal status of the parties involved and the rights of any child produced as a result of treatment services. As always, take care with the names of the characters, do not confuse them with one another! There are not too many people involved here, but it has been known for confusion to creep in, and it is not unknown for a complete stranger to be introduced so that the marker is to be seen bent over scripts demanding 'Who is Godfrey?'

Answer plan
- Relevant area of law—assisted reproduction. Human Fertilisation and Embryology Act (HFEA) 1990.
- Define surrogacy—full/partial. Surrogacy Arrangements Act 1985. Arrangements not enforceable.
- Define legal mother/father. Apply to facts.
- Parental order, s. 30. Adoption. Apply to facts.
- Congenital Disabilities (Civil Liability) Act 1976 as amended by HFEA 1990.
- Local authority intervention?

:Q: Suggested answer

The Human Fertilisation and Embryology Act (HFEA) 1990 regulates treatment services which assist women to carry children. The Act provides definitions of the legal mother and legal father of a child who has been born as a result of artificial methods of conception. Amongst other methods of assisted conception, the Act covers egg donation, embryo donation, *in vitro* fertilisation (IVF) where an embryo is created outside the human body, and gamete intra fallopian transfer (GIFT) where either the sperm or the egg used has been donated.

As the clinic was licensed by the Human Fertilisation and Embryology Authority (HUFEA), Alma will have received counselling before going ahead with the treatment (s. 13(5) and s. 13(6)). Alma is pregnant and involved in a full surrogacy arrangement. A surrogate mother is a woman who carries a child as a result of an arrangement made before she began to carry the child and with a view to the child being handed over to, and the parental responsibility being met (so far as practicable) by, another person or persons (Surrogacy Arrangements Act 1985, s. 1(2) as amended by the Children Act 1989, sch. 13, para. 56).

Alma refers to the 'poor motherless and fatherless child' she is carrying, but the 1990 Act provides that the woman who is carrying or has carried a child as a result of the placing in her of an embryo or sperm and eggs, and no other woman, is to be treated as the mother of the child (s. 27(1)). So, in law, Alma is the mother of the child. The father of the resulting child is defined in s. 28 as being a husband whose wife receives donated sperm, or an embryo created from donated sperm, unless it is shown that he did not consent. Even though Boris did not consent to the treatment, Alma and the child would still be able to rely on the common law presumption that a child born to a wife is that of her husband, that is, until the husband rebuts the presumption. At this stage, that rebuttal seems likely, as Boris wishes Alma to hand the child over immediately after the birth.

Section 28(6) goes on to provide that the donor whose sperm is used to establish a pregnancy, to which a married woman's husband has not consented, is not to be treated as the father of the child. So Alma appears to be partly right at this stage, her child, when born, will be one of the new legally fatherless children, unless Boris changes his mind and does not rebut the presumption of fatherhood. Alternatively, the court may follow *Re B (Parentage)* [1996] 2 FLR 15, where the sperm donor was not anonymous and there was evidence of a joint enterprise in the artificial insemination, which took place at a licensed clinic. The genetic father was held to be the legal father of the child. He had played an essential role in aiding the woman to achieve what they had both been trying for, namely a pregnancy. If the court were to follow *Re B* then Damian would be the legal as well as the genetic father.

Damian cannot be forced to comply with the surrogacy agreement. The common law position adopted in *A v C* (1978) [1985] FLR 445, that no surrogacy arrangement is enforceable by or against any of the persons making it, is put on a statutory footing in s. 1(A) of the Surrogacy Arrangements Act 1985 (as amended by HFEA 1990, s. 36(1)). Hopefully, Boris may change his mind when the child is born, but, if neither Boris nor Alma want the child when he or she is born, they cannot force Cathy and Damian to take the child. If Cathy and Damian were to change their minds they could apply for a s. 30 order, which is a parental order made in favour of commissioning parents where the child was born to a surrogate mother. The court may make the order subject to certain preconditions, amongst them being the situation which applies here, that the gametes of the husband or the wife, or both, were used to bring about the creation of the embryo. Damian and Cathy must apply for an order within six months of the child's birth and the child's home must be with them. Alma and Boris must agree unconditionally to the making of the order and the court must be satisfied that no money or benefit other than expenses has been given or received in connection with the order. As applications for s. 30 orders rank as family proceedings under the Children Act 1989, it is possible that, in addition, or as an alternative, the court could make s. 8 orders, for example it could make a contact order for Alma to visit, or decide that Alma remain the legal parent and grant a residence order in favour of Cathy and Damian.

If Alma refused to agree to a s. 30, HFEA 1990 order Cathy and Damian may wish to seek adoption. All this seems more hopeful than likely, this is not a 'love tug' child beloved by the tabloids, but appears to be a child no one wants, at the moment. The Children Act 1989 does not state when parental responsibility begins, but a child in the Act is taken to refer to a live child, so although Cathy has stated that she wants Alma to have an abortion, no one other than the woman who is carrying the child, the mother, has the right to be consulted in respect of termination of pregnancy (*Paton* v *British Pregnancy Advisory Service Trustees* [1978] 2 All ER 987 (approved by the European Convention on Human Rights, *Paton* v *UK* [1981] EHRR 408), *C* v *S* [1987] 1 All ER 1230; *Kelly* v *Kelly* [1997] 2 FLR 828).

Alma may not be able to enforce the surrogacy agreement against Damian but he may find that the child born as a result of that agreement may be able to sue him where the child is born disabled. The Congenital Disabilities (Civil Liability) Act 1976, s. 1(A) as amended by the 1990 Act, states that such a child may sue if the child has been born disabled following the placing in the woman of an embryo, or sperm and eggs, or following her artificial insemination and, *inter alia*, the disability results from an act or omission in the course of selection of the embryo or the gametes used to bring about the embryo. The clinic, as defendant, would not be answerable to the child, if at the time the embryo was placed in Alma, Damian knew of the particular risk of the child being born disabled. If Damian had failed to reveal the genetic disease, and the condition could not be revealed by testing, then the clinic would not be at fault. The child would have to sue Damian. In cases where the donor is not known, the child may apply to the court for an order under s. 35 requiring the authority to provide identifying information so that the child may sue under the 1976 Act.

In addition to a possible action in negligence against the clinic, could there be an action under the Consumer Protection Act 1987? Would the courts be prepared to regard Damian's sperm as a product? Another difficulty is that under the 1987 Act 'damage' means 'death or personal injury or any loss of or damage to property' (s. 5(1)), but liability is excluded where the defect in the product causes loss or damage to the product itself. Robert G. Lee and Derek Morgan in *Human Fertilisation and Embryology* (2001, Blackstone), acknowledge that the question of whether gametes or embryos could ever amount to a product within the 1987 Act is, to some, evidence of the moral bankruptcy of this whole area.

If none of the adults takes responsibility when the child is born, the local authority will need to intervene. If the child is abandoned at the hospital the local authority would owe the child, who would be a child in need, not only a general duty to safeguard and protect his or her interests, but a duty to accommodate the child (Children Act 1989, s. 20). Care proceedings may be considered with a view to adoption.

Perhaps the characters here, and their reactions to the situation, illustrate why it was felt necessary for those receiving assisted reproduction treatment to receive counselling before they embark on such a course of action, with all its attendant moral, ethical and practical dilemmas.

Q Question 2

'You cannot put genies back into bottles. You can, however, try to make sure that the genies do not go around granting any old wish. You can give the genies some rules.' Ian Kennedy, 'The Moral Status of the Embryo', in *Treat Me Right: Essays in Medical Law and Ethics* (Oxford: Clarendon Press, 1988).

Does the Human Fertilisation and Embryology Act 1990 give the 'genies' some rules and so provide the right balance between the freedom of science to discover methods which assist human reproduction and the protection of society?

Commentary

Address your answer to the problem. This has been said before but it is worth saying again. There appears to be so little time in an examination that you feel under pressure to start writing as soon as you have read the question superficially; read it again, identify what the examiner wants, then and only then, map out short headings or key words which give a logical structure to a directed answer. It may appear time consuming but in the end time will be saved as you avoid discussing the irrelevant and do not become repetitive or forget to include something which is highly relevant.

Does society need protecting from such scientific discoveries? What issues are involved? Do the men in white coats need to be controlled? Consider the possible exploitation of the basic desire for parenthood.

Remember it is a family *law* question with the emphasis on law. Do not lapse into writing your answer in the current style of media communication which appears to show no interest in facts, or what anyone thinks, but instead is obsessed with how they feel.

Answer plan

- Human Fertilisation and Embryology Act 1990. What does the Act cover?

- Discuss reasons for and against regulation.

- Storage.

- Access to treatment.

- Legal mother/father.

- Anonymity of donors.

⚙️ Suggested answer

If assisted reproduction technology can result in good for some people (see Horne, G., *et al.*, 'Live birth with sperm cryopreserved for 21 years prior to cancer treatment: Case report' [2004] *Human Reproduction* 1448), why should there be any legal intervention into what is a very personal and sensitive issue? Should those who are infertile and wish to seek medical treatment for a medical condition be allowed to do so? Should those who object to such treatment, whether it be for moral, ethical or whatever reasons, be given the opportunity to object?

As the Human Fertilisation and Embryology Bill progressed through Parliament it was said by John Hannam MP that legislation was necessary to regulate research on embryos, to protect the integrity of reproductive medicine, and to protect scientists and clinicians from legal action and sanction.

Among the issues at stake is a threat of exploitation of women, particularly in commercial surrogacy arrangements; a possible impact on the relationship of the infertile couple if a child is produced as a result of donor involvement; the rights of children produced to know their genetic origins; the status of early embryonic life created outside the human body and the commercialisation of human reproduction. Human reproduction technology raises highly charged moral and ethical issues.

Assisted reproduction treatment covers such methods as artificial insemination and *in vitro* fertilisation (IVF), where eggs and sperm, either of the couple or donors, are united in a glass dish. Once fertilisation has occurred and the resultant embryo begins to divide, it is then transferred to the woman's womb. If a woman cannot or will not carry a pregnancy, then it could be transferred to another woman as part of a full surrogacy arrangement.

In gamete intra fallopian transfer (GIFT) the egg and sperm are placed in the fallopian tube for fertilisation, and in zygote intra fallopian transfer (ZIFT) the early embryo is transferred into the fallopian tube and allowed to make its progress into the uterus to implant and develop.

High failure rates in IVF resulted in decisions to replace more than one fertilised egg in the woman so increasing the number of multiple births as a result of IVF. The Human Fertilisation and Embryology Authority announced that from 1 March, 2004, women under the age of 40 will be banned from having more than two embryos implanted at one time during fertility treatment. Doctors who breach the new code of practice by implanting more than two embryos could lose their IVF licences, which are issued by the Authority. In some cases, where more than one embryo begins to develop, what are referred to as selective reduction procedures are carried out. What should happen to these surplus embryos—should they be stored for the use of the woman who is undergoing the treatment and then destroyed when no longer required, or should they be available for research? Even where only one fertilised egg is transferred to the woman, the decision has to be made as to what is to be done with the surplus embryos which have been produced *in vitro*. Also a decision will be made as to which embryo should be transferred to the woman. Reproductive technology gives not only the possibility of conceiving a baby, but also conceiving and giving birth to a healthy baby and maybe the possibility of a perfect baby, with anything less than perfection being discarded. In 1985, 1986 and 1987 unsuccessful private members' Bills attempted to make it an offence to create, store, or use a human embryo for any purpose other than to assist a specified woman to become pregnant.

The Human Fertilisation and Embryology Act (HFEA) 1990, s. 5 created a new statutory body called the Human Fertilisation and Embryology Authority. The authority has the power to grant treatment licences, storage licences and research licences (s. 11). The research licence will be granted only where the research is directed to one or more of a defined number of aims and the authority is satisfied that the research is necessary or desirable (sch. 2, para. 3).

The licence cannot authorise keeping or using an embryo after the period of 14 days beginning with the day when the gametes are mixed, not counting any time during which the gamete is stored (s. 3(3)). 'Stored' means keeping while preserved. The reason for the 14-day deadline is that the Warnock Report (Report of the Committee of Inquiry into Fertilisation and Embryology, Cm. 9314 (1984)) noted that embryo research has identified that at about 14 days after fertilisation of the egg, a line appears which is identified as the primitive streak and this is considered to be the time of transformation from molecular matter to a potential human being. Therefore surplus embryos cannot be kept or used beyond the fourteenth day stage of development. Parliament decided to regulate human embryo research rather than have no control over such experimentation, but chose not to go as far as Austria and Germany where such research was prohibited other than for therapeutic use (Eire and Luxembourg where research was implicitly prohibited), or the USA where, although there was no federal legislation imposing a ban, no federal funding was allowed. The freedom of science has been curbed by imposing the 14-day restriction, but whether or not society has been protected, turns on whether or not one believes that life begins at conception, in which case the Act is allowing experimentation on human beings, or whether one adopts the view that life begins to matter morally only on the emergence of the primitive streak, which was the view taken by the Warnock Committee.

In addition to regulating research the Act regulates treatment services which are defined as 'medical, surgical or obstetric services provided to the public or a section of the public for the purpose of assisting women to carry children' (s. 2(1)). The Act does not regulate artificial insemination by husband or partner, or GIFT where the eggs and sperm are from the woman and her husband or partner. As long as there is neither donation of gametes nor fertilisation outside the woman's body, then the Act does not seek to regulate such treatment.

The Act imposes non-clinical criteria in limiting access to treatment and, thereby, parenthood. A treatment service will not be provided to a woman 'unless account has been taken of the welfare of any child who may be born as a result of the treatment (including the need of that child for a father), and of any other child who may be affected by the birth' (s. 13(5)). Robert G. Lee and Derek Morgan in *Human Fertilisation and Embryology* (Blackstone, 2001), point out that this effectively applies a prospective licensing system for parenthood similar to that used in adoption.

Michelle Stanworth in the *Deconstruction of Motherhood, Reproductive Technology* (1987), observed that according to ideologies of motherhood, all women want children; but single women, lesbian women (and disabled women) are often expected to forgo mothering 'in the interests of the child'. The Act appears to reinforce that view by identifying the need for a father. Children of single parents do have problems but those problems are often the result of poverty rather than the lack of a father figure. Is the Act ensuring that there is a father who will have responsibility and who will pay to support the child? The Act does allow for a woman and her male partner, not necessarily a husband, to receive treatment services, but then goes on to provide that the man is to be regarded as the father of the child (s. 28(3)) and therefore responsible for that child (see *Re R (A Child) (IVF: Paternity of Child)* [2003] 2 WLR 1485. However, the House of Lords has given permission for a challenge to the Court of Appeal ruling). The carrying woman is to be treated as the mother of the child even if she is not the genetic mother (s. 27).

If a licensed clinic is prepared to treat a lone woman, then her baby would fall into the category of the legally fatherless child. The anonymous sperm donor is not treated as the father (s. 26(a)). A person's gametes (eggs or sperm) must not be used or received for the purpose of treatment services unless there is an effective consent by that person to their being so used (sch. 3, para. 5; *R v HFEA, ex parte Blood* [1997] 2 All ER 687; and *U v Centre for Reproductive Medicine* [2002] EWCA Civ 565; *Evans v Amicus Healthcare Ltd* (2004) *The Times*, 30 June).

It can be seen that human reproductive technology includes a number of types of interventions, many are still in the developmental or experimental stage, and all of them are carried out on women. According to Andrea Dworkin in *Right-Wing Women* (1983), motherhood is becoming a new branch of female prostitution and disposes of women as women. She goes on to say that the invention of the artificial womb will make women redundant as mothers and lead to general femicide or holocaust. Although that may seem an extreme view, caution must be exercised to prevent reproductive technology being used to subjugate women.

The financial and emotional costs of treatment are high with a low chance of a live birth. It is said that women who present themselves for IVF treatment are often desperate and have reached the end of the line. In an attempt to ensure that hopes are not raised too high, s. 13(6) provides that treatment services which involve the use of donated eggs or sperm, or a donated embryo, or IVF, will not be provided to a woman unless she has been given a suitable opportunity to receive counselling about the implications of taking the proposed steps and has been provided with such relevant information as is proper. It is to be hoped that counselling will be provided if a number of treatment cycles have proved unsuccessful, so that the couple can decide when to stop and come to terms with their situation.

As far as any child produced as a result of treatment services is concerned, if from information held by the Human Fertilisation and Embryology Authority it appears that an applicant aged 18 or over was or may have been born as a result of treatment services, the applicant will be given a suitable opportunity for counselling and then the authority must provide information (s. 31(3)) which, at present, does not identify donors. (See Maclean and Maclean, 'Keeping secrets in assisted reproduction—the tension between donor anonymity and the need of the child for information' (1996) 8 *CFLQ* 3 at 243.) A change in the law is planned which means that children born as a result of sperm, eggs, or embryos donated after April 2005 will be able to access the identity of their donor(s) when they reach the age of 18. It will be 2023 before the earliest 18 year-olds will be able to do this. The new regulations surrounding information on donors will not be retrospective. Anyone donating before April 2005 will remain anonymous.

The 1990 Act cannot be the final word; indeed there have been changes. The Criminal Justice and Public Order Act 1994 amended the HFEA 1990 to include a ban on the use of foetal ovarian tissue in fertility treatment. It was considered that the use of such tissue raised difficult social, ethical, legal and scientific concerns. After the Authority's public consultation in 1994, it was thought that, in the current social climate, it would be difficult for any child to come to terms with being created by an aborted foetus. The Human Reproductive Cloning Act 2001 makes it a criminal offence punishable by up to ten years in prison and/or an unlimited fine to place into a woman an embryo created by any means other than fertilisation. New situations do not always provoke bans, for some people they have brought good news. The Human Fertilisation and Embryology (Deceased Fathers) Act 2003 allows a man (only with his written consent) to be registered as the father of a child conceived after his death using his sperm or an embryo created using his sperm either before or after his death. That Act also enables a man to be registered as the father of a child conceived after his death using an embryo created using donor sperm before his death. However, these provisions do not allow the man to be treated in law for any other purpose and the registration will not confer on the child any legal status or rights, including for example, inheritance or nationality.

This area of rapidly expanding knowledge will surely raise even more questions. New moral and ethical dilemmas will need to be addressed. Recent (and current) issues faced (or to be faced), among others, are non-marital and non-genetic 'fathers'

(*Re R (A Child) (IVF: Paternity of Child)* [2003] 2 WLR 1485); pre-implantation genetic diagnosis and tissue typing (*R (Quintaville)* v *Human Fertilisation and Embryology Authority (Secretary of State for Health Intervening)* [2003] 2 FLR 335); mix-up in IVF treatment (*Leeds Teaching Hospitals NHS Trust* v *A* [2003] 1 FLR 1091); and children who wish to know the identities of gamete donors, their biological parents.

The Act is straining to regulate the genies while trying to recognise, with compassion, the needs of those who want a child of their own.

Further reading

Booth, P., 'Family Law Without the f-word—the Implications of Cloning' [2004] *NLJ* 374.

Brownsword, R., 'Reproductive Opportunities and Regulatory Challenges' [2004] *MLR* 304.

Feast, J., Crawshaw, M., 'Long-term Implications for Families Formed by Surrogacy or Donor Assisted Conception' [2004] *Ad & Fos* 73.

Jackson, E., 'Conception and the Irrelevance of the Welfare Principle' [2002] *MLR* 176.

Lee, R. G., Morgan, D., *Human Fertilisation and Embryology* (London: Blackstone Press, 2001).

Sutherland, E.E., ' "Man not included"—Single Women, Female Couples and Procreative Freedom in the UK' [2003] *CFLQ* 155.

Websites

Department of Health www.doh.gov.uk
Human Fertilisation and Embryology Authority www.hfea.gov.uk
UK Donorlink www.ukdonorlink.org.uk

Adoption

Introduction

Two things about adoption come immediately to mind: they are that it is one of the more segregable topics and that some institutions have examined (and presumably taught) it more than others. Perhaps the one drove the other; adoption is a large chapter in a crowded subject, but its omission does not require too much explanation elsewhere. In our opinion there is one very good reason for 'doing' adoption and that is it is about finding the right parents for the right children; making rather than breaking families, if you like. In any event, the intense parliamentary, media and populist attention surrounding the passing of the Adoption and Children Act 2002 have now made it difficult to ignore in the lecture theatre, seminar room and examination hall.

Adoption can also generate both problems and essays with equal facility. From the candidate's point of view, the attraction of adoption problems is their visibility (not that many family law topics are easy to disguise). If it is examined, some of its components are virtually guaranteed a place: dispensing with parental consent; relative/non-relative adoption. Rather surprisingly, there is also a lot of bureaucracy, and a lot of numbers. These include *inter alia* the role of the adoption agencies and local authorities, social workers, the minimum and maximum ages of the parties, and how long the child must have been placed with the applicants before the court hearing. Despite the comparative conceptual isolation of adoption it is, of course, an example of 'family proceedings' for the purposes of the Children Act 1989 and therefore, e.g. any s. 8 order may be made in lieu, residence or contact, for example.

Because of those perennial policy issues, essay questions are easily constructed. Overseas adoptions, the question of who may adopt (homosexual, unmarried couples) and, in the 1990s, the Government review of adoption, all give rise easily to discussion topics and handy quotations. There has been a steady stream of reviews, from the Report of the Committee on Child Adoption (the Tomlin Report) in 1925, which led to the inaugural Adoption of Children Act 1926, to the reviews instituted by the Department of Health in the 1990s. The last culminated in the White Paper '*Adoption: The Future*' (1993) Cm. 2288 and, in 1996, the then Government produced a draft Adoption Bill. Perhaps influenced by memories of the strife caused by the Child Support Acts 1991 and 1995 and the Family Law Act 1996, neither that Government took, nor did its successor take immediate further action. But once settled into prime ministerial office Mr Blair (whose own father was adopted) returned to the issue. There were two further official documents, *Adoption—the Prime Minister's Review* (2000), plus the ensuing White Paper, *Adoption—a New Approach* (2000) Cm. 5017. One Adoption and Children Bill 2001 fell in the General Election of that year, and in winter 2002 its successor eventually stopped ricocheting between the House of Commons and the House of Lords and received the Royal Assent.

Q Question 1

Five years ago Mary, an unmarried medical student, gave birth to Nick following her affair with Tim (who has since died). During her pregnancy Mary had arranged for Hal and Wendy, a married couple, to give the child a home 'for the time being'. They are now both aged 50; Hal is a labourer and Wendy a shop assistant; they have no children of their own.

Since making this arrangement Mary has qualified as a doctor. During her student days she saw Nick regularly, often offering Hal and Wendy money (for the boy's keep) which they occasionally accepted. Nick understands, as well as his age permits, that Mary is his natural mother, but looks upon Hal and Wendy as his 'mummy and daddy'.

Mary, now aged 24 and recently married to Cecil, a solicitor aged 29, has now told Hal and Wendy that she and Cecil want to bring Nick up as their child. Hal and Wendy want to keep Nick and have applied to adopt him themselves.

Will the law do right by Nick?

Commentary

Note the *question*, i.e. the last seven words. It is not 'Advise Hal and Wendy' or 'Advise Mary and Cecil' and it most certainly is not 'Write all you know about adoption, roughly relating it to this story'. The material needed would be pretty much the same if it were, but what is actually required is child-centredness; child law taking its own precepts to heart. Technically, this question might be described as an essay wrapped up in a problem. The good answer will identify the law and then evaluate it in the manner required.

The examiner has been generous here, throwing in a lot of opportunities for the use of knowledge. In truth, the situation is typically unrealistic in that it would never be possible to summarise such a matter adequately in barely 200 words. Once again, the candidate with good technique is going to score over a classmate with the same amount of knowledge. The former will thread the theme of Nick's welfare through the material supplied. It is not just the welfare principle and dispensing with parental consent. The other aspects include the legality of the placement, the role of social workers and the local authority, and, crucially, the range of orders available. Note that although adoption can be omitted from the course or from your revision without causing much damage to other topics, it cannot itself be dealt with in isolation. The statutory tools are the Adoption and Children Act 2002 and the Children Act 1989, added to which are some decided cases and good practice.

Here, we are going to be partisan, as both law and question require us to be. We are on the side of this little lad, although only goodness knows how best to serve him.

- **Adoption and Children Act 2002**
  - **The welfare principle**
  - **The statutory checklist**
  - **Probationary period**
  - **Age and status**
  - **Parental consent**
- **Children Act 1989—s. 8 orders**

⠜ Suggested answer

This situation will fall to be dealt with under either the Adoption and Children Act 2002 or the Children Act 1989, and in each case the governing principle, s. 1(2) and s. 1(1) respectively, is the paramountcy of the child's welfare—'throughout his life' in the former case. So thus far the law will at least be *trying* to 'do right' by Nick.

Before proceeding, we might note Article 21 of the UN Convention on the Rights of the Child 1989:

> States Parties that recognise and/or permit the system of adoption shall ensure that the best interests of the child shall be the paramount consideration . . .

Section 1(1) of the 1989 Act proceeds to amplify itself in a number of ways. In referring to 'the ascertainable wishes of the child concerned (considered in the light of his age and understanding)', s. 1(3)(a) of the Children Act is identical to s. 1(4)(a) of the 2002 Act. Here, five-year-old Nick understands 'as well as his age permits' that Mary is his mother, but sees Hal and Wendy as his 'mummy and daddy'. It seems that the combination of his extreme youth and the ambivalence of his perceptions renders it difficult to weigh the latter in any appropriate manner.

So far as Nick's immediate future is concerned, it seems that Hal and Wendy could take advantage of sections 36(1)(a) and 40(2)(a) of the 2002 Act whereby a child may not, pending the hearing, be removed from adoption applicants with whom he has had his home (other than by leave of the court). Better for Nick that only one separation occur, if separation there must be. During this period his welfare will be monitored by the local authority (which must be notified of the application) under s.

44 and which will also undertake the investigatory and reporting functions normally undertaken, in 'stranger' adoptions, by the agency responsible for 'placing' the child. These include a health history of the birth parents, an investigation into the applicants' circumstances, and a counselling service. Nick will be medically examined. Because Mary is opposing the adoption, an officer of the Children and Family Court Advisory and Support Service (CAFCASS) will be appointed whose over-all duty will be to safeguard Nick's interests. The guardian will advise, for example, on whether Nick should be present at the hearing.

If it is right for Nick to be adopted, there will be no difficulty with the basic legal requirements. Hal and Wendy are both (well) over 21 and are a couple (s. 50(1) and Nick is under 19 years old (s. 47(9)). The normal position is that the court may be the local bench, the county court (a Family Hearing Centre if the application is opposed) or the High Court. Additionally, there is the suggestion of 'prohibited' payments under s. 95 but, it is unlikely that the money Hal and Wendy 'occasionally' accepted from Mary would be held to be so tainted. Their application would comply with s. 42 in that Nick has lived with them for at least three of the last five years.

Crucial to Nick's future is the designation of adoption proceedings as 'family proceedings' under s. 8(4)(d) of the Children Act 1989. The upshot is that the court, either on its own motion or upon application, can make s. 8 Children Act orders, one or more of which, as we will see, may well be right for Nick. Similarly, the court has the duty, under s. 46(6) of the 2002 Act, to consider whether 'there should be arrangements for allowing any person contact with the child' before making an adoption order.

It is difficult to believe that the s. 1(2) welfare principle—as elaborated by s. 1(4), e.g. (f), the relationship 'which the child has with relatives'—points to the making of the adoption order in favour of Hal and Wendy, with or without conditions. Such an order would sever for all time Nick's legal link with his 24–year-old natural mother, replacing her with a couple who will be in their sixties whilst he is still a schoolboy: in *Re K (A Minor) (Wardship: Adoption)* [1991] 1 FLR 57, a key factor was that the applicant 'mother' would be 57 when the child was 10, and that the mother genuinely wanted her child back. In *Re L (A Minor) (Care Proceedings: Wardship) (No. 2)* [1991] 1 FLR 29, Willis J stated that every child had a right, where possible, to be brought up by 'its' own family and that there must be 'strong, cogent and positive reasons' for denying that right. A labourer and a shop assistant will not be able to offer the same material benefit (a relevant factor in 'welfare'; see *Re A (An Infant)* [1963] 1 All ER 531) as a doctor and her solicitor husband, who may well provide Nick with siblings, unlike, surely, Hal and Wendy. We may admire them and pity their disappointment, but neither the law nor the question permit us to put their feelings before Nick's future. Other things being equal, it is in the interests of the child to be brought up by his parent: *Re W (A Minor) (Residence Order)* [1993] 2 FLR 625.

A fortiori, it cannot be that the court would dispense with Mary's consent under s. 52(1)(b) of the 2002 Act which now applies the welfare principle to the task. Under the previous law (the Adoption Act 1976) such dispensing was governed by whether the consent was being unreasonably withheld, and *not* by the welfare principle (*Re P (An Infant) (Adoption: Dispensing with Agreement)* [1977] Fam 25), although it was 'decisive in those cases where a reasonable parent must so regard it' (*Re W (An Infant)* [1971] AC 682). In *Re F (Adoption: Parental Agreement)* [1982] FLR 101, where the child was also aged five at the time of the application, the court did not dispense with the mother's consent even though she had earlier been guilty of ill-treatment and neglect.

In the short term it *might* be that the law would best serve Nick's interests by taking advantage—in the absence of appropriate private ordering—of the court's ability to make s. 8 Children Act 1989 orders in the adoption proceedings. Surely Nick must live with one couple and see another, his filial link to Mary intact? But with which couple should he make his home? We know little of Cecil, Nick's 'stepfather', other than his apparent respectability. Now that the adoption application (we predict) has been refused and s. 8 orders are being considered, s. 1(5) of the 1989 Act applies, so the court must be sure that 'making an order would be better for the child than making no order at all'. Perhaps Hal, Wendy, Mary and Cecil can come together for Nick's continued well-being, with the former couple becoming invaluable 'social grandparents', Nick seeing them and staying with them as often as possible, to the pleasure and advantage of all concerned. Perhaps we can arrive at that stage consensually and instead of, not after, abortive adoption proceedings. If not, residence orders under s. 8(1) in favour of Mary (who already has 'parental responsibility' as mother under s. 2(2)(a) of the Children Act 1989) and Cecil, with Hal and Wendy able to apply for contact, also under s. 8(1). If these are necessary, let us hope that it will never be in Nick's interests for the court to have to consider any applications for variation. Finally, we must note that Mary and Cecil are eligible to adopt under s. 50(2) as 'a couple where one of the couple is the mother' of the adoptee. But under s. 42(3) such step-parent adoption applications cannot be made until the child has lived with the applicant(s) for at least six months and the local authority has made the investigations required under s. 44 (above). All being well—with the new family—this could prove the culmination of the law's benificent interaction with both Nick *and* the adults in his life.

Since the Children Act 1989, it may be that the law has the tools to do right by Nick. But neither that Act nor any other can give the court the power of foresight, or judgment beyond the merely human.

Q Question 2

The Adoption and Children Act 2002 applies the 'welfare principle' to adoption, extends the categories of those eligible to adopt, and encourages the adoption of children in local authority care. Do you think that these measures meet the needs of a modern adoption law?

Commentary

As ever, a description of the relevant material is not what is asked for (and do note that the rubric rules out the non-adoption aspects of the Act). 'The needs of a modern adoption law' is the key phrase. What reforms were recommended? To what extent were they represented in the Act? Do you approve of the 'extent' involved and would you have preferred a different approach?

So far as the contents of the Act are concerned, you will need to know, e.g., that it applies the 'welfare principle' to adoption, allows adoption by unmarried 'couples', and introduces 'placement' orders. You will also need to deploy other data, particularly the various official documents which led up to the Act, such as, most recently but not exclusively, *Adoption—the Prime Minister's Review* (2000) and the White Paper which followed, *Adoption—a New Approach* (2000) Cm. 5017. What are the differences between the Act and these documents? What do *you* think of the former's contents, particularly where there are such discrepancies? The areas for debate are how far the new law will, as intended, increase the number of adoptions from care, and whether you approve, firstly, of the application of the welfare principle to adoption (also presaged) and, secondly, of the new-found adoptive eligibility of unmarried couples—of the same or different sex—which was not. That last point, in particular, enables us to say again that this module will *not* have been entitled 'What I think about What Was in the Media Today', and that you are expected to use expert materials in your answer and in forming your opinion. On the other hand, a little professional humility goes down well: family lawyers, like any other group, disagree about these matters and some of them enthusiastically espoused such turkeys as the Child Support Act 1991 and the divorce provisions of Part II of the Family Law Act 1996. Finally, even the stuffiest examiner can have no objection to the use of the first person. The question asks what 'you' think.

- Adoption Act 1976

- Children Act 1989

- 1990s Reform Papers

- Welfare principle/statutory checklist

- 'Couples' as adopters

- 'Placement' Orders

- Increasing numbers adopted from care

:Q: **Suggested answer**

In repealing and replacing the Adoption Act 1976, the Adoption and Children Act (ACA) 2002 applies the welfare principle to the dispensing of parental consent, and obliges officialdom to place for adoption many children looked after by local authorities. The ACA's adoption provisions are the culmination of some five official Papers over the last decade and by the Prime Minister's personal initiative to 'place' more children in care. These provisions touch all three of the main domestic routes to adoption in English law—partnering a parent, competing for a child being looked after by a local authority, and 'finding' a child privately.

Section 1 of the ACA 2002 states that 'whenever a court or an adoption agency is coming to a decision relating to the adoption of a child the paramount consideration of the court or adoption agency must be the child's welfare, throughout his life' and is therefore an 'overarching' provision, although whether it merits the self-congratulation it has received since its first mootings under the previous government is a matter to which I return below. To some extent it aligns adoption law with the relevant provisions of the Children Act 1989, but not completely in that (unlike the previous provision in s. 6 of the Adoption Act 1976, under which the child's welfare is only the 'first' consideration) it applies 'throughout his life' and not merely 'throughout his childhood'. Furthermore, whilst s. 1 imports much of the 'checklist' found in s. 1(3) of the 1989 Act (the child's wishes, needs, characteristics, any likely harm) it also refers to the wishes of those with whom the child is currently relating—not merely legally—and their ability to serve him or her.

But none of this is earth-shattering; the upgrading of the child's welfare from 'first' to paramount' in the 1989 Act itself, has cut little ice since it came into force. What *is* important is that the paramountcy principle is extended to the dispensing of parental consent, with specific reference to both the placement and the court order. In thereby abrogating *Re P (an Infant) (Adoption: Parental Agreement)* [1977] Fam 25, Parliament has removed a bulwark against adoption being used to contravene one of the most fundamental of societal principles: that the claims of the birth family, or at least the birth mother, have priority in the absence of proven unsuitability. (Under s. 16(2)(b) of the Adoption Act 1976, the necessary consent(s) of a parent with parental responsibility could be overridden on the basis of, e.g., 'unreasonable withholding' and that a reasonable parent would regard the child's welfare as decisive; *Re W (An Infant)* [1971] 2 All ER 49, HL.) *Review of Adoption Law: Report to Ministers of an Interdepartmental Working Group* (Dep. of Health and Welsh Office, 1992), in recommending that the welfare principle be extended to adoption, referred to 'the important exception' of dispensing with the parent's consent, as otherwise, 'the court would be able to override completely a parent's wishes, which we would consider unacceptable in relation to an order which irrevocably terminates a parent's legal relationship with a child' (para. 7.1). As the 1993 White Paper *Adoption: The Future* (Cm. 2288) pointed out the following year at para. 5.23:

'Uniquely amongst interventions available to protect children's upbringing, adoption involves an irreversible legal separation of the child from his birth parents.... Humane instincts and good child care practice combine to support the principle that the permanent separation of parents from their child is a step to be undertaken with reluctance, particularly if they object'

For that reason the 1993 White Paper followed para. 12.6(c) of the 1992 document in announcing, at para. 5.5, that 'When the court is satisfied that adoption is likely to offer a significantly better advantage to the child than any other option, it will continue to have a power to override a refusal of consent by the birth parties'.

It is important to remember that, in not applying the paramountcy principle, the pre-ACA 2002 law was by no means a minority case. There are at least six different circumstances in which Parliament has disavowed s. 1(1) of the Children Act 1989. In alphabetical order, they are: (international) abduction; ancillary financial relief; child support; divorce; and non-molestation and occupation orders. I suggest that few, if any, of these examples of non-paramountcy are as defensible as it is in adoption, or at least with regard to parental dissent to adoption, and that, in any case, paramountcy is not the key to this Government's actual aim of increasing the number of adoptions from care (see below).

In its original form, the minimum eligibility requirements, which have remained constant since this form of artificial legal parenthood was first introduced into our law by the Adoption of Children Act 1926 would have remained unchanged. So, for example, adoption would still be by married couples or (generally) unmarried individuals. Therefore non-marital couples (same gender or not) would have been unable to adopt which may, or may not, have been justified by the reasons advanced in para. 4.37 of *Adoption: The Future*, Cm. 2288 (1993):

'In spite of high divorce rates in modern society, and the decisions by many adults to enter into other long-term relationships, marriage remains the most common permanent relationship in which the upbringing of children is undertaken; it is the only one registrable under legislation and it is the only one which requires a court to bring it to an end.'

In the event, and after ricocheting between the two Houses of Parliament, the Legislature eventually accepted a Backbench amendment (s. 144(4)) whereby adoption by a 'couple' included:

(a)   a married couple, or

(b)   two people (whether of different sexes or the same sex) living as partners in an enduring family relationship.

I applaud this on the basis that blanket ban on unmarried couples works against the sort of children for whom, previously, only 'joint residence orders' were available.

These orders are the closest that the law came to such adoptions, and in each case the court was satisfied on the facts that such arrangements served the 'welfare principle', usually because there was evidence that they had already been working for some time, and that the couple's relationship was enduring (which is what the Bill requires). Adoption Acts tend to last for a generation or more and such cases are likely to rise in line with the increasing social acceptance of homosexuality—as evidenced by the move to registered civil partnerships since the 2002 Act (as now proposed by the Civil Partnership Bill 2004).

That the aim is to increase adoption from care is made abundantly clear in *Adoption—the Prime Minister's Review* (Performance and Innovation Unit, July 2000) and the ensuing White Paper *Adoption: a New Approach* (Cm. 5017, December 2000). Certainly, the reported fate of children brought up in care is a national disgrace: four times more likely to become unemployed, sixty times more likely to be homeless, and a quarter of the prison population. According to para. 2.5 of the latter Paper, the proportion of looked-after children adopted in 1999/2000 varied by council between 0.5 per cent and 10.5 per cent, and para. 4.16 recorded the Government's belief that an increase of up to 50 per cent was viable, and that there must be a 40 per cent increase by 2005.

The supposed shortfall was due to, e.g.: social workers receiving little training in making decisions for permanence for children; would-be adopters believing that the system is drawn-out, impertinent and arbitrary; an insufficiency of support, both post-placement and post-adoption; the lack of a nation-wide system (a 1999 report found 2,400 children waiting to be adopted and 1,300 approved adopters waiting for children); and court delays. *Adoption: a New Approach* explained how the Government intends to ensure that more 'looked after' children will be adopted. Some measures can be achieved administratively. They include: 'National Standards for Adoption' which standardise the expectations of all concerned; the encouragement of applications by, e.g., outlawing blanket exclusions other than for certain criminal convictions; and the removal of adoption services from failing councils. This last will follow an adverse report from the 'Adoption Taskforce'. The Government also signalled its intent to 'carry out the most radical overhaul of adoption law for 25 years' (para. 3.8), hence the ACA 2002. Some of these statutory measures underpin the following administrative steps: a country-wide Adoption Register for England and Wales to suggest matches between children waiting to be adopted and approved prospective adopters; assessment for post-placement and post-adoption support; and a requirement that councils pay the court fees when its 'looked-after' children are adopted.

Under s. 22(1) a local authority *must* apply for a placement order over its accommodated children, if it is thinks that the care order criteria apply, and that the child should be adopted. Such order is defined as, 'an order made by the court authorising an adoption agency to place a child for adoption with any prospective adopters who may be chosen by the agency' (s. 21(1)), thus acknowledging the current reality whereby, in the general run of cases, the court usually grants the adoption following an earlier, administrative, decision to place a child for that purpose. But surely good practice, as presaged above, can produce the desired 800–1,000 extra each year from a stock of 50,000-plus without having to deprive their natural parent(s) of any real say in the matter? Since the rise of political interest in these matter, successive editions of *Judicial Statistics* have already indicated a growth in the number of children adopted from care—the number of step-parent adoptions, at least, dropped to 26 per cent of the 4,120 total in 2002, 20 per cent less than in 2001—and that in a period in which fewer adoptions orders were made overall.

Further reading

Ball, C. 'The Changed Nature of Adoption: A Challenge for the Legislators' in G. Miller (ed.), *Frontiers of Family Law* (Aldershot: Ashgate, 2003), p. 6.

Choudhry, S., 'The Adoption and Children Act 2002, the Welfare Principle and the Human Rights Act 1998—a Missed Opportunity' (2003) 15 *Child and Family Law Quarterly* 119.

Lowe, N., 'English Adoption Law, Past, Present and Future' in S. Katz, J. Eekelaar, and M. Maclean (eds.), *Cross Currents* (Oxford: Oxford University Press, 2000), p. 314.

Morgan, P., *Adoption and the Care of Children: the British and American Experience*, IEA Health and Welfare Unit (2000).

Children: private ordering

Introduction

Decisions about what should happen to children after separation and divorce of their parents, e.g. where they should live, how much contact they should have with each parent, affect large numbers of families each year. In the first nine months of 1991—i.e. immediately before the Children Act 1989 was activated—38,488 'custody' orders and 73,519 'access' orders were made by the courts (*Judicial Statistics*, 1991).

Major changes were made to this area by the Children Act 1989 not least by s. 8 which replaced the above orders with the more sensitive ones of 'residence' and 'contact' respectively. Many people were surprised by the speed with which the recommendations of the Law Commission (Report: Review of Child Law: Guardianship and Custody 1988 Law Com. No. 172) were incorporated into the Act, becoming law only three years after being proposed. The new system of private ordering encourages continuing parental responsiblity after divorce, with the minimum amount of interference where parents are co-operating. Yet the numbers of orders are climbing again and during 2003 there were an estimated total of 31,966 residence orders and about 67,184 contact orders in private law cases (*Judicial Statistics*, 2003, Cm. 6251, Table 5.3).

This area tends to be popular with students and there is almost certainly going to be a question on the paper. To answer it properly you will need to know not just the s. 8 orders, but also the context in which they operate. The general principles and concepts of the 1989 Act as they relate to private law proceedings will be particularly relevant, i.e. the welfare principle and the statutory checklist, the so-called 'non-intervention' principle and continuing parental responsibility. Other issues which may arise and of which you should be aware include change of child's name; leaving the jurisdiction; and problems with contact. Private orders for children may of course also come up in questions on other areas such as divorce finance and property or the ground for divorce. Questions on private ordering are often problem questions where you are required to advise one of the parents, as in two of the questions in this chapter. In addition there is a further problem question involving the possibility of a minor instituting proceedings, and one essay question.

Q Question 1

While the law can sever the legal bond between husband and wife, the law in family disputes should do nothing that appears to weaken the bond between parent and child. That bond is vital. (Lord Mackay.)

Assess the extent to which the Children Act 1989 accepts and advances this view.

Commentary

First you need to identify what Lord Mackay is talking about. It should be quite clear from the title quotation that the point he is making is that when a husband and wife end their relationship by divorce (sever the legal bond), their relationship with their children should survive intact. Parents divorce each other, not their children. He says that this relationship between parent and child is 'vital' and that the law should not do anything that could be seen as weakening the bond. Is the bond vital? You really need to be aware of some of the research done into the effects of divorce on children to address this. A number of articles were written on this in the mid-1980s when reform of this area was mooted (e.g. Parkinson, 'Child Custody Orders: A Legal Lottery' [1988] *Fam Law* 26). You will also find some useful current information in Hale, Pearl, Cooke and Bates, *The Family, Law & Society*, 5th edn, (London: Butterworths, 2002) chapter 12.

The question asks you to assess the extent to which the Children Act 1989 accepts and advances the view expressed by Lord Mackay. You will need a sound knowledge of the private law provisions of the Act and its underlying philosophy and an appreciation of the approach now taken to private ordering. You are looking for examples of provisions which have an effect on the parent/child bond referred to by Lord Mackay. Do not just give a list; assess each one in terms of the title quotation.

- Empirical research findings

- Parental responsibility ('PR')

- Continuing 'PR' post-divorce

- The 'non-intervention' principle and s. 41, MCA 1973

- s. 8, residence and contact orders

☼ Suggested answer

The view being expressed by Lord Mackay—Lord Chancellor at the time of the 1989 Act—in the title quotation is that when a couple divorce, it is their spousal relationship which ends, not their parental relationship with their children, and that the law, when dealing with children after the divorce of their parents, should be seen to support this continuing parent/child relationship. We are asked to assess the extent to which this view is accepted and advanced by the Children Act (CA) 1989. Before looking at the Act's response to this view, it is useful to consider briefly whether the parent/child bond is 'vital' as Lord Mackay states.

Court decisions on 'custody' affect many children every year—and not just on parental divorce, but upon parental separation (if, indeed, they have ever lived together at all). In recent years a lot of research has been done, particularly in the United States, into the effects of divorce on children, and an early British study of children's experience of divorce was conducted in Edinburgh in the mid-1980s (A. Mitchell, 'Children in the Middle', 1985). This research indicates that the most important factor in a child's adjustment to divorce is the quality of post-divorce arrangements for all the family members, a view espoused with enthusiasm in the official papers which led to the 1989 Act, e.g. Law Com. No. 172, 'Review of Child Law—Guardianship and Custody' (1988). A vital element in a child's adjustment is a continuing relationship with both parents. Children want two active and involved parents (Lisa Parkinson, 'Child Custody Orders: A Legal Lottery?' [1988] *Fam Law* 26). This would appear to confirm that the parent/child bond is very important and should be preserved wherever possible. There are obviously always going to be cases where it will not be in the child's best interests to maintain the bond (e.g. in cases of serious abuse) and (perhaps) cases where the absent parent does not wish to preserve the relationship.

No law can make someone be an active involved parent (for a contrary view see Helen L. Conway, 'Forced contact—a child's right or an impossibility?' [1997] *NLJ* 374), but it can at least encourage those who would like to continue in that role even after separation and divorce to do so. Prior to the 1989 Act, under the old system of private ordering there was very little to encourage joint responsibility or to preserve a real relationship between a child and the non-custodial parent. Two orders which did go some way towards achieving this were joint custody orders and access orders; with the former the benefit was often symbolic and with the latter the parent/child relationship was often artificial and unnatural. One parent would often feel redundant or inferior when the other got 'sole custody' and would stop playing any useful part in the child's life as a result.

So what stance is taken by the Children Act 1989? Does it support the view expressed by Lord Mackay and if so, to what extent? Generally, it is true to say that the Act does accept that on separation and divorce both parents should continue in their role as parents, and a number of its provisions support this view: first, the concept of parental responsibility. Where parents are married, both have parental responsibility for their children (s. 2, CA 1989) and this is totally unaffected by separation or divorce. Court intervention is not seen as lessening a parent's duty to continue to play a full role. If a s. 8 order is made, parental responsibility is limited only to the extent that the order settles a particular issue (e.g. where the child should live) between the parties. For many items, parental responsibility runs with the child; either parent can exercise it when the child is with him, each can act independently in meeting his responsibility and there is no consultation requirement in the Act (s. 2(7). (Although in *Re G (Parental Responsibility: Education)* [1994] 2 FLR 964 it was said that the non-resident parent, having parental responsibility, should have been consulted about sending the child to boarding school.) One statutory limitation is that neither must act incompatibly with any order made (s. 2(8)). In the absence of an order, if one parent objects to what the other is doing, then application must be made to the court, although third parties, such as the child's school, should deal with the absent parent on an equal footing with the residential parent. Thus, perhaps more than any other provision of the Act, this concept of continuing parental responsibility goes some way to ensuring that no matter what happens to the marital relationship, the parent/child relationship continues.

One of the most innovative principles in the 1989 Act is the non-intervention principle (s. 1(5)). It is relevant in all family proceedings but in practice the most important situation in which it operates, and where it was, initially at least, believed to be working well (Children Act Advisory Committee: Annual Report 1991/92), is on divorce. The principle reflects the basic philosophy of the 1989 Act that responsibility for children rests with their parents and state intervention is only justified when it is best for the child. There is a 'presumption' (no order 'unless . . . better for the child than making no order at all') of no order which, in this context, discourages parents from expecting a court order in every case simply as part of a package. Wherever possible, parents should be left to make their own arrangements for their children. An order will always have to be justified on the basis of the child's welfare. An order will be desirable where there is a dispute, vital where there is the possibility of abduction and practical where housing is a problem and the local authority requires an order for the purpose of points allocation but unlikely to be made, just because a parent will feel more secure. Otherwise, perhaps lawyers deter order-seeking estranged parents—and the court can actually make 'orders of no order': 1,522 following private law contact applications in 2003 (Judicial Statistics, 2003, Cm. 6251, Table 5.3).

Section 41 of the Matrimonial Causes Act 1973 (as amended by sch. 12, CA 1989) is in line with the non-intervention principle. There is no longer a requirement of judicial approval of private agreements regarding children on divorce; the court's duty is the more modest one of considering what order, if any, to make. Scrutiny of the arrangements made for children is a paper exercise; there is only a hearing when the form seems to indicate something is amiss, and the discretion to direct that the decree is not to be made absolute until further order, is exercised in exceptional circumstances only. Again, the procedure leaves the parental responsibility to the parents wherever possible and does not interfere unnecessarily.

The private orders available under s. 8 also help to advance the view that the bond between parent and child is vital, and recognise the potential psychological impact on a parent of 'labelling'. The two principal orders, i.e. residence and contact, reflect the issues most likely to need resolving namely: where the child should live and how much the child should see of both parents. The court is no longer concerned with wholesale reallocation of rights; each parent retains parental responsibility and does not lose parental status. The opportunity for conflict is reduced and, most importantly, the 'winner takes all' situation, which led many absent parents to feel redundant under the old system, is avoided. The orders provide practical solutions to questions which arise in relation to a child's upbringing; they are flexible and intended to be less emotive than the old orders. The re-partnering of either party does not of itself affect the issue.

If a residence order is made, the two automatic conditions contained in the order relating to change of the child's surname and removal of the child from the UK (both only being possible with the consent of every person who has parental responsibility for the child or leave of the court) emphasise the importance of a continuing link with the non-residential parent (s. 13, CA 1989). (The 'residential' parent is not prevented from removing the child from the UK for less than one month. A parent of a child under 16 may be commiting an offence if he takes or sends the child out of the UK without the appropriate consent (s. 1, Child Abduction Act 1984).) In addition, s. 11(4) makes shared residence possible. In *D* v *D* *(Shared Residence Order)* [2001] 1FLR 495 the Court of Appeal held that, contrary to earlier case law, it is not necessary to show that exceptional circumstances exist before a shared residence order may be granted. Nor, probably, is it necessary to show a positive benefit to the child. What should be demonstrated is that the order is in the interests of the child, in accordance with s. 1 of the Children Act 1989. The court should exercise its discretion on the facts and with the 'checklist'. Both *D* v *D* and *Re F (Shared Residence Order)* [2003] 2 FLR 397 illustrate that shared residence does not require an evenly alternating pattern between homes. Even though the parents' homes might be separated by a considerable distance, that did not preclude the possibility that the child's year would be divided between the two homes in such a way as to validate the making of a shared residence order.

Fully contested disputes over children after divorce are fortunately rare. In all cases where the central issue is the upbringing of a child, the welfare of that child is, of course, paramount (s. 1, CA 1989). Where a s. 8 order is opposed the welfare checklist applies (s. 1(3)) and focuses on the needs and views of the child. The checklist is clearly influenced by the research evidence on the effects of divorce on children, and enables the court to justify, on the basis of the child's welfare, the extent to which the bond should be preserved. Where parents are in agreement, the checklist does not apply as otherwise the court might feel obliged to order a welfare report which would be seen as an unnecessary intrusion.

Many parents (perhaps the majority) after divorce need information and short-term help to organise their shared responsiblities, and mediation is consequently a feature of many of these cases. It aims to civilise the consequences of marriage breakdown, to diffuse a potentially acrimonious situation and to help pave the way for good, working relationships, particularly with the children, after divorce. In addition the court may of its own motion make a family assistance order (s. 16, CA 1989) to help a family resolve the conflicts flowing from breakdown and to smooth the transition period. This short term order (six months) has to be voluntary, the child's welfare being paramount. The Code of Practice of the Solicitors' Family Law Association (SFLA) advocates that solicitors should explain to their clients how the attitude of parents towards each other in negotiations involving children may affect their relationship with the children. Thus mediation, family assistance orders and the SFLA Code of Practice recognise the importance of trying to preserve the parent/child bond and of avoiding doing anything which may weaken it.

The Children Act 1989, therefore, adopts as the norm the view that ex-spouses remain parents and ought to retain a commitment to their children. One can never legislate for human nature; no legal provision can make an unwilling parent be an active and involved parent and there will always be situations where it is not in the child's best interests to preserve the bond. The Act clearly recognises, however, the importance of the parent/child relationship and through a number of its provisions seeks to encourage its preservation where practicable, thus advancing the view expressed by Lord Mackay—which is now being re-iterated by FAINS (Family Advice and Information Network Services) to its 'customers', i.e. those contemplating divorce.

Q Question 2

Ruth is a 15-year-old girl whose parents are in the throes of a very acrimonious divorce. Ruth's father has moved away, and was happy for Ruth to stay with her mother, so that she could remain at the same school. Ruth does not get on with Bill, the man with whom her mother is now living. He constantly finds fault with Ruth and makes it very plain that he would prefer it if she were not around. Ruth's mother always takes his side. Ruth is a very intelligent and sensitive girl and the stressful situation at home has started adversely to affect her school work. Last week when her mother told her that she was going to marry Bill, Ruth left home and moved in with her aunt and uncle, who are happy for her to stay with them indefinitely. Ruth's mother is not happy with the situation and is insisting that Ruth returns home immediately. Yesterday she turned up at Ruth's school and tried to bundle Ruth into the back of her car to take her home. Ruth wants to stay where she is.

Discuss.

Commentary

Student reaction to this might be: what a super question. There was a very similar story in the daily paper when I was her age (or my daughter was). Indeed the issues raised by this question have been given rather emotive press coverage on a number of occasions since the implementation of the Children Act 1989, under such misleading headlines as 'Boy divorces mother without her knowledge'; 'Girl, 11, first in England to "divorce" parents'. The High Court has made it clear, however, that it is a mistake to use 'divorce' in this context.

The student who is desperate for a last question may see such a question as a real gift from the examiner, but it would be a mistake to think that it can be answered by relying solely on what you have read over your cornflakes. It will not go down well if your answer comprises nothing more than uninformed comment and subjective opinion. This is, in fact, quite a nice, compact question, but do remember that it is on a family law paper and that the examiner will, not unreasonably, be looking for some law. The facts do raise several legal issues, and there are specific statutory provisions which are relevant and need to be discussed. Look for example at the child's right to apply for orders; the types of order available, the welfare principle, the relevance of the child's wishes and feelings. In addition, as you are asked to 'discuss', rather than advise a particular party, you can take the opportunity to assess the situation from the mother's point of view as well as Ruth's. Such cases as there are in this area are unreported as they are heard in chambers, but by all means refer to such cases by way of illustration and try to incorporate the 'guidelines' given by the President of the Family Division into your answer.

- s. 8 Orders—Leave to apply (s. 10(8))

- 'Instructing' a solicitor and legal aid

- Welfare principle: the 'checklist'

- '*Gillick*-competent' minors

- Inherent jurisdiction and wardship

:Ọ: Suggested answer

A number of issues are raised by the given facts. Clearly there is a dispute between a mother and her teenaged daughter over where the daughter should live. It is, therefore, necessary to examine how the matter might be resolved. Can the mother insist that her child returns home to live with her? Can the daughter take any steps to ensure that she can stay where she is?

One of the principal aims of the Children Act was to give the child a voice, and one way in which it seeks to achieve this is by empowering the child to make application to the court. (Similarly, Art. 12 of the 1989 UN Convention on the Rights of the Child gives the child the right to express an opinion, and to have it taken into account in judicial proceedings.) Under s. 8 of the Children Act, Ruth can apply for a range of orders; residence, contact, prohibited steps and specific issue. She cannot apply as of right, however; leave is required (s. 10(8)) which *may* be granted if the court is satisfied that the child has sufficient understanding to make the proposed application. The level of understanding required is high (*Re S (A Minor) (Independent Representation)* [1993] Fam 263). Ruth will have to convince the judge that she is able to understand the consequences of her action. Age is obviously relevant, though no minimum age is specified in the Act. As Ruth is 15 years old, the court is likely to listen very carefully to what she has to say. In *Re P (A Minor) (Education: Child's Wishes)* [1992] 1 FCR 145 where the child involved was 14, the court emphasised the importance of listening and paying respect to the views of older children who are mature enough to make up their own minds as to what they think is best for them. In *M v M, The Times*, 12 August 1992, the Court of Appeal expressed the view that considerable weight should be given to the wishes of intelligent and articulate children of 10 and 11. Hence leave may well be granted. In *Re H (Residence Order: Child's Application for Leave)* [2000] 1 FLR 780, it was held that the court may consider the likely success of the proposed application, and that the child's welfare is an important, but not paramount, consideration.

Ruth will be able to instruct her own solicitor, if the court gives leave or the solicitor agrees to act (s. 41). She must have sufficient understanding to instruct and be able to give rational, coherent and consistent instructions (*Re H (A Minor)* [1991] 2 FCR 330). She will also be able to apply for legal aid and she will be assessed on her own means, making funding easier to secure so long as she can meet the 'merits test'.

What orders is she likely to apply for? What she wants is to be allowed to live with her aunt and uncle and to prevent her mother taking her away from their home. Hence she should apply for a residence order which is an order settling the arrangements to be made as to the person with whom a child is to live, and a prohibited steps order which is an order that no step which could be taken by a parent in meeting his parental responsibility for a child and which is of a kind specified in the order, is to be taken by any person without the consent of the court. The residence order would allow her to stay where she wants, at least for the time being. The court may decide to make an interim residence order pending final determination of the matter, but in any event residence orders are subject to review. The effect of the order would be to vest parental responsibility in Ruth's aunt and uncle, though Ruth's parents would, of course, retain parental responsibility. The prohibited steps order would be used to prevent Ruth's mother taking her away from her aunt and uncle's home; this will be the issue specified in the order which has to be referred to the court. Both the orders will cease when Ruth reaches 16.

In the circumstances described Ruth should be entitled to seek help through the courts. A number of young people have already brought proceedings in similar circumstances but the cases are, of course, unreported as they are heard in chambers.

Sir Stephen Brown, President of the Family Division of the High Court, has given some guidance as to how these applications should be treated (*Re AD (A Minor)* [1993] Fam Law 405). He has emphasised that the Act only intends to open the courtroom door to genuine cases of last resort, where there has been a severe breakdown in a child's relationship with his parents, and not, for example, in cases where a child is peeved because he is not getting his own way at home (*Re C (A Minor) (Leave to Seek Section 8 Order)* [1994] 1 FLR 26). Applications should be made in the High Court or transferred there if made in the lower courts.

Ruth has obviously had problems at home: her parents' divorce is described as 'acrimonious', her father has moved away and she does not get on with Bill, her mother's new partner. We are told that she is an intelligent and sensitive girl whose school work is being adversely affected by the stressful situation at home. As she is 15 years old she is obviously at an important stage of her education. It is not a case of her not getting her own way at home, there is obviously a breakdown in her relationship with her mother because of her mother's new partner. Her welfare will be the paramount consideration in any application (s. 1, CA 1989) and the court's task is to assess her best interests. In an opposed s. 8 order application (as this is likely to be) the checklist applies (s. 1(3)) and Ruth's wishes and feelings will be taken into account, commensurate with her age and understanding. It seems likely that the court would make the orders applied for as they represent the best solution for Ruth.

As we are asked to 'discuss' the scenario rather than to advise Ruth, we should also consider the mother's position in all this. Perhaps understandably she is trying to enforce her right, as she sees it, to 'custody' of her daughter. Even before the implementation of the Children Act it was recognised that a wise parent would not try to force his views on a mature child and since the House of Lords decision in *Gillick v West Norfolk and Wisbech Area Health Authority* [1986] 1 FLR 224, the child's level of intellectual or emotional development has been relevant in deciding the extent of parental authority. Ruth is Gillick-competent and would be regarded as sufficiently mature to decide for herself what she wants to do. There is no doubt that she will fully understand all the issues involved here.

The mother could turn to the inherent jurisdiction of the High Court and make Ruth a ward of court under s. 41, Supreme Court Act 1981 (as happened in *Re AD (A Minor)* above). Legal control over Ruth would then vest in the court which takes over ultimate responsibility for her welfare. All important decisions about her upbringing must subsequently be referred to the court including, of course, where and with whom she should live. In wardship, Ruth's welfare will be considered 'first, last and all the time' (*per* Dunn J in *Re D (A Minor) (Justices' Decision: Review)* [1977] Fam 158). The High Court may well ask that a guardian *ad litem* be appointed for Ruth and give directions that 'he' should investigate the case. Ruth will be able to retain her own solicitor however and the two separate applications, both being 'family proceedings' will be heard together in the High Court. However, in *Re CT (A Minor) (Wardship: Representation)* [1993] 2 FLR 278, the Court of Appeal in discharging wardship proceedings brought by the adoptive parents of a 13-year-old girl who had applied for a s. 8 residence order to enable her to live with an aunt, said that wardship could not be invoked in such cases for the purposes of introducing a guardian *ad litem*, and should rarely be used to challenge a solicitor's view of the ability of a minor client to instruct. Waite LJ saw no need for separate wardship proceedings in such cases and no need to give the girl the status of a ward, a status which he described as 'exceptional under the modern law as it must now be applied'. Hence, relying on *Re CT*, Ruth's mother will not be encouraged to use wardship and the application will proceed as one for s. 8 orders.

In *Re W (Contact: Joining Child as Party)* [2003] 1 FLR 680, it was said that the appropriate way to deal with a difficult case, where the child needed separate representation, was to invite the Children and Family Court Advisory and Support Service (CAFCASS) Legal to provide a guardian to represent the child and take over the child's case. (See *CAFCASS Practice Note (Officers of CAFCASS Legal Services and Special Casework: Appointment in Family Proceedings) (March 2001)* [2001] 2 FLR 151.) Only if CAFCASS did not feel able to represent the child would it be appropriate to appoint a local guardian (and only exceptionally would private law cases require a guardian) and a local solicitor to do so. The amendments to the Children Act 1989 in Part 2 of the Adoption and Children Act 2002, in s. 122 effectively adds s. 8 orders to the list of proceedings which may be specified in s. 41 CA 1989 (implementation of these provisions promised by the end of 2004). Children involved in disputes about residence and contact will have the possibility of separate representation by both a children's guardian and a children panel solicitor, in the same way as children in specified public law proceedings.

Finally, it should be noted that in this context, where a child applies to the court against a parent's wishes, it is wrong to talk in terms of the child 'divorcing' its parent. There cannot be divorce from a parent with parental responsibility and Ruth's mother can be reassured that the only way in which her relationship with her daughter can be totally severed is by adoption. Assuming that Ruth successfully obtains a prohibited steps order and a residence order, it is likely that some continued contact with her mother will be maintained and encouraged.

Q Question 3

Caroline and Robin were divorced two years ago after an eight-year marriage. The divorce was largely due to Robin's involvement with a somewhat extreme religious sect whose beliefs he tried to impose on all the family. Robin is a strict disciplinarian and expects very high standards of his family. The two children, Debbie, now aged seven and Linda, now four, stayed with Caroline after the divorce but see their father regularly.

For the past six months, Philippa, an engineer, has been living with Caroline and they are involved in a lesbian relationship. Robin has only just discovered the nature of Caroline and Philippa's friendship and is horrified. He says that Caroline is not fit to bring up children and that his daughters are not staying in that immoral environment. He intends to apply for a residence order and to ensure that Caroline sees the girls as little as possible. He lives alone but says that his sect friends will look after the girls when he is at work.

Caroline only works part-time to enable her to look after the girls, who are both at school.

Advise Caroline.

Commentary

Solicitors should encourage the attitude that a family dispute is not a contest with a winner and a loser, but a search for fair solutions (Solicitors Family Law Association Code of Practice). In cases such as this one, this may take some doing.

The facts indicate the likelihood of a fully contested application for residence: fortunately in practice such cases are rare. They may generate a great deal of bitterness, as each parent perceives the other's unfitness as the main issue. An opposed s. 8 application does however provide you with the opportunity to use the statutory checklist in s. 1(3), Children Act 1989. The welfare principle (s. 1) is going to be central to your answer. Use the information given in the question to identify which factors on the checklist are relevant and make use of case law too, particularly decisions subsequent to the CA 1989. Technically decisions prior to the Act should not be regarded as binding, but they are highly persuasive unless clearly at odds with the Act's principles. Do not forget that the non-intervention principle (s. 1(5)) is also relevant in such cases.

- Welfare report

- Both have PR

- s. 8—Residence and contact

- The welfare principle—s. 1

- Statutory checklist, s. 1(3)

- The homosexual parent—relevant

- The 'religious' parent—relevant

Suggested answer

One assumes that Caroline wants the two girls, Debbie and Linda, to continue to live with her, but that she is concerned, in the light of Robin's outburst about her lesbian relationship with Philippa, that he will be allowed to take them away from her. Is this in fact the case? Obviously on such facts there is likely to be a full blown dispute over the children. Mediation may be considered but is perhaps unlikely to be successful, and the court will order a welfare report to be prepared (s. 7, CA 1989).

As married parents, Caroline and Robin both have parental responsibility for Debbie and Linda (s. 2, CA 1989) and this has not been affected by their divorce. They may both exercise their responsibility independently of each other when the girls are with them. Any s. 8 order will only affect parental responsibility in so far as it deals with a concrete issue concerning the girls' upbringing, and neither parent must act incompatibly with such an order. Robin says that he intends to apply for a residence order—Caroline will oppose any such application. In private family disputes such as this one, it is not automatic that an order will be made. The court will be influenced by the non-intervention prinicple (s. 1(5), CA 1989) and will only make an order if satisfied that there is a demonstrable need for one. Robin and Caroline will have to justify an order being made, but where there is a dispute, as here, an order is probably going to be desirable.

In deciding with whom Debbie and Linda should live, their welfare will be the court's paramount consideration (s. 1, CA 1989). As the s. 8 application for a residence order is opposed, the checklist in s. 1(3), CA 1989 is applicable to assist the court with the balancing exercise necessary to assess the children's welfare. It is not necessary for the court to consider every guideline in every case, merely the relevant ones: *B v B (Minor: Residence Order: Reasons)* [1997] 2 FLR 602. Applying the checklist to the given facts, as appropriate, first on the list (though this does not give them priority over other factors (*Re J (A Minor)* [1992] Fam Law 229)) are the ascertainable wishes and feelings of the children, considered in the light of their age and understanding. Children can be influenced by all sorts of things when expressing a view and the court will not be constricted by a child's wishes particularly if they appear to be at odds with the child's welfare; at the end of the day it is the court's decision. The court may well listen to and pay respect to the views of older children (*Re S (Contact: Children's Views)* [2002] 1 FLR 1156, children of 16, 14 and 12), but the girls here are only seven and four, and the court is most unlikely even to hear them directly, relying instead on the welfare officer's interview. In *Re A (Specific Issue Order: Parental Dispute)* [2001] 1 FLR 121, the court was influenced by the psychological evidence that it is harmful to require children to choose between parents. Incidentally, there is evidence that children prefer to be brought up by the parent of the same sex after divorce.

The girls' physical, emotional and educational needs must also be considered. Here the fact that Debbie and Linda are girls and also so young will weigh in Caroline's favour. As a general rule it is better for young children to be with their mother (*M* v *M* [1982] 4 FLR 603), but maternal preference does not have the status of a legal presumption and the weight attached to it is a matter of judicial discretion. In the Scottish case of *Brixey* v *Lynas* [1996] 2 FLR 499 the House of Lords referred to 'the workings of nature . . . where a very young child has been with its mother since birth and there is no criticism of her ability to care for the child only the strongest competing advantages are likely to prevail'. The more recent English case of *Re A (Children: 1959 UN Declaration)* [1998] 1 FLR 354 suggests that the court will be more easily persuaded that the child is better cared for by the mother than by the father, and the younger the child(ren) the more so. Yet any presumption to that effect might constitute sexual discrimination and thus contravene the Human Rights Act 1998. Certainly there should be no question of separating the two girls (*C* v *C (Custody of Children)* [1988] 2 FLR 291; siblings should be brought up together in same household), particularly in view of the age proximity. A further factor in Caroline's favour is the fact that since she and Robin divorced two years ago the girls have lived with her. In practice, preservation of the *status quo* tends to be the most important factor (s. 1(3)(c)). Continuity of care is important and the court will be reluctant to disturb the girls' settled environment, unless there is good reason for doing so (*Re B (Residence Order: Status Quo)* [1998] 1 FLR 368).

In considering any harm suffered or likely to be suffered by Debbie and Linda (s. 1(3)(e)) the court will look at their parents' lifestyle and behaviour, such behaviour being relevant if it reflects on the individual as a parent. In this particular case two aspects of parental behaviour require discussion as being very relevant to the outcome of the case.

First we are told that Robin is involved with an extreme religious sect and that the marriage broke down because of his attempts to impose his beliefs on the rest of the family. He is also described as being a strict disciplinarian with very high standards, factors which will not necessarily work against him (*May* v *May* [1986] 1 FLR 325). His religion is, however, a different matter. Usually a parent's religious beliefs will not be of particular relevance in such cases but, if the parent's beliefs are extreme and result in social isolation, psychological damage or physical suffering for the children, then they will be relevant (*Re B and G (Minors) (Custody)* [1985] FLR 493; father a member of Church of Scientology which set out to indoctrinate children making them 'unquestioning captives and tools of the cult, withdrawn from ordinary thought, living and relationship with others'; custody to mother). In *Hoffman* v *Austria* (1993) 17 EHRR 293 ECtHR, it was held permissible to deny 'custody' to a parent because of the *effect* of any religious practices on the child. If the court found that there was a risk of any sort of harm to Debbie and Linda as a result of their father's involvement with what is described as an extreme sect, Robin would not be given a residence order.

Secondly we are told that Caroline is involved in a lesbian relationship with Philippa. Now that Robin has found out about this, Caroline is obviously very concerned that the court will share his opinion that she is not fit to bring up the girls. But is this going to be the case? This is always a sensitive issue and Caroline's sexual orientation will have to be discussed because of the possible impact on the children's own sexual identity and the possible stigmatisation of the girls by their peers. Despite changes in attitude over the last twenty years or so, a lesbian relationship is still regarded as an unusual background in which to bring up a child (*C v C (A Minor) (Custody: Appeal)* [1991] 1 FLR 223). However, the fact that Caroline is a lesbian is not in itself conclusive and does not *per se* render her unfit to care for Debbie and Linda as Robin contends. It is, though, a factor which obviously cannot be ignored by the court when weighing up the options of what is best for the girls (*C v C (A Minor) (Custody: Appeal)* above). In *B v B (Minors) (Custody, Care and Control)* [1991] 1 FLR 402, Callman J, when giving a lesbian mother care and control of a two and a half year old, was influenced by expert evidence that the dangers of living in a lesbian household tend to be overestimated. Indeed, in the past, there has been a tendency to make assumptions about the effects on children of living in such an environment. Empirical evidence, however, demonstrates that a mother's sexual orientation does not appear to influence the child's well-being; it is the quality of parenting which is important (Barton, 'The Homosexual in the Family' [1996] *Fam Law* 625).

Each case depends on the evidence available. If, for example, Caroline and Philippa are 'militant' lesbians and tend to advertise their relationship, this may adversely affect Caroline's case as the risks of harm to Debbie and Linda will be greater (*B v B* (1991) above). However, if as a mother, Caroline is found to be good enough, the court may well decide that a 'sensitive, loving lesbian relationship is a more satisfactory environment for the children than a less sensitive or loving alternative' *per* Glidewell LJ in *C v C* (1991) (above) in which, on a subsequent rehearing, care and control was given to a lesbian mother by Booth J. But, since the Human Rights Act 1998, even these distinctions may be passé: in *Da Silva Mouta* v *Portugal* (unreported 21.12.99 ECtHR) it was held contrary to Arts. 14 and 8 to deny residence or contact on the ground of sexuality *per se*.

Caroline only works part-time and is able to look after the girls herself when they are not at school. Robin, on the other hand, intends to leave the girls with other members of the sect whilst he is at work. Child care arrangements are another relevant factor and the court may well be reluctant to see Debbie and Linda being looked after by sect members at times when they could be with their own loving mother. (One of the factors which went against the lesbian mother in *B v B* (above) was that the father had remarried and was living in a 'classic husand and wife relationship'.)

On balance, taking all relevant factors into account, it would seem likely that the court will decide that Debbie and Linda's welfare demands that they stay with Caroline, and make an unconditional residence order in Caroline's favour. A joint residence order (s. 11(4)) would appear unlikely and impracticable in the circumstances and it has been said that such orders would only be appropriate where there is a good relationship between the parents (*Re R (A Minor) (Residence Order: Finance)* [1995] 2 FLR 612). Robin would, however, undoubtedly be allowed regular and frequent contact with his daughters. In *Re S (Contact: Promoting Relationship with Absent Parent)* [2004] EWCA Civ 18 [2004] Fam Law 387, it was recognised that no parent was perfect, but 'good enough' parents should have a relationship with their child, for their own benefit and, even more, in the interests of the child. It was therefore, most important that the attempt to promote contact between a child and the non-resident parent should not be abandoned until it was clear that the child would not benefit from continuing the attempt.

Q Question 4

Matthew and Liz divorced amicably 18 months ago. They have two sons, Tom, now eight and Jack, now ten, and Matthew has always been happy for them to stay with Liz. No orders were made in relation to the boys on the divorce.

Matthew tries to see the boys two or three times a week and they frequently spend weekends with him. These arrangements worked well until recently, but Matthew is now experiencing a number of problems.

A few months ago Liz met Bruce, a New Zealander living over here, and there is now talk of marriage. On a number of occasions in the last few weeks, Matthew's arrangements to see Tom and Jack have been cancelled at the last minute, as the boys were going out with Bruce. Last week when Matthew actually got to see the boys, Tom was talking excitedly about a possible trip to New Zealand with Bruce. Matthew feels that Bruce is trying to replace him as the boys' father. Liz refuses to discuss this, or indeed anything to do with Tom and Jack, with Matthew.

The boys are happy living with Liz, and Matthew does not want to change this, but he is concerned about being increasingly excluded from Tom and Jack's lives. He seeks your advice as to his position.

Commentary

Here you are asked to advise the divorced father of two young boys on his position in relation to a number of problems which have recently arisen in relation to the boys. The divorce took place 18 months ago, but the arrival on the scene of a third party in the form of Bruce, seems, as is sometimes the case, to have complicated matters and to have upset the apple cart somewhat. You should note that the father is happy for the boys to continue to live with their mother, i.e. residence is not in dispute. The welfare principle is obviously going to be relevant, but emphasis should be on the two problem issues raised by the facts, i.e. contact, and the 'New Zealand connection', remembering that to date, no orders have been made in relation to the boys. To advise the father fully, you should consider in relation to the two issues what might happen in the future (contact further restricted; the boys being taken to New Zealand for long periods, or even permanently). Try to deal with each issue as thoroughly as possible, using relevant case law and not forgetting the relevance of the general principles and philosophy of the Children Act (CA) 1989.

- Parental responsibility

- s. 8—Contact Order

- The welfare principle

- Statutory checklist

- Leaving the jurisdiction—PSO, s. 8

:Ọ́: Suggested answer

At the time of their divorce 18 months ago, Matthew and Liz were able to settle things amicably and it was agreed that their two sons, Tom and Jack, should stay with Liz. Matthew has seen his sons several times each week and they have spent many weekends with him. Obviously the agreed arrangements have worked well and despite their parents' divorce, Tom and Jack have had two active and involved parents, in keeping with the underlying philosophy of the Children Act 1989. Unfortunately, as sometimes happens, problems have arisen since Liz acquired a new partner, and it is about these problems that Matthew is seeking advice.

There seem to be two areas of concern, namely problems with contact and the possibility of the boys being taken to New Zealand for a trip or longer.

So what is Matthew's position? Ideally, of course, he should try to talk to Liz about the children and to see whether these matters can be sorted out on an amicable basis. However if, as we are told, she will not discuss the boys with him at the moment, then he may feel that he needs to take some formal steps to safeguard his position. As a married father, Matthew shares parental responsibility for Tom and Jack with Liz (s. 2, CA 1989) and this has not been affected by their separation or divorce (or by the arrival of Bruce). No s. 8 orders have been made to date so that when Matthew has Tom and Jack with him he may exercise his parental responsibility as he sees fit and may act independently, in the best interests of the boys, (s. 2(7)). Liz may do the same. As the non-resident parent Matthew retains the right to be involved in, and to have opinions on the boys' upbringing. In a situation where one parent is unhappy with what the other parent is doing (as here), then it may be necessary to make application to the court. Matthew does not wish to change the residence arrangements as he believes that it is in Tom and Jack's best interests to stay with Liz; he simply wants to ensure that he is not in practice replaced as the boys' father by Bruce. However, if Liz and Bruce were to marry then it would be possible for Bruce to acquire parental responsibility (PR) by way of agreement to that effect with everyone who has PR for the child. However, if Matthew were to refuse to consent, then Bruce could acquire PR by a court order (s. 112 of the Adoption and Children Act 2002 inserts s. 4A into the Children Act 1989). Step-parents will no longer need to apply for a residence order, adopt or be appointed as a guardian to enable them to acquire PR. Matthew, of course, would not lose his PR, he would share it with Liz and Bruce and, should Matthew marry again, his spouse could acquire PR too.

We now turn to deal with the two problem areas, first contact. Matthew is experiencing problems with contact and cannot reach a satisfactory agreement with Liz, he may apply as of right (as a parent—s. 10(4)(a), CA 1989) for a contact order (s. 8). An order for reasonable contact would include staying contact, and leave the specific arrangements to Liz and Matthew. This type of order is to be preferred but if agreement cannot be reached, then the court may define contact in terms of duration and frequency. Defined orders tend to be restrictive and do little to encourage ordinary, natural relationships between parents and children. When deciding whether and, if so, what order to make, the court will be influenced by the non-intervention principle (s. 1(5), CA 1989) and the welfare principle (s. 1). The checklist (s. 1(3)) applies in the event of a dispute and it is likely that the court will attach weight to the wishes and feelings of Tom and Jack on the matter (*Re P (A Minor) (Education: Child's Wishes)* [1992] 1 FCR 145). On the facts given, there seem to be no reasons why Matthew should not have regular contact, there is nothing to indicate that he is no longer a fit and proper person to have contact with his sons and no apparent reasons why physical contact would be considered undesirable. It is clear from both *Re L (A Child) (Contact: Domestic Violence)* [2000] 2 FLR 334 and Article 9(3) of the UN Convention on the Rights of the Child 1989 that parental contact is appropriate except where it is not in his interests. Jonathan Herring concludes that, 'Despite the ambiguity of the research, the law has been willing to accept that contact promotes the welfare of the child' (*Family Law* (Longman, 1991)). The boys are eight and ten, and obviously have a well-established relationship with their father which should be preserved. Tom and Jack's best interests will be served by having continued contact with their natural father. However, Matthew should be warned that even where a residential parent's opposition is irrational, the court may (exceptionally) conclude that her distress may harm the children (*Re C (Contact: Supervision)* [1996] 2 FLR 314).

What, however, if Liz still makes it difficult, without genuine reasons, for Matthew to see Tom and Jack as he would like; or worse, tries to stop contact altogether? If the original order is for reasonable contact, then Matthew would have to return to the court to have contact defined, and if there are still problems, consider taking steps to enforce the order. It is rather simplistic to suggest that enforcement proceedings are the answer in such a situation, where the real problem is a breakdown in communication. The aim is to get the order working, not to punish. However, Liz could be warned by the court of the sanctions which may be applied, given some time in which to comply and then the case could be reviewed (*V-P* v *V-P* [1980] Fam Law 20). More constructively, the court may make a family assistance order (s. 16, CA 1989) in the hope that a welfare officer can produce a solution. As a last resort, and to encourage compliance with the order Liz could be imprisoned, though such a Draconian step is usually considered inappropriate in such cases and of course would adversely affect the boys' welfare. In *Re L* [1989] 2 FLR 359 Hollis J said that it might serve the long-term interests of children if their mother went to prison to make her comply with an order in the future, and in *Z* v *Z* [1996] 1 FCR 538, the mother was committed for six weeks but was released after two days when she purged her contempt. However, in *Re F (Contact: Enforcement: Representation of Child)* [1999] 1 FLR 810, the Court of Appeal noted that treatment rather than imprisonment is better where contact orders are disobeyed. Nonetheless, failure to enforce contact decisions may violate the European Convention of Human Rights: *Hokkanen* v *Finland* [1996] 1 FLR 289 (see also *Re K (Contact: Committal Order)* [2003] 1 FLR 277). In intractable contact disputes the court may transfer residence *(V v V (Children) (Contact: Implacable Hostility)* (2004) *The Times*, 28 May), or even transfer residence and make a supervision order in favour of the local authority *(Re M (Intractable Contact Dispute: Interim Care Order)* [2003] 2 FLR 636. See also *Re D (Intractable Contact Dispute: Publicity)* [2004] 1 FLR 1226 where, in the view of Munby J, the two great vices of the present family justice system were (1) that the system was almost exclusively court-based, and (2) that the court's procedures were not working as speedily and efficiently as they should be.

The second area of concern is that Liz's new partner is Bruce, a New Zealander, and there is 'talk of marriage'. We are told that he is living here, but we do not know whether this is a permanent or temporary arrangement. Matthew is obviously not very happy at the prospect of his sons going on a trip to New Zealand with Bruce but, even in the absence of a residence order in her favour, it is possible that Liz may take the boys out of the country with impunity. A residence order in Liz's favour would be subject to the automatic condition that Liz could remove the boys from the jurisdiction for up to one month only, without Matthew's written consent or leave of the court (s. 13(2)). (In the absence of any residence order, Liz *might* be open to prosecution under the Child Abduction Act 1984. She could, however, claim (s. 1(5)(c)) that Matthew is unreasonably refusing to consent. If there is 'sufficient evidence' of that, then the onus switches to the prosecution: s. 1(6).) If Matthew does not want Tom and Jack to leave the UK at all, he should apply for a prohibited steps order (s. 8, CA 1989) which will specify that before the boys can be taken out of the UK, the issue must be referred to the court.

It may be that Matthew would not really object to Tom and Jack merely having a holiday in New Zealand, but that his fear is that Liz and Bruce may decide to live permanently in New Zealand. A prohibited steps order would ensure that the matter would have to be referred to the court. Would the court give leave for Tom and Jack to leave the jurisdiction permanently? The Court of Appeal has in a number of such cases granted leave if the request was reasonable, on the basis that to refuse leave would cause distress and frustration within the new family unit, which in turn could adversely affect the welfare of the children. In *Belton* v *Belton* [1987] 2 FLR 343 leave was granted to the mother of a three-year-old girl to emigrate to New Zealand, the home of her new husband. Since the implementation of the Children Act, such decisions are harder to justify as they clearly fly in the face of the concept of continuing parental responsibility, but the courts have, since the Act, indicated that they are likely to continue to take the same approach to these cases and refuse leave only if it can be clearly shown that the move would be contrary to the child's interests: in *Re T (Removal from Jurisdiction)* [1996] 2 FLR 352 Thorpe LJ referred to 'the general proposition that the parent with primary care is entitled to select the place and country of residence of the child unless that selection is shown to be plainly incompatible with welfare'. In *Payne* v *Payne* [2001] 1 FLR 1052 (the first case in which the impact of the European Convention for the Protection of Fundamental Rights and Fundamental Freedoms 1950 (European Convention) on relocation cases was considered by the Court of Appeal in a substantive appeal), Thorpe LJ warned against the danger of elevating the reasonable proposals of the primary carer into a legal presumption. Then, there would be an obvious risk of the breach of the respondent's rights, not only under Art. 8 (right to respect for his private and family life) but also his rights under Art. 6 to a fair trial and the too ready assumption that the mother's proposals are necessarily compatible with the child's welfare. (Note also *Re B (Removal From Jurisdiction; Re S (Removal From Jurisdiction* [2003] 2 FLR 1043 particularly where the child's stepfather is a foreign national, and *L* v *L (Leave to Remove Children from Jurisdiction: Effect on Children)* [2003] 1 FLR 900, where the educational opportunity in the US, for a child with a learning disability, was a key factor for a family where the husband had been offered a major career advancement in the US, even though that would involve moving away from a father who was having frequent and regular contact. Given that the mother and her husband viewed the father as morally blameworthy in having left the family originally, the consequences for them of having their perfectly reasonable expectations now thwarted by him would go beyond ordinary disappointment. The children would detect their bitterness and hence the emotional security and stability would be badly and seriously impaired.) Yet the operation of the welfare principle cannot be fettered, and as recently as 1997, leave was denied in 9 of the 18 cases reported since 1885 (C. Barton, 'When Did You Next See Your Father', CFLQ Vol. 9 No. 1 (1997), p. 82). The need to retain paternal links, the planned emigration being ill-thought out, the views of competent children, the motives of the emigrating parent: all have come to the father's aid—just as the fact of her new partner has come to the mother's.

If Liz were to seek the court's leave to go to New Zealand permanently with Tom and Jack, as Bruce is from New Zealand and the request therefore reasonable, the court may well take the view that they should be allowed to get on with their lives without the court's interference, and grant leave. Matthew will have to hope that the situation does not arise.

Having advised Matthew as to his position, it is to be hoped that the problems he is experiencing are merely hiccoughs in his post-divorce relationship with his ex-wife. Perhaps court intervention may prove unnecessary once the importance of the concept of continuing parental responsibility, and of acting in Tom and Jack's best interests has been emphasised to Liz, and it has been made clear to her that the Children Act 1989 firmly takes the view that on their divorce Matthew ceased to be her spouse, but did not cease to be Tom and Jack's father.

Further reading

Bailey-Harris, R., Davis, G., Barron, J., and Pearce, J., *Monitoring Private Law Applications Under the Children Act* (Bristol: University of Bristol, 1998).

Bainham, A., 'Contact as a Fundamental Right' (1995) *Cambridge Law Journal* 54, p. 255.

Barton, C., and Douglas, G., *Law & Parenthood* (London: Butterworths, 1995).

Douglas, G., and Murch, M., 'Taking Account of Children's Needs in Divorce' (2002), CFLQ, Vol. 14, p. 57.

Murray, C., ' Same-sex Families: Outcomes for Children and Parents' [2004] *Fam Law* 136.

Richards, M., 'The Interests of Children at Divorce', in M. Meulders-Klein (ed.) *Families et Justice* (Bruylant, 1997).

Richards, M., and Connell, J., 'Children and the Family Law Act', in L. J. Thorpe and E. Clarke (eds) *No Fault or Flaw* (Bristol: Jordans, 2000).

Smart, C., *et al.*, *Residence and Contact Disputes in Court, Department for Constitutional Affairs Research Series No. 6/03* (DCA, 2003).

Spon-Smith, R., 'Relocation Revisited' [2004] *Fam Law* 191.

Children and the local authority

Introduction

This chapter deals with Parts III, IV and V of the Children Act 1989. Although each of these Parts deals with a different aspect of child care law, the Act must be read as a whole. The former Lord Chancellor, Lord Mackay of Clashfern, stated that the Act 'brings together the public and private law concerning the care, protection and upbringing of children and the provision of services to them and their families'.

In the same way that the Act brings together public and private law, so must you be willing, and able, to discuss the private law orders when you are considering intervention by the local authority. The Act provides a set of remedies which are available in all courts in all family proceedings. Although applications for residence orders are made mainly in divorce proceedings, an application could be made when a child is in care. The care order would be discharged if a residence order were to be granted. A care order discharges any s. 8 order (s. 91(2)) so ending the parental responsibility of non-parents (s. 12(2)).

It can be seen therefore that it would be unwise to attempt an answer to a problem question in this area if all you intend to do, or if all you are able to do, is confine yourself to a narrow consideration of part of the Act in isolation. Consider all the options.

Parents have primary responsibility for their children, however, on occasions they may need the help and support of the local authority. Other situations may demand local authority intervention to protect children.

During 2003, a total of 22,725 public law applications were made (a decrease of nearly 4 per cent from 2002). In 2003 there were 7,387 care orders, 2,383 supervision orders and 2,061 emergency protection orders made (*Judicial Statistics*, 2003, Cm. 6251, Table 5.2). The most significant trend was the increase (16 per cent) in the number of emergency protection orders (against the trend of the previous year) and the large increase (35 per cent) in supervision orders (up again). The number of care orders increased again (14 per cent).

The Act aims to provide a comprehensive code of the law affecting children. It may not be all you need to know, but if you can find your way around the Act you will impress the examiner.

Q Question 1

Les, a trainee local authority social worker, would be grateful for your advice on one of his current cases.

Molly, who is 21 and unmarried, has two children, Norman aged five and Oscar aged one. Six months ago Peter, aged 18 years, moved in with them and Molly is expecting their child. Staff at the local health centre are concerned that Oscar is underweight and failing to thrive. Norman's teacher, Miss Quinn, is concerned that he has become rather withdrawn in the last few months. Her view, when he started school a year ago, was that he was small for his age and not very clean. When she attempted to discuss the matter with Molly she was told cheerfully 'All kids hate washing, don't they?'. Les thinks that Molly loves her children and cares for them, albeit in a rather haphazard manner, and although she has serious learning difficulties she has managed to cope until recently. Molly no longer attends the clinic at the health centre and when the health visitor called recently Peter refused to let her into the house. Neighbours have contacted the social services department reporting that the children were out in the garden late at night in cold weather wearing thin clothes and no shoes.

Miss Quinn has informed Les that as a result of talks with Norman she suspects he is being sexually abused by Peter. Molly screamed at her to 'keep out of it' when Miss Quinn suggested that Norman should have a medical examination.

Les thinks that the time has come to take immediate action.

Commentary

Not quite a cast of thousands, but almost! Molly is not the 'perfect mother' but then again, who is, apart from the wonder-women of the television detergent 'ads'?

This is a problem question which requires you to consider the powers given to a local authority for the emergency protection of children, the clues are provided in the facts of the problem and the statement that Les wishes to take 'immediate action'. Les should heed the words of Butler Sloss LJ, speaking at the King's College—LSE Child Protection Course in February 1993 where she warned that:

> If the child is removed on insufficient information, a court may not make an order and the child will go home. If the child was not abused, he will have had all the drama of being taken away with its attendant disruption. If he has been abused and you cannot prove it, he will still go home and what will he think of the system? It is better not to have gone away. Perhaps the most difficult thing you have to do is live with uncertainty and not be able to give sufficient protection to some children you feel are at risk.

Answer plan

- Local authority duty to investigate, s. 47, Children Act 1989.

- Protection of children—Part V, Children Act 1989.

- Child assessment order, s. 43.

- Emergency protection order, s. 44.

- Exclusion requirements, s. 38A and s. 44A.

- As always apply relevant cases and statutes to facts.

:Ọ: Suggested answer

Les is aware of the concern that has been expressed about the welfare of the children by staff at the health centre, the health visitor, Molly's neighbours and Miss Quinn, and although Molly has not lived up to the ideal of the perfect mother, she has coped in the past. The situation appears to have deteriorated since Peter's arrival and Les, understandably, wishes to do something; the question is what can he do, or being child-centred, what should he do?

Where a local authority has reasonable cause to suspect that a child is suffering, or is likely to suffer significant harm, it must investigate before it decides what action to take (s. 47 Children Act (CA) 1989, see *Re S (sexual Abuse Allegations: Local Authority Response)* [2001] 2 FLR 776).

Action under s. 47 'should be seen as the usual first step when a question of child protection arises' (Department of Health's Guidance and Regulations). Les should attempt to work in partnership with the family and, except in emergencies, case conferences should be held before anyone contemplates removing a child. 'Case conferences provide a forum for the exchange of information and allow for inter-agency, multi-disciplinary discussion of allegations or suspicions of abuse; . . . an action plan for protecting the child and helping the family' (Department of Health and Social Security, Working Together (1988)).

In the Report of the Inquiry into Child Abuse in Cleveland in 1987 (Cm. 412, 1988) it was noted that local authority lawyers rarely attended case conferences. The early involvement of the local authority lawyer would allow evaluation of the evidence and consideration of the options available. Early morning removal of a child from its home by the police, even though effected in conjunction with the social services, should only be carried out when there are clear grounds for believing significant harm would otehwise be caused to the child or vital evidence is available only by such means (*Re A and Others (Minors) (Wardship: Child Abuse: Guidelines)* [1992] 1 All ER 153). Any intervention by the local authority must be looked at from the child's point of view, i.e. is it going to do more harm than good? If Les acts on insufficient information the children may be removed from a home where they are not in danger, or removed and returned to a home where they are in danger. The questions that must be asked are, is this an emergency situation where immediate action must be taken, is there enough evidence to initiate proceedings and if not, how can such evidence be obtained?

A child assessment order (CAO) may be able to provide the evidence that Les requires. A CAO was described by David Mellor as 'a multi-disciplinary assessment in non-emergency situations' (Hansard (HC) vol. 158, col. 596). Only the local authority or the National Society for the Prevention of Cruelty to Children (NSPCC) can apply. This evidence-seeking order (*per* David Hinchcliffe MP, Hansard (HC) vol. 158, col. 604) may be granted by the court if the applicant has reasonable cause to suspect that the child is suffering or is likely to suffer significant harm, an assessment is necessary to determine this and is unlikely to be made without such an order (s. 43(1)). The court must be satisfied with the reasonableness of the applicant's belief, whereas for an emergency protection order (EPO) the court must be satisfied that there is reasonable cause to believe the child is likely to suffer significant harm if he is not removed from, or does not remain in, his present accommodation (s. 44(1)(a)). Anyone can apply for an EPO. In the case of an application by a local authority, the court may only make an order if it is satisfied that enquiries in respect of the child are being made under s. 47(1)(b) and that those enquiries are being frustrated by access to the child being unreasonably refused to a person authorised to seek access and that the applicant has reasonable cause to believe that access to the child is required as a matter of urgency (s. 44(1)(b)). This lowers the hurdle considerably in many cases as where s. 44(1)(b) is satisfied, no other threshold test applies. The local authority will not have to prove that the removal must be immediate for an EPO to be granted. Peter may promise to leave the home, the power to remove the child who is the subject of the order would continue for the duration of the order and if Peter were to return, the child could be removed.

New powers have been given to the court to exclude an alleged abuser when making an interim care order (s. 38A) or an EPO (s. 44A) (as amended by s. 52 and sch. 6, Family Law Act 1996). The exclusion requirement can be made where the grounds for an interim care order or an EPO have been made out and there is reasonable cause to believe that if Peter is excluded from the home, the child will cease to suffer or cease to be likely to suffer significant harm and that Molly is able and willing to give the child the care it would be reasonable to expect a parent to give him. Additionally, and here lies the problem, Molly must consent to the inclusion of the exclusion requirement. A power of arrest may be attached to the exclusion requirement (s. 38A(5)) or the court may accept an undertaking from Peter, instead of making an exclusion requirement.

Molly could apply under Part IV of the Family Law Act 1996 for a non-molestation or occupation order against Peter, to protect Norman from abuse; the local authority could not apply for such orders. Molly may have to make a choice in the near future between living with Peter or living with her children.

If, during s. 47, CA 1989 enquiries, access to a child is refused, the local authority has a duty to apply for an EPO if the child's welfare demands it (s. 44(1)(b)). An EPO is designed to give immediate short-term protection to children in emergencies.

If the local authority decides that a CAO is appropriate it must take reasonably practicable steps to give notice of the application to Molly; the children's father; Peter (if he has parental responsibility, or is regarded as another person caring for the child) and Norman and Oscar (s. 43(11)). As the notice period is seven days, this order is not suitable where there is a need for urgent action. The local authority may take the view that it is Norman only who is in immediate danger and apply for an EPO in respect of Norman and a CAO in respect of Oscar. A CAO imposes a duty to produce the child to the person named in the order for assessment. The local authority would not acquire parental responsibility on the granting of a CAO; it would if an EPO were granted.

As a CAO can last for no longer than seven days and cannot be extended, Les should ensure that arrangements for the assessment have been carefully planned so that the time available is not wasted. A CAO does not allow a child to be removed from home unless the court makes a direction to that effect (s. 43(9)) and the child must be returned home as soon as possible. The results of the assessment should give enough information for the authority to decide whether or not to apply for an emergency protection order, or a care or supervision order. It may be that the fears were unfounded or it may be that the problem, if there is one, could be dealt with in another way, for example with local authority support for Molly and the provision of child care classes. That may seem somewhat naive and optimistic in view of the fact that as Molly is carrying Peter's child he is likely to be around for the foreseeable future, even though the chances of a long-term relationship may seem unlikely.

Les may be concerned to hear that if Molly were to fail to comply with a CAO there is nothing that can be done to enforce it. However the local authority would be unlikely to allow the matter to rest there and would almost certainly apply for, and get, an EPO.

The court must not make a CAO if there are grounds for making an EPO (s. 43(4)) and may treat a CAO application as an EPO application (s. 43(3)). It may be that a thorough and complete assessment could not be carried out in seven days, so Les may think it necessary to apply for EPOs, which can be for up to eight days. A local authority is entitled to apply for an EPO to be extended for one further period of seven days (s. 45(4)). By then there should be enough evidence to allow the authority to decide whether or not to proceed with a care order.

Conditions may be satisfied for either the making of an EPO or a CAO but the court is not bound to make an order. The child's welfare must be the court's paramount consideration (s. 1(1)) and the court must be satisfied that it would be better to make an order than no order at all (s. 1(5)). Applications for a CAO or an EPO do not come within family proceedings, so the court has no power to make s. 8 orders even where an EPO or a CAO is refused.

If an EPO were to be granted, the local authority must allow reasonable contact between the child who is the subject of the order and Molly. The Cleveland Report emphasised the danger of denying contact to parents who were the victims of unsubstantiated allegations; suffering is caused to the parents and to the children who are taken away. The court could give directions for assessment and prohibit contact between the children and Peter, or allow supervised contact so that neither Molly nor Peter are allowed to put pressure on the children to persuade them to withdraw any allegations. Care must be taken to prevent faulty interviewing techniques from persuading the children to make allegations which are not true. Butler Sloss LJ recognised the importance of listening to children but was of the opinion that what is said should be examined critically. 'Why are children believed when they say abuse has occurred but not believed when they say it hasn't? They may be right or wrong in saying either' ((1993) 143 *NLJ* 275).

Les should be aware that an EPO application must be carefully prepared, especially if the local authority wants the children to be medically examined or if it wants contact restricted. An application for an EPO can be made on a without notice basis; cf. the notice requirements of a CAO. After 72 hours Molly or Peter, as a person with whom the child was living prior to the order, could apply to discharge the order (s. 45(8), (9)) unless they had notice of the original hearing and were present, or the order had been extended (s. 45(11)).

If Les is concerned about the care a new born baby would receive from Molly and Peter, he could advise the local authority to make an application for a care order (s. 31), or an EPO, immediately after the birth of the baby, on the basis that the child is likely to suffer significant harm.

However, following the European Court of Human Rights decision in *P, C and S v United Kingdom* [2002] 2 FLR 631 the removal of a baby at birth under an EPO may breach the parents' right to respect for family life under Art. 8 of the European Convention for the Protection of Human Rights and Fundamental Freedoms 1950 (see also *K and T v Finland* [2001] 2 FLR 707; *Venema v The Netherlands* [2003] 1 FLR 551; and *KA v Finland* [2003] 1 FLR 696). Local Authorities should, when managing a perceived risk, try to find a way to allow mother and child to remain together. Otherwise they could face a challenge under Art. 8 and an injunction to prevent removal under s. 8, Human Rights Act 1998. In *Re M (Care Proceedings: Judicial Review)* [2003] 2 FLR 171, it was stated that it is inappropriate to seek to prevent a local authority from bringing substantive proceedings where it will be possible to challenge the authority's approach in those very proceedings. This is in line with *Re L (Care Proceedings: Human Rights Claims)* [2003] 2 FLR 160, where it was said that complaints about a proposed care plan should normally be raised in the substantive proceedings and not by way of action under ss. 7 or 8 of the Human Rights Act (HRA) 1998. This view was reiterated in *Re V (Care Proceedings: Human Rights Claims)* [2004] 1 FLR 944. Apart from a declaration of incompatibility under s. 4 of the HRA 1998, all family courts have the jurisdiction to take, and deal with, human rights arguments. Applications for proceedings to be transferred to the High Court, so that discrete human rights issues might be determined by a High Court judge, were to be strongly discouraged and could amount to an abuse of process. The *Protocol for Judicial Case Management in Public Law Children Act Cases (June 2003)* [2003] 2 FLR 719 should ensure that these issues are identified at the outset and dealt with in the court's management of the proceedings.

Q Question 2

During the course of their turbulent marriage, Stan has left his wife Rose and their three children (aged 14, 12 and 9) on numerous occasions. Last year, on one of these occasions, it all became too much for Rose and she attempted suicide. She was admitted to hospital and voluntary arrangements were made for the children with the local authority. The children were looked after for almost a year by Mr and Mrs Taylor who are experienced foster parents. Contact between the children and their mother was maintained by visits and letters.

Rose and the children returned to the family home three months ago, Stan joined them a month later. Last week Stan walked out 'never to return' and Rose has become extremely depressed fearing that she cannot cope on her own. The hospital is willing to take her as a voluntary patient. Rose contacted the local authority with a view to making a voluntary arrangement for the children and much to her relief was told that Mr and Mrs Taylor were able and willing to look after the children again. The children are distressed about their mother's health but feel reassured that they will be able to be accommodated in familiar surroundings with people they know and like.

Rose was due to go into hospital tomorrow, but yesterday Stan telephoned her, stating that he did not think that she should abandon the children in this way and that he intended to oppose the arrangement. Stan has a job as a long distance lorry driver making deliveries around Europe, which involves him being out of the country for three weeks in every month. Rose is concerned that even if the children go to Mr and Mrs Taylor's home, Stan will remove them when he returns to this country.

Can the other parties involved ensure that their plans will not be disrupted by Stan?

Commentary

The main area that you are required to consider in this answer is local authority support for children and families under Part III of the Children Act 1989.

As yet, there is no general test for competency in parenting; Stan has parental responsibility but does not appear to be behaving very responsibly. There is nothing short of adoption that can be done to take away his parental responsibility, but as this question and answer illustrate, parental responsibility may have to be shared or, it could be argued, restricted. Residence orders take away the right of the parent without the order to object to the child being accommodated by the local authority. When a child is in care parents share parental responsibility with the local authority which has the power to determine the extent to which the parent may meet his parental responsibility.

Answer plan

- Local authority support for children and families—Part III, Children Act 1989.

- LA Duty to children in need s. 17, CA 1989.

- Parental responsibility, s. 2, s. 3.

- Provision of accommodation, s. 20.

- Removal from jurisdiction, s. 13(1)(b), CA 1989. Child Abduction Act 1984.

- Wardship. Residence order s. 8. LA intervention.

☼ Suggested answer

Rose wishes to make a voluntary arrangement with the local authority so that her children can be accommodated by them while she is in hospital. Every local authority has a general duty to safeguard and promote the welfare of children in its area who are in need and, so far as is consistent with that duty, to promote the upbringing of such children by their families (s. 17(1), Children Act 1989). It appears that the local authority was supportive the last time Rose went into hospital and that there was a successful voluntary partnership which safeguarded the welfare of the children. Rose and Stan each have parental responsibility as they are the natural parents of the children and they are married to each other (s. 2(1)). 'Parental responsibility' means all the rights, duties, powers, responsibilities and authority which by law a parent of a child has in relation to the child and his property (s. 3(1)). Rose and Stan will have the responsibility for raising their children, but the local authority has a duty to accommodate children in need in its area when the person caring for them is prevented from looking after them. Where there is a voluntary arrangement the local authority does not acquire parental responsibility. Even where children are taken into care and a local authority acquires parental responsibility (s. 33(3)), the parents do not lose parental responsibility, they share it with the local authority (s. 2(6)).

Before providing accommodation under s. 20 the local authority must, so far as is reasonably practicable and consistent with the child's welfare, ascertain the child's wishes regarding the provision of accommodation and give due consideration (having regard to his age and understanding) to such wishes. As far as these three children are concerned, living with the Taylors appears to be the next best thing to living with their mother when she is well.

Where there is more than one person with parental responsibility for a child, each of them may act alone and without the other in meeting that responsibility (s. 2(7)). Therefore Rose may make arrangements with the local authority without waiting to consult Stan. Nevertheless the Act acknowledges the continuing nature of parental responsibility and allows Stan, as a person with parental responsibility, to object to the local authority providing accommodation. Stan must be able to show that he is willing and able to provide or arrange alternative accommodation for the children (s. 20(7)). It seems unlikely that Stan can provide accommodation if he continues with his present job, and as he made no arrangements the last time the children were accommodated by the local authority, this may suggest that he may not be able to do so on this occasion. If Rose were to apply for and be granted residence orders in respect of the children, this would prevent Stan objecting to the voluntary arrangement (s. 20(9)(a)). Before making a residence order, which is an order settling the arrangements to be made as to where the child is to live (s. 8(1)), the court would need to be satisfied that doing so would be better than making no order at all (s. 1(5)). When considering whether to make a residence order, the child's welfare must be the court's paramount consideration (s. 1(1)), and where the making of the order is opposed by any party to the proceedings, the court must have regard to the welfare checklist (s. 1(3)), which includes a consideration of the capability each of the child's parents has in relation to meeting that child's needs. Although Rose has problems of her own, her children appear to be her first concern whereas Stan, from the most benevolent viewpoint, could at best be described as feckless or, more realistically, uncaring for his wife and children and totally selfish, in other words an unfit father. Stan may argue that a residence order would take away his right to object to the children being accommodated; so in his view it should not be granted. He does not appear to have been a responsible parent when times were hard and in the final analysis it is not Stan's 'rights' which are important but the welfare of the children.

However, Stan could wait until the children are living with the Taylors and then, without notice, remove them (s. 20(8)) provided no person with a residence order objects. Unlike s. 20(7) there is no requirement in s. 20(8) for the parent to be able to accommodate the child. Stan may not remove the children if Rose has a residence order (s. 20(9)). Where a residence order is in force with respect to a child, no person may remove him from the United Kingdom without either the written consent of every person who has parental responsibility for the child or the leave of the court (s. 13(1)(b)). Stan should be warned that the Child Abduction Act 1984 makes it a criminal offence for anyone with parental responsiblity for a child under sixteen to take the child out of the United Kingdom, without the consent of all those with parental responsiblity, or leave of the court.

If the Taylors are concerned about Stan taking the children away, they could apply to the wardship jurisdiction of the High Court. This may be getting more involved than they contemplated when they agreed to foster children for the local authority. As the children lived with them for less than three years, the Taylors cannot apply for leave to apply for a residence order unless they have the consent of the local authority (s. 9(3)). If the court were to grant the Taylors a residence order, then they would have parental responsibility while the order was in force (s. 12(2)). Parental responsibility would be shared with Rose and Stan. Even if the Taylors do not acquire parental responsibility, they, as persons with care of the children, may (subject to the provisions of the Children Act 1989) do what is reasonable in all the circumstances of the case for the purpose of safeguarding or promoting the child's welfare (s. 3(5)).

The children could apply to court for leave to make applications for residence orders, if they did not wish to go with their father. The court may only grant leave if it is satisfied that a child has sufficient understanding to make the proposed application for the residence order (s. 10(8)) (*Re C (Residence: Child's Application for Leave)* [1995] 1 FLR 927; and *Re H (Residence Order: Child, Application for Leave)* [2001] 1 FLR 780). The court could make residence orders stating that the children are to remain with their foster parents.

If no one has residence orders in respect of the children, the local authority could apply for an emergency protection order (EPO) or for a care or supervision order. An EPO would appear to be an extreme reaction to the situation and would require the local authority to satisfy the court that there is reasonable cause to believe that the children are likely to suffer significant harm if they do not remain with the Taylors (s. 44(1)(a)). For a care or supervision order to be granted the court would have to be satisfied that the children would suffer significant harm if they were to be taken away from the Taylors by Stan and that the harm is attributable to some deficiency in parental care (s. 31(2)). Any s. 8 orders would be discharged automatically by the making of a care order (s. 91(2)) and any non-parent would lose parental responsibility. Rose could apply for a discharge of the order (s. 39) when she returns home. With local authority support providing a range and level of services appropriate to the children's needs (s. 17(1)), she should be able to cope without Stan.

The Department of Health has estimated that each week more than 200,000 families receive family support services (DoH, *Children Act Report 2001* (DoH, 2002) at p. 21).

It is up to the local authority, considering its own circumstances and resources, to determine how to respond to the needs of children in its area (*R (G)* v *Barnet London Borough Council; R (W)* v *Lambeth London Borough Council; R (A)* v *Lambeth London Borough Council* [2003] 3 WLR 1194). In *Re T (Judicial Review: Local Authority Decisions*

Concerning Children in Need) [2004] 1 FLR 590, it was said that although the court could direct the local authority to reconsider the services it should provide for the claimant, it could not direct the local authority to take a particular course. In terms of inter-agency working and co-operation, reference was made to *The Victoria Climbié Inquiry*, Cm. 5730 (2003), which addressed, *inter alia*, the way in which agencies decided what services to provide. It was stated in that report that agencies ought to be providing services that met a person's needs rather than the person in need receiving only those services that were available, the expectation should therefore be of a needs-led, rather than service-led, practice.

If the local authority is concerned that the children may be in and out of accommodation, and is of the view that this would be unsettling for the children, it should clarify the legal position to the parents and explain that it, the local authority, may decide to instigate care proceedings. This may make Stan come to his senses and stop him using the children to punish Rose for their failing marriage. One of the main aims of the Act is to make decisions about children more child-centred and in the best interests of the children. Hopefully Stan may be brought round to this point of view before more drastic action needs to be taken by the local authority.

Q Question 3

Adam, aged 12, was found by the police yesterday after his mother, Barbara, had reported him missing. He was found at the railway station attempting to board a train to where his father lives with his new family. Adam has run away from home on numerous occasions since his mother married Clive a year ago. Barbara and Clive are partners in a very successful interior design consultancy.

Diane, a local authority social worker was allocated to Adam's case six months ago but does not feel she has made much progress. Barbara and Clive always listen politely and benignly to the advice that Diane offers but do nothing about putting her advice into practice. Diane is finding their attitude rather patronising.

The headmaster of Adam's school is very concerned about Adam's persistent absenteeism.

Diane feels that anything that money can buy is lavished on Adam but that he lacks time and attention from Barbara and Clive. Diane is convinced that Adam should be taken into care.

Advise Diane.

Commentary

Adam may think that he does not belong with his mother and her new husband and may feel that he is the odd one out in his father's new family. The problem for Diane is for her to satisfy the court that the threshold criteria for a care order have been satisfied. As a result of the Children Act 1989 there is now only one route into care. It may appear that in such an affluent family a child could not be neglected but the Act recognises that a child's emotional development can be impaired by lack of emotional care.

Answer plan

• Removal and accommodation of children by police in cases of emergency, s. 46, Children Act 1989.

• Education supervision order, s. 36.

• Welfare of the child, s. 1.

• Application for care order—threshold criteria, s. 31. Is suffering or is likely to suffer significant harm—attributable to . . . Cases.

• Guardian, s. 41.

• Effects of care/supervision orders.

☼ Suggested answer

If the police had reasonable cause to believe that Adam would be likely to suffer significant harm, they could have removed him to suitable accommodation and kept him there for up to 72 hours (Children Act 1989, s. 46). The police do not acquire parental responsibility but are given the power to apply on behalf of the appropriate authority for an emergency protection order under s. 44. Diane should note that it would appear that the police did not regard any of the incidents as an emergency as they returned Adam to his home rather than taking him into police protection.

Diane should consider an education supervision order (ESO) as a first step to ensure Adam's attendance at school. If the local education authority is considering applying for an ESO to deal with Adam's truancy, it must consult the social services committee (s. 36(8)). On the application of the local education authority, the court may make an ESO (s. 36(1)) where it is satisfied that the child is of compulsory school age and is not being properly educated (s. 36(3)). A child requires efficient full-time education suitable to his age, ability and aptitude and any special educational needs he may have. Where he is a pupil at a school which he is not attending regularly, it will be assumed that he is not being properly educated unless it is proved otherwise (s. 36(5)). Adam's welfare must be the court's paramount consideration (s. 1(1)) and the court must have regard to the statutory checklist (s. 1(3)) and the no order principle (s. 1(5)). A care order could be made if everything that could have been done under an ESO had already been tried (*Re O (A Minor) (Care Order: Education: Procedure)* [1992] 2 FLR 7).

An ESO is intended to transfer the primary obligation to ensure that the child is educated from the parent to the local education authority. While the ESO is in force it is the duty of the supervisor to advise, assist, befriend and give directions to the child, his parents and any person with parental responsibility for him, in order that the child is properly educated. Initially an ESO will be for one year although the court may extend the order. Adam, his parents, anyone with parental responsibility and the local education authority may apply to discharge the ESO. Clive, on his marriage to Barbara, will not have automatically acquired parental responsibility for Adam, although he would acquire it if he is granted a residence order in respect of Adam.

Truancy alone is not a ground for a care order, although if the truancy is a symptom of a wider problem a care order could be available. Application for a care order can be made only by the local authority or the NSPCC. Before the local authority makes a decision with respect to Adam it has a duty under s. 22 to ascertain his wishes, the wishes of his parents and anyone else with parental responsibility.

In any application for a care or supervision order, the court should appoint a Children's Guardian unless satisfied that it is not necessary to do so in order to safeguard the child's interests (s. 41(1)). The Children's Guardian will wish to establish the grounds for the local authority's application. The Children's Guardian will meet Adam and establish what he wants to happen; see Adam's father and hopefully discuss Adam's feelings of rejection and the need for contact in the future; meet Barbara and Clive and Adam's headmaster and hear their views. A solicitor will be appointed and instructed to act for Adam by the Children's Guardian.

The only way that a local authority can take a child into care is by going to court and satisfying the threshold criteria set out in s. 31. It must be established that the child is suffering or is likely to suffer significant harm (s. 31(2)(a)). The words 'is suffering' refer to the period immediately before the process of protecting the child is first put in motion (*Re M (A Minor) (Care Order: Threshold Conditions)* [1994] 3 All ER 298; and *Re G (Children) (Care Order: Evidence of Threshold Conditions)* [2001] 2 FLR 1111). The burden of proof of showing to the court's satisfaction that the child is likely to suffer significant harm lies on the applicant and the standard of proof is the ordinary civil standard, i.e. the balance of probabilities. However, the more serious or improbable the allegation of abuse, the more convincing is the evidence required to prove the allegation. A conclusion that the child is suffering, or is likely to suffer harm has to be based on facts, not just suspicion (*Re H and others (Minors) (Sexual Abuse: Standard of Proof)* [1996] 1 All ER 1). If the evidence is insufficient to prove sexual abuse in the past, and if such abuse is the only basis for asserting a risk of sexual abuse in the future, there is no basis, other than suspicion or mere doubt, for finding a risk of future sexual abuse (*Re M and R (Minors) (Sexual Abuse: Expert Evidence)* [1996] 4 All ER 239; *Re H (Care: Change in Care Plan)* [1998] 1 FLR 193; *Re ET (Serious Injuries: Standard of Proof)* [2003] 2 FLR 1205; *Re U (A Child) (Serious Injury: Standard of Proof)*; and *Re B (A Child) (Serious Injury: Standard of Proof)* [2004] 2 FCR 257. In *Re U* it was stated that, in *Re ET* too high a standard of proof had been applied. Therefore, the principles in *Re H* 1996 should continue to be followed).

'Harm' means ill treatment or the impairment of health or development (s. 31(9)). There is no definition of 'significant' in the Act but the Department of Health's Guidance indicates that not every minor deficiency in a child's health or development will justify the making of an order. However, 'significant' should not be equated with 'substantial'. It was identified as 'considerable', 'noteworthy' or 'important' in *Humberside CC* v *B* [1993] 1 FLR 257.

Impairment of health or development will cover cases of neglect of emotional care; in such circumstances the court is directed to compare the child's health or development with that which could reasonably be expected of a similar child. According to Lord Mackay this means a child with the same physical attributes not a child of the same background (Hansard (HL) vol. 503, col. 354–355). In the case of a truant of average intelligence, 'similar child' was held to be a child of equivalent intellectual and social development who has gone to school and not merely an average child who may or may not be at school (*Re O (A Minor) (Care Order: Education: Procedure)* [1992] 2 FLR 7). To assess if Adam's development has been impaired he will be compared with an average 12-year-old who does attend school regularly. Where truancy caused the child's intellectual and social development to suffer she was thereby suffering significant harm (*Re O (A Minor) (Care Order: Education: Procedure)* (above)).

The harm or likelihood of harm must be attributable to the lack of reasonable care by the parent, or to the child being beyond parental control (*Lancashire County Council and Another* v *B and Another* [2000] 2 AC 147; *North Yorkshire County Council* v *SA* [2003] 2 FLR 849) (s. 31(2)(b)). In addition to a finding of significant harm, the court must evaluate the care given to Adam and then ask itself whether that care meets the required standard or whether Adam is beyond parental control. It is immaterial whether the lack of parental control is the fault of the parents or the child (Department of Health's Guidance). 'Where a child is suffering harm in not going to school and is living at home it will follow that the child is beyond her parents' control or that they are not giving the child the care that it would be reasonable for a parent to give' (*Re O (A Minor) (Care Order: Education: Procedure)* (above)).

Even if the s. 31 threshold is crossed, the court has a discretion whether to grant a care or a supervision order or not, and if it decides not to do so it may either make a s. 8 order or it may decide to make no order; Adam's welfare is the paramount consideration (s. 1(1)). The court will consider the welfare checklist which includes a duty to listen and ascertain the wishes and feelings of the child. The weight placed on Adam's wishes will depend on his age and understanding; the court will be guided by the Children's Guardian. While the court has a duty to listen to Adam's wishes, it will not be constricted by those wishes and will disregard them if his future welfare appears to diverge from them. It is the decision of the court and not the child (*Re P (A Minor) (Education)* [1992] 1 FLR 316).

An assessment of what the local authority has done before instigating proceedings will have been carried out by the Children's Guardian, followed by an exploration of the possibility of an agreement between the local authority and Adam's parents to avoid court proceedings. It may be that the Children's Guardian will be more successful than Diane in persuading the parties to face their responsibilities when they realise the potential consequences of their thoughtlessness. Hopefully, Adam's mother and father will make an arrangement, taking into consideration Adam's wishes, as to where he should live, with sufficient contact with the non-residential parent. If the matter proceeds to court the Children's Guardian will advise whether any order is necessary to protect the child's interests.

The court will need to be satisfied that the making of an order is better for Adam than making no order (s. 1(5)). The court may make a s. 8 order as an alternative to a care or supervision order, whether or not the threshold criteria are proved.

On the granting of a care order the local authority acquires parental responsibility, which is shared with the parents. Where a care order is made the responsibility for the child's care is with the authority rather than the court. The court retains no supervisory role monitoring the authority's discharge of its responsibilities (*Re S (Minors) (Care Order: Implementation of Care Plan); Re W (Minors) (Care Order: Adequacy of Care Plan)* [2002] 1 FLR 815). After care proceedings have come to an end and the local authority is implementing the care plan, the requirements of Art. 8 of the European Convention still apply. Parents must be involved in the decision-making process, even when proceedings have come to an end and the care plan is being implemented (*Re G Care: Challenge to Local Authority's Decision)* [2003] 2 FLR 42; *Re M (Care: Challenging Decisions by Local Authority)* [2001] 2 FLR 1300; and *C v Bury Metropolitan Borough Council* [2002] 2 FLR 868).

If a supervision order were to be made, Adam would be placed under the supervision of the local authority or a probation officer (s. 31(1)). Neither the supervisor nor the local authority would acquire parental responsibility. It is the duty of the supervisor to advise, assist and befriend the child. This may seem more appropriate than a care order because if any child needs assisting or befriending it would appear to be Adam (*Re O (Supervision Order)* [2001] 1 FLR 923).

Q Question 4

Are the wishes and feelings of the child presented to the court satisfactorily in care proceedings?

Commentary

Answer the question asked. This has been said before, but it is worth repeating. The temptation here may be to launch into a detailed discussion of *The Victoria Climbié Inquiry*, Cm. 5730 (2003) and the inadequacies, or otherwise, of proposals in the Children Bill 2004, which deals with, among other matters, the introduction of a Children's Commissioner and a duty of co-operation among agencies working with children. Resist. By all means, let the examiner know that you are aware of these developments but do not get bogged down in the detail and so run out of time. You are asked to consider whether the 'voice of the child' is heard satisfactorily in the context of care proceedings.

In your essay you would be expected to evaluate the provisions of the Children Act 1989 which allow a child's voice to be heard in care proceedings. This would include a consideration of the statutory checklist and the role of the Children's Guardian.

Answer plan

- *Gillick.*

- **Welfare principle, s. 1, Children Act 1989. 'Checklist' s. 1(3)(a).**

- **Guardian, s. 41. Appointment. Duties.**

- **Appointment of solicitor.**

☀ **Suggested answer**

After the decision in *Gillick* v *West Norfolk and Wisbech AHA* [1986] 1 FLR 224, there was a recognition that children should have more influence over decisions which affect them and in the Cleveland Report it was said that 'the child is a person and not an object of concern' (Report of the Inquiry into Child Abuse in Cleveland 1987 (1988) Cm. 412).

In response, the Children Act 1989 recognises that the views of a child should be taken into account and in the checklist contained in the Act the court is directed to have regard, amongst other matters, in particular to the ascertainable wishes and feelings of the child concerned (considered in the light of his age and understanding) (s. 1(3)(a)). The statutory checklist is designed to assist the court in operating the welfare principle which must be applied in certain specified proceedings.

In care proceedings, once the court is satisfied that the grounds for an order exist, the principle that 'the child's welfare shall be the court's paramount consideration' will be applied (s. 1(1)).

There has become an increasing awareness of the importance of listening to the views of older children and taking into account what they say, not necessarily agreeing with what they want nor doing what they want, but paying proper respect to older children who are of an age and maturity to make up their minds as to what they think is best for them. It should be borne in mind that older children very often have an appreciation of their own situation which is worthy of consideration by, and the respect of, adults and particularly including the courts (*Re P (A Minor) (Education: Child's Views)* [1992] 1 FLR 316; (*Re S (Contact: Children's Views)* [2002] 1 FLR 1156, children of 16, 14 and 12)).

Although the wishes and feelings of the child are first on the checklist of factors to be taken into account, that does not give them priority over other items on the checklist, including any harm the child is suffering or is at risk of suffering (*Re J (A Minor)* [1992] 2 FCR 785).

In care proceedings the court must appoint a Children's Guardian for the child concerned, unless it is satisfied that it is not necessary to do so in order to safeguard his interests (s. 41(1)). The Children and Family Court Advisory and Support Service (CAFCASS) has a duty to ensure that there are sufficient officers of the service for appointment as guardian to meet fully the requirements imposed by statute and Rules of Court (s. 12(2) Criminal Justice and Courts Services Act 2000). In *R v Children and Family Court Advisory and Support Service* [2003] 1 FLR 953, the applicants sought judicial review of the duty and obligation of CAFCASS. The court took the view that CAFCASS was not under a duty to provide a guardian immediately upon request. The 'no delay' principle in s. 1(2) CA 1989 did not, of itself, found a conclusion that all steps had to be taken immediately or that CAFCASS had to make an officer available immediately on request. However, it was stressed that CAFCASS was under a statutory duty to make appropriate provision for the performance of its functions and should make officers available for appointment as soon as possible, taking into account prioritisation and resource considerations. It was important that CAFCASS received sufficient funding to enable it to meet its obligations.

The independence of the guardian is important. A local authority cannot interfere with the manner in which Children's Guardians consider it necessary to carry out their duties (*R v Cornwall County Council ex parte G* [1992] 1 FLR 270).

Although there is a power to appoint a welfare officer in public law proceedings, such an appointment should not be made when a Children's Guardian has been appointed, save in exceptional circumstances. It is not a sufficient reason that a parent believes a guardian to be biased because his views coincide with that of the local authority (*Re S (A Minor) (Guardian ad Litem/Welfare Officer)* [1993] 1 FLR 110). Many parents are confused and regard the Children's guardian as the representative of the local authority and concerns were expressed to the Children Act Advisory Committee that independence might be compromised by being a paid employee of a local authority.

The primary duty of the Children's Guardian is to safeguard the interests of the child (s. 41(2)(b)). The Children's Guardian will wish to establish the grounds for the local authority application for a care order and examine and take copies of local authority social services records in relation to the child (s. 42) (*Re T (A Minor) (Guardian ad Litem: Case Record)* [1994] 1 FLR 632). The foundation policy is that of inter-agency co-operation. Where documents fall within s. 42, public interest immunity will not arise so far as the guardian's inspection is concerned (*Re R (Care Proceedings: Disclosure)* [2000] 2 FLR 751 and *Re J (Care Proceedings: Disclosure)* [2003] 2 FLR 522). The child's wishes and feelings should be ascertained by the Children's

Guardian and it should be ensured that the child understands that, although his views will be communicated to the court, the Children's Guardian may recommend that the court does not follow his wishes.

Parents, anyone with parental responsibility and anyone who is felt to be important to the child, for example teachers, doctors or relatives or anyone whose information can assist in safeguarding the interests of the child, must be seen by the Children's Guardian. After these investigations the Children's Guardian produces a written report which advises on the interests of the child. The report should be filed with the court seven days before the hearing and copies are served, by the court, on the parties.

A solicitor will be appointed and instructed, by the Children's Guardian, to act for the child. Where a solicitor is satisfied that the child wishes and is able to give instructions which conflict with the Children's Guardian, then instructions are to be taken solely from the child (*Re H (A Minor) (Care Proceedings: Child's Wishes)* [1993] 1 FLR 440). In *Re O (Care Proceedings: Evidence)* [2004] 1 FLR 161, a teenage boy had been given leave to be separately represented, having been regarded by the court as having sufficient understanding to participate as a party in the proceeding. However, the court exercised its discretion and refused to hear oral evidence from the boy. Courts were sensitive to the potentially harmful impact of court attendance on a child (*Re W (Secure Accommodation Order: Attendance at Court)* [1994] 2 FLR 1092). They had to balance the rights of children to participate and be heard against their need to be protected from exposure to material that might be damaging (*Re A (Care: Discharge Application by Child)* [1995] 1 FLR 599). The Children's Guardian will continue with his duty to safeguard the interests of the child and provision is made under the Family Proceedings Rules 1991 for the Children's Guardian to be separately represented.

The framework within which the Children's Guardian has to operate is set out in the Family Proceedings Rules 1991. The Children's Guardian will have a duty to advise and work with the court and the clerk to the justices in regard to timetabling in the child's best interests. There is a general principle that any delay in determining the question is likely to prejudice the welfare of the child (s. 1(2)). It may be that the child could benefit from a constructive delay, but what should not happen is that the proceedings be allowed to drift without control. If the delay is purposeful it should be encouraged (*C* v *Solihull Metropolitan Borough Council and Others* [1993] 1 FLR 290).

The court will look to the Children's Guardian to advise on the appropriate court to deal with an application. The criteria for transfer are governed by the Children (Allocation of Proceedings) Order 1991. The main criteria justifying a transfer are that the proceedings are exceptionally grave, important or complex, it is appropriate for the proceedings to be heard together with other pending family proceedings and it would significantly accelerate the determination of the proceedings. Lengthy issues should be transferred upwards (*L* v *Berkshire County Council* [1992] Fam Law 544). Cases involving serious and unexplained injuries to a baby should be transferred upwards (*C* v *Solihull Metropolitan Borough Council and Others* (1993) above). Where an intelligent adolescent blighted his prospects of achievement because of grossly disturbed behaviour, it was thought to be one of those acutely difficult family cases which was more appropriately dealt with in the High Court where the services of the Official Solicitor could be used (*Re H (A Minor) (Care Proceedings: Child's Wishes)* [1993] 1 FLR 440).

As magistrates' clerks cannot allocate a case to the High Court, public law cases will only be allocated at that level following a second allocation by the district judge.

At each hearing the Children's Guardian has to advise the court of the options available from the range of orders, and their suitability. The wishes of the child and the weight to be given to those wishes must be conveyed to the court and the court should be advised on whether the child should attend each hearing.

The report of the Children's Guardian is not binding on the court but it has a considerable influence on the court's decision and the court should give reasons if the recommendations are not to be followed (*S* v *Oxfordshire County Council* [1993] Fam Law 74).

The Children Act 1989 has recognised that children's wishes and feelings should command serious attention and provides a structure and personnel (the Children's Guardian in care proceedings) to allow that voice to be heard. It is nevertheless acknowledged that children are vulnerable and impressionable, lacking the maturity to weigh the longer term against the shorter (*Re S (A Minor) (Representation: Child's Wishes)* [1993] Fam Law 244). The duty of the Children's Guardian is to safeguard the interests of the child; that is achieved not only by ascertaining the wishes of the child but also taking into account the wider issues and recognising that a child can be manipulated by adults and is not necessarily mature enough to appreciate what is in his own best interest. The court has a duty to listen to and ascertain the wishes and feelings of the child, but the court will not be constricted by those wishes and should disregard them if the child's future welfare appears to diverge from his expressed wishes. It has to be the decision of the court and not the child (*Re P (A Minor) (Education)* [1992] 1 FLR 316).

Therefore the wishes of the child will be presented to the court but not necessarily followed by the court. This may not satisfy the child but the court's decision will be consistent with one of the main aims of the Act which is that the welfare of the child is paramount.

Improving the position, to allow children and young people to be heard properly, should result from the findings of *The Victoria Climbié Inquiry*, Cm. 5730 (2003). Also, providing further support are the proposals in the Children Bill 2004, which deals with, among other matters, the introduction of a Children's Commissioner (who will carry out formal investigations at the direction of a government minister (as set out in the Green Paper, *Every Child Matters*, Cm. 5860 (2003)) and a duty of co-operation among agencies working with children. Apparently, as evidence that that the commitment to children goes beyond merely listening to them to giving them a voice, children will be invited to sit on the selection panel for the appointment of the Children's Commissioner.

Additionally, s. 119 of the Adoption and Children Act 2002 provides access to an independent advocacy service for 'looked after children' making complaints under s. 26 of the Children Act 1989. These provisions aim to increase children's access to, and status in, the family justice system.

Further reading

Bailey, S., *et al*, The Rt Hon Lord Justice Thorpe and C. Cowton (eds), *Delight and Dole: The Children Act 10 Years on*, (Family Law, 2002).

Department of Health, *The Children Act Report 2001*, DoH, 2002. www.doh.gov.uk/quality protects/index.htm and

www.doh.gov.uk/scg/childrenactreport2001.htm

Law Society, *Family Law Protocol* (London: The Law Society, 2002).

Lyon, C. *Child Abuse*, 3rd edn (Jordans/Family Law, 2003).

Scoping Study on Delay in Children Act Cases, 2002, Lord Chancellor's Department. LCD website: www.lcd.gov.uk

Tolson R., *Care Plans and the Human Rights Act*, (Family Law, 2002).

White, R., Carr, A. P., and Lowe, N., *The Children Act in Practice*, 3rd edn (London: Butterworths, 2002).

Other websites

For children in care www.carelaw.org.uk

International child abduction

Introduction

International parental child abduction has become a widespread problem owing to the growth in international relationships (both marital and non-marital) and the increase in family breakdown world-wide, coupled with cheaper and easier travel (e.g. free movement of persons within the European Community). The Child Abduction Unit of the Lord Chancellor's Department now claims to consider the position of some 500 children annually. This includes both preventions *and* complaints that children have been wrongly brought *to* as well as taken *from* the UK Note also that by 1998, and in an unanticipated development, c. 70 per cent of abductions were by resident mothers (of whom a high proportion may well have been escaping violence).

The United Nations Convention on the Rights of the Child 1989 (Art 11) requires those states which are parties to the Convention to take measures to combat the illicit transfer and non-return of children. Part I of the Child Abduction and Custody Act (CACA) 1985 implemented the Hague Convention on the Civil Aspects of International Child Abduction 1980, and Part II of CACA implemented the European Convention on Recognition of Decisions Concerning the Custody of Children 1980.

The Hague Convention and the European Convention determine the treatment of children abducted to (or from) the UK from (or to) Convention countries. Thankfully, the number of safe havens available to child abductors is being reduced as additional states ratify the Conventions (some 64 countries were contracted to one or both Conventions by Summer 2004). The aim is to protect children by preventing their abduction. The Conventions make it more difficult for parents to succeed in abducting their children; they also encourage the prompt return of children to their home country. So the welfare principle has no direct application. The European Convention only applies where there has been a court order and its aim is to ensure the recognition or enforcement of judgments concerning the custody of children. Should both Conventions apply in a case, then the Hague Convention application takes precedence over the European Convention application (s. 16(4)(c), CACA 1985). According to *Reunite (National Council for Abducted Children)*, only Liechtenstein and Lithuania are signatories only to the latter at the time of writing.

If a child has been taken to a non-Convention country, then proceedings will have to be taken there in the absence of an extradition treaty. Conversely, if the child has been brought to the UK from such a country, then the child is likely to be warded and the welfare principle will apply (*Re L (Minors) (Wardship: Jurisdiction)* [1974] 1 All ER 913), coupled with a presumption that the courts of the country whence the child was abducted are best placed to judge the matter: *Re S (Minors) (Abduction)* [1994] 1 FLR 297.

Today, when so many children are non-marital and so much litigation involves them, note *Re W; Re B (Child Abduction: Unmarried Father)* [1999] Fam 1 which states the various circumstances in which an unmarried father may invoke the Hague Convention, e.g.: when he has parental responsibility; where a current court order prohibits removal; relevant proceedings are pending here; or the mother has delegated primary care to him (or has accepted that he has as 'inchoate' right to determine residence: *Re H (Child Abduction) (Unmarried Father: Rights of Custody)* [2003] EWHC 492 (Fam)).

Child abduction is a criminal offence under the Child Abduction Act 1984, and may be kidnapping at common law. Other deterrents and preventative measures include applications to the civil courts for wardship or under the Children Act 1989, passport control, 'All Ports' warnings, and the seeking of security for a child's return. (Children over 12 months old can now only travel on their own UK passport.) However, this chapter is primarily concerned with the civil application and construction of the Hague Convention, together with the approach taken with non-Convention countries, as most of the reported cases are on that area.

It should be noted that the Conventions and the CACA 1985 refer to 'rights of custody' rather than the concepts of residence and parental responsibility to which we have become accustomed under the Children Act 1989.

There are two questions in this chapter: one problem and one essay. Both are vehicles, in part, for the basic approach to Hague Convention cases: habitual residence; rights of custody; wrongful removal or retention; application to the 'central authority' of each country; and the presumption of return qualified by the exceptions of consent, acquiescence, grave risk of harm, and the child's objection.

Q Question 1

Rhett, born in the USA, met and married Sylvia in North Carolina, USA, ten years ago. Their son Tod was born there a year later. Six months ago Sylvia brought Tod to England for a two-month visit to her parents' (and her childhood) home. At the end of the holiday she decided to remain in England and eventually to divorce Rhett. She informed Rhett and her parents of her decision. Tod is attending the local junior school. He is flourishing there, away from his domineering father. The severe facial twitch which Tod suffered from when he lived in the USA has disappeared in England. Rhett agreed to his wife's and son's two-month trip, although he did not wish to join them as it coincided with his local hunting season. Rhett is president of the local Guns in Hunting Club.

Rhett has consulted lawyers in the USA and he has told Sylvia that there will be court proceedings unless she brings Tod home 'pronto'. Rhett is concerned that Tod is becoming an English 'cissy'. Tod is a vegetarian, as are his mother and grandparents.

Sylvia seeks your advice.

Commentary

The USA is not a signatory to the European Convention and no court order exists in relation to Tod, making any detailed discussion of the European Convention doubly irrelevant. In your answer you would be expected to apply the Hague Convention to the facts set out in the question. Sylvia needs to know whether she is likely to be ordered to return Tod to the USA under the Hague Convention. Therefore, the key elements of habitual residence, wrongful removal or retention and the grounds for refusing an order to return must be considered.

- 1980 Hague Convention on 'child abduction'

- Habitual residence

- Rights of custody and central authority

- Presumption of return

- Unlawful retention

- Risk of harm and child's objection

⨀ Suggested answer

Sylvia should be alerted to the fact that the Hague Convention on the Civil Aspects of International Child Abduction may be used to secure the prompt return of Tod to the USA. Although Rhett's home country, the USA, is not, of course, a signatory to the European Convention on Recognition of Decisions Concerning the Custody of Children, it is a signatory to the Hague Convention. (Additionally, the European Convention applies only to cases where there is an existing court order and no orders exist in relation to Tod.) The Hague Convention is incorporated into UK law by Part I of the Child Abduction and Custody Act (CACA) 1985. The whole purpose of the Convention is to ensure that parties 'do not gain advantage by either removing a child from the country of its usual residence, or having taken the child, with the agreement of any other party who has custodial rights, to another jurisdiction, then wrongfully to retain that child' (*Re E (A Minor) (Abduction)* [1989] 1 FLR 135).

Every Convention country has a Central Authority which deals with the administrative action required to operate the remedies under the Conventions. The Child

Abduction Unit acts as the Central Authority for England and Wales. Responsibility for the Unit rests with the Official Solicitor. Central Authorities must co-operate with each other to promote the objects of the Hague Convention, one of which is to secure the prompt return of children wrongfully removed to, or retained in, any contracting state (Art 1).

Rhett may contact the Central Authority in the USA which, in turn, would deal with the Central Authority here, in an attempt to secure a voluntary return of Tod to the USA. However, if Sylvia will not agree to a voluntary return then the Central Authority will initiate proceedings. Again, Sylvia must be warned that, should the Convention apply to Tod's circumstances, the courts cannot investigate the merits of the case and must order his return unless one of the grounds in Articles 12 or 13 apply (see below). 'The courts of the country of habitual residence should determine their future . . . The interests of the child in each individual case are not paramount since it is presumed under the Convention that the welfare of children is best met by return to their habitual residence' *(Re M (A Minor) (Child Abduction)* [1994] 1 FLR 390).

The Hague Convention applies where a child under 16 who is habitually resident in one contracting state is wrongfully removed to, or retained in, another (Art 4). Let us consider whether Rhett can invoke the Hague Convention. Clearly, Tod is under 16, but where is his habitual residence? Nowhere in the Convention is the term defined. However, in *Re J (A Minor) (Abduction: Custody Rights)* [1990] 2 AC 562, it was said by Lord Brandon at 578–9 that the expression is not to be treated as a term of art—it is a question of fact to be determined by all the circumstances of the case. Lord Brandon went on to say that it is possible for habitual residence in a country to end in a single day, by leaving with an intention not to return, but it is only acquired after an appreciable time with a settled intention to remain. When a child lives with his parents, the child's habitual residence will normally be that of his parents *(Re A (Wardship: Jurisdiction)* [1995] 1 FLR 767). In *Re A (Abduction: Habitual Residence)* [1998] 1 FLR 497 it was held that a short visit to a country—there, a three-week visit to Greece for what was akin to a holiday—does not initiate a period of habitual residence, although in *Re R (Abduction: Habitual Residence)* [2003] Fam Law 860 it was held that one could acquire habital residence in country B without a settled intent not to return to country A. It seems likely that, immediately before his retention, Tod was habitually resident in the USA. Where both parents have parental responsibility neither can unilaterally change the child's habitual residence *(Re B (Minors) (Abduction) (No. 2)* [1993] 1 FLR 993).

Rhett agreed to a two-month visit to England but after that time elapsed, Tod was being retained against Rhett's wishes. Removal or retention of a child is wrongful where it is in breach of 'rights of custody' attributed to a person or any other body under the law of the state in which the child was habitually resident before the removal or retention (Art 3). 'Rights of custody' include rights relating to the care of the person of the child and, in particular, the right to determine the child's place of residence (Art. 5). The law of the country of the child's habitual residence determines the existence of rights of custody, which includes rights which would have been exercised but for the retention (Art. 3). It is then a matter of English law whether there is a breach of those rights (*Re F (Abduction: Custody Rights Abroad)* [1995] 3 All ER 641). By her retention of Tod in England, Sylvia frustrated Rhett's equal and separate rights of custody. Where a child has been wrongfully removed or retained for less than a year the court must order the return of the child (Art. 12). Even where a year has elapsed such return is mandatory unless it is demonstrated that the child is 'settled in its new environment' (Art. 12). However, Art. 13 gives the court a discretion whether to order return if the person who opposes the return can establish that the applicant, at the time of the removal or retention, was not exercising custody rights or consented to it, or subsequently acquiesced in it, or there is a grave risk of physical or psychological harm if the child is returned, or a mature child objects. There is a heavy burden on a person alleged to have abducted a child if she is to bring herself within the provisions of Art. 13 (*Re E (A Minor) (Abduction)* [1989] 1 FLR 135). It would need to be an exceptional case for the child's return to be refused.

Acquiescence is a question of fact and the weight to be attached to the evidence is a matter for the judge's discretion (*Re H (Abduction: Acquiescence)* [1997] 1 FLR 872). Rhett has made it clear that he does not consent to, or acquiesce in, the wrongful retention of Tod. Again, there would be a heavy burden on Sylvia if she claimed that there is a grave risk that return would expose Tod to physical or psychological harm or place him in an intolerable position. In *N v N (Abduction: Article 13 Defence)* [1995] 1 FLR 107 the court ordered that three children should be returned to Australia even though there was some evidence that the father had sexually interfered with one of the children. The court was entitled to weigh the risk of psychological harm of return against the psychological harm of refusing return. However, in exercising its discretion the court must give due weight to the primary purpose of the Convention. A less stringent approach would undermine the spirit and purpose of the Convention, which is the speedy return of children so that a court in the country of their habitual residence can decide what is best for the child. Some harm may be inevitable: *E v E (Child Abduction: Intolerable Situation)* [1998] 2 FLR 980. However, to refuse return, the harm must be grave or there must be a high degree of intolerability (*Re C (Abduction: Grave Risk of Psychological Harm)* [1999] 1 FLR 1145). Article 12 requires the child to be returned to the state of its habitual residence and not to the other parent (*B v K (Child Abduction)* [1993] FCR 382). However, under Art. 13 it is possible to consider the objections of the child to returning to the parent and not to the state (*Re M (A Minor) (Child Abduction)* [1994] 1 FLR 390). In *S v S (Child Abduction) (Child's Views)* [1992] 2 FLR 492, the court refused to order the return of a 10-year-old girl to France as there was a grave risk that return would result in physical or psychological harm. She objected to being returned and had reached the age and degree of maturity where it was appropriate to take account of her views. The girl had a severe stammer and behavioural problems in France but these had disappeared in England. A court welfare officer would assess whether Tod is of sufficient maturity to object to being returned; if so, he would then convey Tod's views to the court. (Although it is 'highly unusual' a mature 12-year old was given separate representation in *Re J (Abduction: Child Appellant)*, *The Times*, 12 April 2004.) In exercising their discretion, the courts have been influenced by the fact that a child returned to the country of habitual residence would be more than likely to be allowed to leave again by a court of that country (*Re A (Minors) (No. 2) (Abduction: Acquiescence)* [1993] 1 FLR 396; *Re K (Abduction: Consent)* [1997] 2 FLR 212). In *Re T (Abduction: Child's Objections to Return)* [2000] 2 FLR 193, the court heeded the objections of an 11-year old to being returned to Spain, to a mother with drink problems.

This case may appear to be on the borderline, bearing in mind that we have not heard Tod's views from the court welfare officer. A two-stage process is required under Art. 13. The establishment of one of the Art. 13 'defences' gives a court a discretion whether or not to order the child's speedy return and in *H v H (Abduction: Acquiescence)* [1996] 2 FLR 570 it was held that the court must consider, e.g., the extent to which refusal would frustrate the purpose of the Hague Convention. Were the court to decide—as seems likely on balance—that this is not a case where it should exercise its discretion, then Sylvia must return Tod. If she wishes Tod to live with her in England, she must apply for an order for custody, in a court in the USA, and an order that Tod should be allowed to leave that country with her—and in the event of parental disagreement about his diet, etc., a court of the appropriate country could decide the issue.

Q Question 2

In cases of international child abduction from a 'non-Hague Convention' country, which principle should the court apply—welfare or comity?

Commentary

It would be a grave mistake for anyone to attempt to answer this question if they did not know the meaning of the word 'comity'. Such a lack of knowledge of one of the current 'buzzwords' would display an unfamiliarity with the continuing debate of the principles to be applied in non-Convention international child abduction cases.

You may have been directed to certain articles or your lecturer may have chosen to set an examination question which can be answered perfectly adequately from lecture notes and the set textbooks, but which allows you to display that you have engaged in wider reading and have kept up to date with recent cases and developments.

- Abduction to and from non-Convention countries

- The Hague Convention—once the model

- Re-assertion of the welfare principle?

- Attitude of other country's courts

- The future

:Ọ: Suggested answer

Applications for the return of children from England and Wales to a country which is not a signatory to the Hague Convention on the Civil Aspects of International Child Abduction are decided by the High Court in wardship, where the welfare of the child is paramount. The court has a duty to promote and protect the interests of the child. The leading authority on non-Convention cases is *McKee* v *McKee* [1951] AC 352 where the Privy Council stated that the court has a complete discretion to select from options ranging from a peremptory return order of the child to, itself, undertaking a full consideration of the merits of the case. It is possible that the welfare of a child may require that the dispute be settled in a foreign court. However, abduction cases, under the wardship jurisdiction, raise no presumption of prompt return. All the circumstances of each case must be considered. That is the theory. In practice what happened after the Hague Convention was incorporated into English law by the Child Abduction and Custody Act 1985, was a line of cases where the courts appear to have felt constrained to apply Hague Convention principles to non-Convention cases.

The objects of the Convention are to secure the prompt return of children wrongfully removed or retained in any contracting state and to ensure that rights of custody under the law of one contracting state are effectively respected in the other contracting states. 'The courts of the country of habitual residence should determine their future . . . The interests of the child in each individual case are not paramount since it is presumed under the Convention that the welfare of children is best met by return to their habitual residence' (*Re M (A Minor) (Child Abduction)* [1994] 1 FLR 390).

Such a presumption of prompt return and comity between nations is supportable in Convention cases, because the preamble to the Hague Convention confirms that the signatories are 'firmly convinced that the interests of children are of paramount importance in matters relating to their custody'. However, as Beevers, 'Child Abduction—Welfare or Comity?' [1996] *Fam Law* 365, points out, this is not true of many countries of the world. Assumptions cannot be made that the safeguards which are built into the system between contracting states will be applied in non-Convention countries.

In the non-Convention cases of *Re F (A Minor) (Abduction: Jurisdiction)* [1991] 1 FLR 1 and *G v G (Minors) (Abduction)* [1991] 2 FLR 506, the Court of Appeal took the view that Parliament was not departing from the welfare principle when it incorporated the Hague Convention into English law in the Child Abduction and Custody Act 1985. Rather it was giving effect to a belief 'that in normal circumstances it is in the interests of children that parents or others should not abduct them from one jurisdiction to another, but that any decision relating to the custody of children is best decided in the jurisdiction in which they hitherto have normally been resident'. Immediate return to non-Convention countries was ordered in each case.

There appears to have been escalation from a discretion to a legal principle of international comity in *Re S (Minors) (Abduction)* [1994] 1 FLR 297 where the Court of Appeal ordered the return of a child to Pakistan, a non-Convention country. The Court of Appeal, referring to the earlier cases of *G v G (Minors) (Abduction)* and *Re F (A Minor) (Abduction: Jurisdiction)* said it rendered it 'settled law that although Pakistan is not a signatory to the Hague Convention, we must apply the philosophy of the Convention to the case before us'. Hayes and Williams, *Family Law—Principles, Policy and Practice* (Butterworths, 2nd edn, 1999 at p. 404) identified that the reality in applying the Hague Convention philosophy to this non-Convention case was that the Court of Appeal was 'preserving comity between nations' by ordering the return of children to a 'system which would take account of matters which an English court would regard as incompatible with the welfare principle'.

In *D v D (Child Abduction: Non-Convention Country)* [1994] 1 FLR 137 there was a reminder that 'the articles of the Convention are not to be applied literally in the wardship jurisdiction and the court retains the discretion to consider the wider aspects of the welfare of the wards'. McClean and Beevers, 'International child abduction—back to common law principles' [1995] *CFLQ* 128, noted that the Court of Appeal did not appear to be speaking with one voice, as in *Re M (Abduction: Non-Convention Country)* [1995] 1 FLR 89 no mention was made of the welfare principle when summarising the effect of *D v D (Child Abduction: Non-Convention Country)* and the 'discretion to consider the wider aspects' was re-worded to direct that the court can take 'account of those matters which it would be relevant to consider under Article 13'.

It could be said that a step too far was taken in *Re M (Abduction: Peremptory Return Order)* [1996] 1 FLR 478. The Court of Appeal considered that the underlying purpose of the Hague Convention applies by analogy to non-Convention cases. 'Underlying the whole purpose of the peremptory return order is a principle of international comity under which judges in England will assume that facilities for a fair hearing will be provided in the court of the other jurisdiction' and very exceptional circumstances would be needed to justify departure from this general principle.

The welfare principle was reasserted by the Court of Appeal in *Re P (Abduction: Non-Convention Country)* [1997] 1 FLR 780. Allowing the appeal against a peremptory return order, it was said that the judge had misdirected himself and had wrongly considered himself bound by the authorities to apply the spirit of the Hague Convention in a non-Convention case. Under s. 1 of the Children Act 1989 the child's welfare is the sole consideration in an application for a child's return to a non-Convention country. The judge had fallen into error by applying Art. 13 literally. He had gone so far as to say that had the child's welfare been the only test the application would have been refused.

Further support to the welfare principle was given in *Re JA (Child Abduction: Non-Convention Country)* [1998] 1 FLR 231 where the mother had abducted the child from their country of habitual residence, the United Arab Emirates. The Emirates was not a party to the Hague Convention. The Court of Appeal said the authorities before the advent of the Child Abduction and Custody Act 1985 seemed clearly to establish that it was an abdication of the responsibility and an abnegation of the duty of the court to the ward under its protection, to surrender the determination of its ward's future to a foreign court whose regime might be inimical to the child's welfare. If necessary the Court of Appeal was prepared to say that the decision in *Re M (Abduction: Peremptory Return Order)* [1996] 1 FLR 478 was decided *per incuriam*. No violence was done to this approach in *Re Z (Non-Convention Country)* [1999] 1 FLR 1270 where the child was ordered to be returned to Malta on the basis that its courts would apply the welfare principle. But in *Re E (Abduction: Non-Convention Country)* [1999] 2 FLR 642, Thorpe LJ said that effective reaction to cross-border child abduction involved respect for different cultures, and that even in non-Convention cases, the English Court should not gainsay the approach of other systems other than in exceptional cases such as persecution or ethnic discrimination. Accordingly, the mother was ordered to return her children to Sudan (whence she had abducted them), where the dispute within this Muslim family would, it was held, be more appropriately resolved. *Re H (Child Abduction: Mother's Asylum)* [2003] EWHC 1820 (Fam) balanced the competing considerations—the father's undertakings to support mother and son, the mother's fears for her safety there—and held that the child's interests would be better decided by the Pakistani courts.

So return seems to be the more likely outcome even in non-Convention cases and those observers who, perhaps, find succour for their perceived cultural superiority in 'our' welfare principle will point to the fact that such countries may well not take a reciprocal approach to children abducted to them, nor advance legal aid to their litigants. On the other hand, in *Outcomes for Children Returned after Hague Orders* (Reunite, 2003) Marilyn Freedman found that the fate of all concerned tended to confirm the wisdom of the courts' policy in returning a very high proportion of children.

Further reading

Lowe, N., and Perry, M., 'The Operation of the Hague and European Conventions on International Child Abduction between England and Germany', *International Family Law* 1: 8 (1998).

Websites

www.offsol.demon.co.uk/caumenu.htm (The Child Abduction Unit, based in the Official Solicitor's Department of the Lord Chancellor's Department).
www.reunite.org/ (National Council for Abducted Children).

Property rights

Introduction

We have yet to see a family law exam without a question on property rights. It usually concerns the family home. Unfortunately, there are two other ever-present questions which deal with the same item, namely the questions on domestic violence and property adjustment respectively (although two or more of these topics may come together). The profusion comes about like this. First, the couple fall out with one another, the woman wanting the man removed from the home so that she (together with the children, if any) can live in peace. That is the domestic violence/occupation rights question. Subsequently, ownership matters naturally arise. This will be a declaratory issue if the couple are unmarried (property rights); but more likely a discretionary one if they are married (property adjustment on divorce). Perhaps the most important thing is to distinguish between these last two. Normally this is a simple matter of whether the couple are married or not, with the latter pair being forced to rely on the declaratory position, whilst the former pair (or one of them) gains instead from the divorce court's ancillary relief jurisdiction. But do remember those residuary cases where even spouses are forced back on to the *status quo*, such as: death; third party rights as on, e.g. insolvency; divorce not wanted or not available; and after remarriage. Although it is difficult to confuse the two, it would be very expensive to do so in an exam.

There are two further advantages of including this topic in your revision programme. First, apart from the strong likelihood that it will appear in the family law exam, it may well do double duty for you by reappearing in the land law/equity and trusts paper(s) as well. Secondly, there is more to it than the 'matrimonial' home, even though it is the examiners' favourite: there is also law on personal property, e.g. money, bank accounts, shares, furniture, pets. The comparitive rarity of questions on these matters reflects the comparative lack of modernity in their law, together with the fact that 'in practice' the question of who ends up with the three-piece suite is likely to be a matter of agreement. There is still extant law in this area, however, and unrequited Law Commission Reports on both real and personal property.

Q Question 1

Tony and Mei became a couple six years ago and shortly afterwards Tony bought a house (he tells you) 'in his own name'. The house cost £75,000 of which Tony paid £25,000 which he had won in the National Lottery. He raised the rest on a mortgage. The couple moved into the house, having agreed that they would take equal responsibility for household expenses (excluding the mortgage payments which Tony paid) and maintenance costs. Two years ago they made equal contributions towards a £10,000 extension. Mei has always done the cooking and cleaning as well as looking after the garden and performing do-it-yourself jobs around the house. There are no children.

Now, the relationship has foundered and Mei has left. She is claiming that Tony owes her half the net value of the house, in which the equity is now £100,000.

(a) Advise Tony, eliciting from him any further information you may require. [14 marks]

(b) How, if at all, would your answer differ were Tony the woman and Mei the man? [4 marks]

(c) If Tony and Mei were husband and wife, in what circumstances would the court be required to apply declaratory, rather than adjustive, principles? [7 marks]

Commentary

Do note the mark allocations. Supplying this information is fast becoming *de rigueur* in multi-part questions; the number of words you devote to each part will normally be in direct proportion to the marks available. Usually (as here) it will also be indicative of the amount/importance of the law concerned, but not always; the examiners may simply be warning you of their priorities. A further advantage of this style of question is that it does a lot of the analysis for you; it may take a little longer to absorb, but it tells you what to do more clearly than a simple 'Advise' or 'Discuss'. You might choose the question even if you feel you know next to nothing about the 4-mark part. Incidentally, it is better to structure your answer in the same way as the question, with 'a' and 'b' etc. in the margin, so as to make it easy for the examiner. The only exception might be where you really are bereft of knowledge on one or more of the points, when one integrated answer might just persuade the examiner to award an holistic mark, but do not count on it!

Note also the simple announcement that, 'There are no children'. Such exclusion is likely to become increasingly common in this sort of question in order to eliminate consideration of the Child Support Acts 1991 and 1995, the Child Support, Pensions and Social Security

Act 2000 and s. 15 and sch. 1 of the Children Act 1989, the last of which Acts empowers the court to make property adjustment orders in favour of non-marital children.

Finally, do not ignore the 'eliciting any further information you may require' instruction in 1. This becomes very easy to milk for marks when you consider the inadequacy of what has been volunteered—'He tells you'; 'in his name', etc. As you begin to consider the law you need to deploy, you will see that its application is dependent on much that the question omits. It puts you in the position of an actual adviser, whose skill will be to know what questions to ask after the client has told you what he thinks you need to know.

Answer plan

- **Property ownership. Formalities. Legal ownership.**

- **Beneficial ownership. Trusts—implied/resulting/constructive.**

- **Common intention—cases. Detrimental reliance—cases.**

- **Apply relevant law to facts.**

- **Relevance of declaratory principles to spouses, e.g. death, third party rights, remarriage etc.**

☼ Suggested answer

(a) We had better obtain the 'further and better particulars' from Tony before we presume to advise him. First, we will check that the relationship is non-marital. There is no mention of a wedding and the rubric in (c) below would seem to suggest that in this part of the question they are cohabitants.

We need to discover, from the actual document and not merely by asking Tony, just what is meant by 'in his own name'. Section 52 of the Law of Property Act 1925 requires a deed for the conveyance or creation of any legal estate in land. So if the house was indeed taken in Tony's name only, it follows that Mei will have no claim to the legal estate. Crucially, if it also contains an express declaration of beneficial interests, e.g. that these are wholly vested in Tony, such will be conclusive in the absence of fraud or mistake (*Goodman* v *Gallant* [1985] Fam 106). On the other hand, if what 'he tells you' proves inaccurate to the extent that Mei's name is also on the title, then that will be similarly conclusive as to what it relates. (If, as in *Bernard* v *Josephs* [1982] 2 WLR 1052, the conveyance does not state the proportions in which the beneficial entitlements are held, it may be argued that they are different. But given the date of the purchase, i.e. after *Bernard*, the solicitor is likely to have addressed this issue expressly.)

Writing is also necessary to create other interests in land: s. 53 of the Law of Property Act (LPA) 1925 requires a signed written document in order to create, e.g. an express trust. In *Gissing* v *Gissing* [1971] AC 886, the house had been conveyed into the husband's sole name. When the marriage broke up he told his wife, 'It's yours', but she was held to have no claim merely on that basis. Similarly, s. 2(1) of the Law of Property (Miscellaneous Provisions) Act 1989 requires that all contracts concerning property rights be written, and signed by the parties. Should the deed, however, vest only the legal interest in Tony, then he needs to be warned that s. 53(2), LPA 1925 states that s. 53 does not affect the 'creation or operation of resulting, implied or constructive trusts'. (There is a corresponding exception in s. 2(5), LP(MP)A 1989.) Could Mei turn this to her advantage? We should start with the warning given by Mustill LJ in *Grant* v *Edwards* [1987] 1 FLR 87, 101 that it is not yet 'possible to state the law in a way which will deal with all the practical problems which may arise . . . consistently with everything said in the cases'. Happily for Tony, 'under English law the mere fact that A expends money on B's property does not by itself entitle A to an interest in the property' (*per* Slade LJ in *Thomas* v *Fuller-Brown* [1988] 1 FLR 237, 240). (Mei would, of course, be entitled to the return of her £5,000 contribution to the extension.)

Mei would need to show a common intention that they should both be beneficial owners and that she relied on this to her detriment. What is meant by 'common intention'? There is nothing here like *Grant* v *Edwards* (1987) (above), where the claimant was told that her name was not going on the title deeds because if it did there might be problems in her then pending divorce proceedings. Nor has Mei provided part of the purchase price, unlike *Sekhon* v *Alissa* [1989] 2 FLR 94, where a mother, having contributed £22,500 to the £36,500 purchase price of a house conveyed into the sole name of her daughter, was subsequently held entitled to an interest in equity in the property by way of resulting trust. From such contributions, the court may infer the necessary intention; the same result may flow from helping with the mortgage, e.g. *Re Gorman (a Bankrupt)* [1990] 2 FLR 284. We are expressly informed, however, that Tony took exclusive responsibility for the repayments.

Mei's chances would seem best advanced by reference to *Cooke* v *Head* [1972] 1 WLR 518, and *Eves* v *Eves* [1975] 1 WLR 1338. They provide some authority for the proposition that non-financial contributions might demonstrate the necessary intention (using sledge hammer and cement mixer in the former, and breaking up concrete/demolishing a shed/carrying out expensive decorations in the latter). Yet more recent decisions (Tony will be glad to hear) would seem to militate against drawing the vital inference from such contributions. In *Burns* v *Burns* [1984] FLR 216 a couple had lived together for 19 years, the woman giving up her job to look after the man and (their) two children; she had put her earnings into the housekeeping, bought goods for the house including a washing machine and tumble-dryer, and laid a patio and done decorating work. She did not, however, show the 'necessary intention'. In *Lloyds Bank* v *Rosset* [1990] 2 FLR 155 Lord Bridge, with whom the other Law Lords agreed, was 'at least extremely doubtful' that anything other than a direct contribution to the purchase price would be sufficient. Cases since *Rosset* have applied Lord Bridge's dictum. They include *Midland Bank* v *Cooke and Another* [1995] 2 FLR 915 where the Court of Appeal held that *if* a claimant has established *some* beneficial interest, the court may be able to quantify it by reference to the dealings between the parties during their whole relationship.

Even where there has been a direct contribution to the purchase price, that does not mean that the proportion of the beneficial interest acquired will be limited to the proportions given by a resulting trust. *In Oxley* v *Hiscock* [2004] 2 FCR 295 a property had been purchased with unequal contributions made by the two former cohabitants and yet registered in the name of only one of them. The Court of Appeal inferred a common intention that the beneficial interest of the property should be held on trust for both of them. The Court then went on to consider what was fair, rather than apply resulting trust principles of apportioning shares in proportion to contributions to the cost of acquisition. The proper course was to apply the principles of a constructive trust or proprietary estoppel to assess the respective shares after the sale of the property, having regard to the conduct and contributions of each party relating to the property after its acquisition.

Tony may feel himself well served by these authorities. Even if Mei does satisfy a court of 'common intention', it seems unlikely that she would be able to demonstrate the further requirement of 'detrimental reliance'. In *Hyett* v *Stanley* [2004] 1 FLR 394 the property was in the man's sole name. The woman agreed to execute a legal charge in the bank's favour and the couple gave a joint and several covenant to discharge their liabilities to the bank, secured against the property. It was held that the woman became entitled to an immediate and absolute beneficial interest in the property by way of a constructive trust. The Court of Appeal concluded that the couple could only reasonably have intended that they should each take a half share in the beneficial interest in the property. Also, she had acted to her detriment in reliance on that understanding by assuming the risk of joint liability on the mortgage. In *Midland Bank* v *Dobson and Dobson* [1986] 1 FLR 171, the Court of Appeal, having found the common intention, would not accept her purchase of domestic equipment/doing the decorating as sufficient evidence of such reliance. Mei's cooking, cleaning, gardening and DIY may prove similarly unhelpful to her cause. But it is Lord Bridge's words (above) which seem fatal to her claim. So far as one can be confident of anything in this area, Tony should be advised that her claim for half (or less) of the equity seems doomed to failure. Even the quarter-share granted in *Eves* would seem out of her reach today. Finally, there seems to be no evidence to sustain a claim based on either contract (*Tanner* v *Tanner* [1975] 1 WLR 1341) or proprietary estoppel (*Pascoe* v *Turner* [1979] 1 WLR 431).

(b) There would be strictly no change. In *Pettit* v *Pettit* [1970] AC 777 the husband had increased the value of the family home (bought by the wife) by over £1,000, but gained nothing by it in the absence of an express agreement. In *Thomas* v *Fuller-Brown* (above) a bricklayer was provided with accommodation by a divorced woman. He did a considerable amount of work on the house, including a two-storey extension, but it was held that there was no common intent that he should have a beneficial interest, merely that he was a kept man, provided with board, lodging and pocket money in return for his work. The governing principle here is that these are matters of land law, equity and trusts and not family/gender issues.

(c) Normally, as the question implies, if spouses are falling out with each other to the extent of litigation over home ownership, divorce (or separation order/ annulment) is likely, in which case the discretionary, adjustive jurisdiction of the divorce court will obtain under Part 2 of the Matrimonial Causes Act (MCA) 1973. There are still any number of circumstances, however, where the question of beneficial ownership may be relevant. The parties may not seek divorce, or any other matrimonial cause, or the ground(s) may not be available. The divorce court's powers may no longer be exercisable; a former spouse loses the right to apply for a property adjustment on remarriage: MCA 1973, s. 28(3).

A dispute about the use, rather than the ownership of the house might still involve declaratory issues where a third party is involved. An example is where a creditor seeks to enforce a judgment against a spouse's share in property by way of a charging order against the debtor's interest in the family home. The involvement of a third party will also be significant in so far as the husband's creditor will not be able to attack property beneficially owned by the wife, unless she has made herself liable; *Lloyds Bank plc* v *Rosset* [1990] (above) was concerned with this situation. The bankruptcy of one spouse naturally brings this issue into sharp relief, with the other spouse's property not vesting in the trustee in bankruptcy. Another possibility is illustrated by *Harwood* v *Harwood* [1991] 2 FLR 274. The firm in which the husband was a partner contributed to the cost of the matrimonial home, and the court could not resolve matters until the extent of the other partner's interest had been established; the divorce court wanted to exercise its powers under s. 24A, MCA 1973 to order the house to be sold.

Death, of course, terminates more marriages than does divorce. If a spouse has left his or her property elsewhere, the survivor may apply for reasonable provision from the estate under the Inheritance (Provision for Family and Dependants) Act 1975. Where the court is balancing the relict's claims against those of others, she might claim that she actually owned the house, which, therefore, did not pass under the will anyway.

A final possibility is that the legal and equitable interests might be relevant in the actual exercise by the divorce court of its discretion: the existing position is the necessary starting point, after all (*Tebbutt* v *Haynes* [1981] 2 All ER 238).

In conclusion, it should be noted that the relevant declaratory principles might well favour the married claimant over the unmarried: since *Midland Bank* v *Cooke* (above) the court may be readier to infer a joint beneficial ownership where the relationship is supposedly life-long.

Q Question 2

Consider the property interests generated by the activities of H and W, a married couple, in each of the following situations. How far would your answers differ if they were unmarried?

(a) H and W keep a cache of gold under their mattress. It all comes from H, who receives the metal by way of income payments. One day, with H's knowledge, W has some of it made into a necklace for her to wear.

(b) One Christmas, W, a businesswoman, buys two sportscars, one red and one green, with her own money and gives H a set of keys to the green one. W nearly always drives the red one, and H the green one, although both cars are insured in her name. Now, some years later, W is bankrupt.

(c) One of them gives the other a monthly housekeeping allowance from which the recipient manages to save £2,000 which the latter spends on clothes before dying in a road accident.

N.B. Maximum marks available for each part of this question are *equal*.

Commentary

This is another multi-parter, but this time with segregated data. This is more common in other subjects than it is in family law, where the tendency is to use one integrated narrative which depicts the vagaries of family life. Although the relevant area has remained unchanged for some time, it has become something of a backwater, family law having more important things to consider. Of the standard texts, *Bromley's Family Law* (Lowe and Douglas, 9th edn, 1998, pp. 106–133) is probably the most detailed treatment, although *Family Law* (Standley, 4th edn, 2004) has a useful overview.

What the examiners have done here is to take three issues of property rights, i.e. common funds, gifts, housekeeping allowances, and weave a separate story around each. Those who know the material, which is fairly short and straightforward, can score heavily provided they note the following. First, do not do it if you are bereft of knowledge on one of the parts: arithmetically, a bare lower second average on the rest will be a bad fail, as half of 66.6 is only 33.3! If it is a forced choice, do find something to say about each bit. A blank will earn no marks at all. Secondly, do not forget the opening instruction about cohabitation. Finally, however brief and one-dimensional they seem, the parts all have something which give the better student the chance to prove it.

You will see that we have started with a short introduction, designed to show the examiners that we have understood their plan and to make some points which apply throughout. This should engender goodwill from the start, hopefully to be represented in a little extra something by way of marks. Do not assume that the equality of marks *per* part necessarily means equality of length. In such questions, there may be less legal material in some parts which nonetheless involve tricky analyses, *viz* **(c)** here.

Answer plan

- **Common fund—joint interest. Contributors—rebuttable presumption of advancement. Relevant cases.**

- **Gift of a chattel—intent and deed/delivery. Insolvency. Insolvency Act 1986.**

- **Housekeeping allowance. Spouses—Married Women's Property Act 1964.**

- **Cohabitants—common law—agreement.**

:Ọ: Suggested answer

The theme which runs thorugh this question is partnership 'rights' over property other than the family home. The various aspects are, respectively: the 'common fund'; gifts between the partners; and housekeeping allowances. Normally the declaratory position between spouses will not be decisive because of the divorce court's discretionary adjustive powers. There is, however, still scope for proceedings under s. 17 of the Married Women's Property Act 1882, and the declaratory position may still be determinative where third parties are involved (insolvency and death) or where the couple are unmarried. In *Pettit* v *Pettit* [1970] AC 777, the House of Lords held that s. 17 did not give the court the power to vary existing interests. Finally, it should be noted that in *Hammond* v *Mitchell* [1991] 1 WLR 1127, Waite J stated that former cohabitants should be encouraged to settle disputes about chattels, on the basis that otherwise the court might well divide them equally. Standley (above) suggests that the court could adopt this approach even where the partners had not been cohabitants.

(a) The question here is who owns the gold, both under the mattress and around W's neck. *Prima facie*, the income of either spouse remains his/hers, as in *Heseltine* v *Heseltine* [1971] 1 All ER 952 where the wife received income from her own investments. Where there is a 'common fund', however, the couple may be taken as acquiring a joint interest in it. This arose in *Jones* v *Maynard* [1951] Ch 572 where the husband authorised his wife to draw on his bank account, after which they both paid in and both drew out. Occasionally he used such withdrawals to pay for investments in his own name. It was held that the wife was entitled to a half share in the account and in her husband's investments, even though his inputs had exceeded hers and they had made no express arrangements about the matter.

It thus seems that where both spouses contribute, however unequally, such an intention will be imputed in the absence of contrary agreement. Here, of course, H is the sole contributor and so any claim by W would have to be based upon the (rebuttable) presumption of advancement, as in *Re Figgis* [1969] 1 Ch 123. Since *Pettit* this is a much weaker presumption, and in the latter case Lord Diplock even questioned whether the presumption had survived at all. We are told that 'H and W' keep the gold under 'their' mattress, yet gold is not a liquid commodity and such cases as do exist involve bank accounts.

If, as seems doubtful, the cache is a 'common purse', the question of the necklace arises. *Jones* v *Maynard* (1951) was distinguished in *Re Bishop* [1965] Ch 450, where each spouse made withdrawals from the common fund, because in the earlier case they had agreed that the fund money should ultimately be invested. Here, of course, the item is conspicuously one of personal use and so, even were the cache held to be a common purse, the necklace might be taken as being hers alone. Irrespective of the common purse issue, questions of valid executed gifts from H to W might conceivably arise, see the answer to **(b)** below.

Were H and W cohabitants, the same reasoning would apply because the idea of the common purse is based on the purpose for which it was formed, and not on the nature of the parties' relationship (*Paul* v *Constance* [1977] 1 All ER 195).

(b) The question nakedly exposed by this story is whether ownership of the green car, as well as the red one, will vest in W's trustee in bankruptcy. Has W managed to make an earlier, binding, gift of it to H? It should be acknowledged at the outset that there is no presumption of undue influence as between husband and wife (*Howes* v *Bishop* [1909] 2 KB 390). There is nothing here reminiscent of *Simpson* v *Simpson* [1992] 1 FLR 601, where the presumption arose because one spouse had become particularly dependent on the other. There, the husband's mental capacity had been reduced by a cerebral tumour, and the effect of the transfer would have been to deny his children by an earlier marriage.

In order to perfect the gift of a chattel, there must be intent on the donor's part plus either a deed (not in issue here) or delivery. It may be that the giving of the keys (at Christmas, a time for presents) will be sufficiently symbolic, as in *Lock* v *Heath* (1892) 8 TLR 295, where the husband's delivery of one chair to his wife was held to cover all his furniture. Thus there may be enough evidence here to overcome the twin difficulties which bedevil the proof of delivery as between spouses, i.e. the fact that spouses frequently use each other's property and that the goods in question may already have been used by both parties before the gift.

A further difficulty may be less easily overcome. English law is reluctant to infer delivery where to do so would be a vehicle for the deprivation of the 'donor's' creditors. *Re Cole* [1964] Ch 175 has dangerous parallels to the present case. There the husband completely furnished a new house before his wife ever set foot in it. 'It's all yours' said he, after she had completed her tour, which began when he took his hands from her eyes after she had entered the first room. Nonetheless the furniture (which he used, as here) remained insured in his name (again as here). It was held that the gift was not perfected and the trustee was held entitled to the goods. Further, it is at least arguable that as it is the wife, and not the husband, who is the alleged donor, there was (still) a presumption of resulting trust in her favour, as in *Mercier* v *Mercier* [1903] 2 Ch 98.

Finally, s. 423 of the Insolvency Act 1986 must not be overlooked. It enables any transaction at an undervalue (e.g. a gift) to be avoided by the trustee in bankruptcy, if it was made with the intention of defeating the claims of creditors. Given that there was a gap of 'some years', this is clearly unlikely here. Overall, however, it seems likely that the green car will join the red one in the hands of W's trustee in bankruptcy.

It is further suggested that there would be little, if any, change in the position were the couple not married to one another, as the 'delivery' difficulty would be equally applicable. (Section 423 of the Insolvency Act 1986, above, applies to an insolvent cohabitant as to any bankrupt.)

(c) We are not told which spouse is the giver and which the receiver. This may be crucial. If the matter is one of 'role-reversal' and W is the supplier, then the allowance and any savings made from it are presumed H's as head of the family, according to the old case of *Edward* v *Cheyne* (No. 2) (1888) 13 App Cas 385. It seems doubtful whether this would apply today, according to *Bromley's Family Law* (9th edn, 1998 at p. 122). Anyway, if H is the allowance-giver then the situation would seem to be covered by s. 1 of the Married Women's Property Act (MWPA) 1964 whereby the savings or any property acquired from them 'shall be treated as belonging to the husband and wife in equal shares'. This applies in the absence of contrary agreement, of which there is no evidence here.

A difficulty unanticipated by the couple, and, indeed by the legislators, may arise as a result of the recipient's unfortunate demise. 'Equal shares' means that the whole beneficial interest will not automatically pass to the survivor (as does the 'common purse') but will go to the personal representatives instead. So there is the danger that half the value of the clothing could end up elsewhere, perhaps under a residuary bequest. Parliament overlooked the fact that many marriages survive. Indeed, the fact that the money was spent on items of so personal a nature might even suggest a tacit agreement (were the other to have known of it) that they belong wholly to the buyer, in which case the personal representatives could end up with the lot.

If the couple are 'mere' cohabitants, the MWPA 1964 is inapplicable and on the face of it the common law rules will apply. Whichever partner was the supplier, any unspent balance, here represented by the clothes, would belong to that partner. On the other hand, these things always give way to contrary agreement (e.g. that it should belong to them both jointly) which itself can always be inferred by a court. The truth is that we await a decision.

Q Question 3

'There were two consistent themes running through all the Commission's earlier work. The first was the persistent observation that the present rules for determining the ownership of property during marriage were arbitrary, uncertain and unfair. The second was that ownership of property whilst a marriage continues is important and that it is not right to consider marital property only in relation to what happens when a marriage ends.' ((1988) Law Com. No. 175 para. 1.4, Family Law, Matrimonial Property)

'The prevalence of cohabitation must be kept in mind when considering the case for the reform of family property law since a property regime which conferred interests on the basis that a couple were married might, yet again, fail adequately to consider social realities.' (Cretney and Masson, *Principles of Family Law*, 6th edn, 1997 at p. 220)

How, if at all, should matrimonial property law be reformed?

Commentary

When examiners turn (unenthusiastically) into mere markers, they often produce a grid called a 'mark analysis sheet'. It produces, amongst other things, a graphic demonstration of the comparative 'popularity' of the questions asked. The column applicable to this type of question often remains untroubled by entries, for which candidates, strong and weak alike, are to be congratulated.

One purpose of including this question here is to show that examinations sometimes include difficult questions which are best avoided. Whether this is merely bad examining or a legitimate means of encouraging wise selection by candidates is another matter. Here, there are a number of good reasons why discerning, and other students are quite right to shudder and move on. All that we can make of this question at first sight is that it requires a critical approach to partnership property law. The closest most students (and most courses) come to that is question 1 above, i.e. problems about the declaratory position in the family home. This one, on the other hand, covers property generally, requires knowledge of difficult and contentious proposals on the table, brings in a value judgment about partnership differentials, and requires the student to hold the ring between such luminaries as the Law Commission on the one hand and Professors Cretney and Masson on the other. It is also pretty boring, although older students with homestead experience tend to find it less so.

This commentary, therefore, is not going to be one of those exhortations which begin, 'We are always surprised that students make such heavy weather of this question, it is really quite simple if only . . .', etc. Instead, we are going to confirm that they are best ignored. Not, of course, that the question is impossible to address, just very difficult, requiring a lot of reference to a lot of extra reading. Even Hale, Pearl, Cooke and Bates, *Family Law & Society*, 5th edn (London: Butterworths, 2002), collators of materials to the Upper Second Classes, would need to be swallowed whole to make something out of this one, and the student texts which deal with it properly are Cretney, Masson and Bailey-Harris *Principles of Family*

Law, 7th edn, 2002 and Herring J. *Family Law* (Longman, 2001). It could be tackled as coursework, perhaps. In the exam, however, even the aspiring First is best advised to find an easier way to achieve that grade even if, as one would hope, the course had covered this sort of thing.

Answer plan

* Property ownership during marriage—brief history—declaratory. Reform— Matrimonial Proceedings and Property Act 1970—divorce courts' discretionary powers of adjustment. Part 2, Matrimonial Causes Act 1973.

* Law Commission Reports. Joint ownership/restraint on dealings/presumption of ownership. Use/benefit.

* Community of property—California.

* Money—common fund.

* Own views/recommendations.

:Q: Suggested answer

In *Sen* v *Headley* [1991] Ch 425, it transpired that a family home bought for £1,100 in 1936 had been valued at 'several hundred thousand pounds' by 1986; more incrementally, the spouses in *McHardy and Sons (A Firm)* v *Warren and Another* [1994] 2 FLR 338, were able to buy their third home for £42,000 in 1982, having bought their first home for £3,691 in 1968 (when the only cash involved was the £650 deposit provided as a wedding present by the groom's father). It is against this background that the question is set. We are concerned not only with the family homes of married couples (although about one-third of the net wealth of the personal sector is made up of dwelling houses), but also with issues such as which partner owns the furniture, the car or the dog? What about the bank account(s)? For the 70 per cent of the adult population who are presently expected to marry (see Cretney, Masson, and Bailey-Harris, 7th edn, 2002), some relief may subsequently be obtained by way of the divorce courts' discretionary adjustment powers, yet for the two million or so who are estimated to be in extra-marital partnerships (the 'social realities' referred to in the second quotation) no such mitigation is available.

   Until the Matrimonial Proceedings and Property Act 1970, the law most certainly merited the first criticism, i.e. 'arbitrary, uncertain and unfair', mentioned by the 1988 Law Commission Report. The wife gained nothing for her contribution to the family, as her rights were solely dependent on declaratory questions of land law, contract, equity and trusts. In *Pettit* v *Pettit* [1970] AC 777 the House of Lords held that property disputes between husband and wife had to be decided by these 'ordinary principles'. Yet since the 1970 Act (now Part 2 of the Matrimonial Causes Act 1973) the divorce court, at least, has the all-important power of discretionary adjustment, and 'virtually all' marital homes are anyway vested in husband and wife jointly, according to Law Com. No. 175, para. 4.3. It could also be said that married couples differ in their attitudes to ownership of property and that, for all these reasons, there is no need for reform.

There are, however, powerful counter-arguments. They apply with equal force to all types of property. To the partner with no separate income, the present rules for determining ownership may appear as unfair during the marriage as they do when it ends. It is anyway a false distinction to divide marriages into the happy and the unhappy, and to say that when they are happy, ownership is unimportant. Many marriages do not end in divorce, and there may be occasions when who owns what is important to one or both spouses. A clear law which reflects the intentions of both parties would do more to encourage marital stability than one which does not. Bankruptcy and death also bring property rights into focus, with the latter terminating more marriages than divorce. Even where the court has to reallocate property on divorce, known existing rules could provide a better basis for adjustment and could reduce acrimony, cost and delay in reaching a settlement. It is remarkable that English law does not give spouses the right to know what each other owns (at least not until matrimonial proceedings are commenced).

In the First Report on Family Property—A New Approach (Law Com. No. 52 (1973)) the Commissioners recommended that the home be treated as jointly owned in the absence of contrary agreement. Amongst other arguments, it was thought that that would reflect the reality of marital life, whereby spouses regard the house as 'theirs'; act as recognition of joint contribution to the marriage; and eliminate the uncertainties of litigation in which the outcome is based on financial contribution. In the 1988 Report, the one referred to in the question, the Commission has abandoned the scheme, regarding it as 'too controversial'. Earlier it had become clear (Hansard (HL) 18 July 1979, vol. 401, col. 1432) that Government support would not be forthcoming. Perhaps the Scottish Law Commission, in Scot Law Com. No. 86 (1984), produced the most damning criticisms of a joint ownership scheme. Were one spouse to opt out, it could exacerbate marital dispute; it could go too far if applied to gifts or inheritances during marriage; it would benefit the undeserving as well as the deserving; and the supposed benefits of fixed equal rights would be illusory, in view of property adjustment on divorce, i.e. it would be most useless when most needed.

Other ideas have been floated as regards the marital home. A 'restraint on dealings' has been suggested whereby the husband could not mortgage, or even sell, the home over his wife's head. But how would a purchaser be put on notice? First, the registration system of the Matrimonial Homes Act 1983 is a hostile step, and one which the other spouse may not wish to take. Secondly, there could be a 'presumption of ownership', effectively reversing the maxim that equity follows the law, but again raising the question of third party rights.

The family home is often by far the most significant marital asset. The idea of a 'community of property' which is sometimes suggested would, however, be of general application. The principle is that, by marriage, the parties' property would at some stage be subject to joint ownership. Any given scheme might best be tested by reference to the criticisms raised by the Scottish Law Commission (above). Perhaps most importantly of all, would it be subject to variation on divorce? In her book, *The Divorce Revolution* (1985), Professor Weitzman demonstrates that the Californian community regime leads to divorced wives being worse off post-divorce where there is insufficient capital in the community pool, particularly if there are young children. (The Child Support Acts 1991 and 1995 might now militate against that here, of course.) One (pre-Child Support Act 1991) suggestion here has been a 'mixed community of gains'. This was suggested by Freedman *et al.* in their book *Property and Marriage—An Integrated Approach* (1985), in which an holistic approach is recommended, breaking down barriers between property law, family law, tax law, social security and pensions, bankruptcy, succession and intestacy. The upshot would be that all gains and liabilities during marriage would be shared equally on termination or bankruptcy, with certain assets, such as the marital home and pensions, being co-owned. On divorce, the continuing needs of children would be taken into account and would be weighed in the balance on the division of the community of property.

In the 1988 Report, above, the (English) Law Commission proposed that the beneficial ownership of property acquired during marriage should depend upon whether it was for the use/benefit of just one, or both, of the spouses. Even though the scheme was subject to a number of qualifications, e.g. it would apply only in the absence of contrary intention known to the other spouse and would not apply to land, life insurance policies and business purchases, other difficulties may still be observed. The dissenting Commissioner pointed out that assumptions made about household goods do not necessarily apply to such as cars or securities, which are generally more valuable. It is significant that the Family Law (Scotland) Act 1985, s. 25, in raising a rebuttable presumption of equal rights in household goods, is careful to exclude money and securities, cars and caravans (and pets). (Scot Law Com. No. 86 (1984) suggested that such animals are normally regarded as belonging to one or other of the spouses.)

In 2002, the Law Commission abandoned attempts to devise a scheme providing certainty and consistency in the evaluation of beneficial interests in the shared home (The Law Commission, *Sharing Homes: A Discussion Paper*, 2002, London: Law Commission). 'Ultimately, the complexity of fine-tuning a scheme so that it would apply fairly across the whole range of diverse relationships rendered the aims of the project unattainable', said Stuart Bridge, Law Commissioner for England and Wales in 'The Property Rights of Cohabitants—Where do we go from here?' [2002] Fam Law 743. He went on to say that, although the rules of implied trusts and proprietary estoppel might be imperfect they at least gave the courts some flexibility to cater for individual circumstances. The cautious view of the Law Commission was—better to let matters alone—and that any modification of the common law should be left to the judiciary rather than the legislature. However, it may soon be impossible to avoid grappling with a community of property regime. It may be imposed on us from Europe (see Barlow, A., Callus, T., and Cooke, E., 'Community of Property—A Study for England and Wales' [2004] Fam Law 47). Better then, it is suggested, to create or negotiate a regime that would be acceptable in England and Wales.

On the specific issue of money, the present law remains predicated on the idea of the 'common fund', whereby a spouse's income remains his or her own except where funds are pooled, in which case they both acquire a joint interest in the whole fund. Section 1 of the Married Women's Property Act 1964 deals (rather inadequately) with savings made by wives from housekeeping money supplied by husbands; it belongs to them both in 'equal shares'.

In conclusion, it seems that the more thought is given to the reform of matrimonial property law, the less agreement is reached as to the form it should take, or even whether any (further) intervention is desirable. The Law Commission alone produced some nine Papers/Reports between 1971 and 1988, the last contributing the first quotation used in this question. We have seen that the 1988 proposals were comparatively modest, yet were not unanimous, were not followed in Scotland, and did not seem to have attracted Government (or public) support. Community of property systems from, e.g., California have not proved to be attractive models either.

Although the Law Commission's discussion paper *Sharing Homes* (2002) accepted that marriage is a status deserving of special treatment, the change in living arrangements in the UK overtook their deliberations. They recognised the need to consider the wide range of present day personal relationships. However, their conclusion was that it was not possible to devise a statutory scheme for the determination of shares in the shared home which can operate fairly and evenly across all the diverse circumstances which are now encountered. The Law Commission expressed a belief that further consideration should be given to the adoption, necessarily by legislation, of broader based approaches to personal relationships outside marriage, following the lead given by jurisdictions such as France, Australia and New Zealand. This may be by formal registration of certain civil partnerships (for same sex couples see the Civil Partnership Bill 2004) and the conferment on the courts of an adjustive power to reallocate the rights of individuals who are, or have been, living together for a defined period or in defined circumstances. The Law Commission took the view that it was not for them to attempt to define a status which would lead to the vesting of rights and obligations. However, the Law Society have risen to the challenge, in *Cohabitation—The case for clear law* (July 2002) they have put forward ideas to give legal protection for unmarried couples after they have lived together for two years, or have a child together, but which stop short of the safeguards offered to married couples on relationship breakdown.

Further reading

Bailey-Harris, R., 'Law and Unmarried Couples: Oppression or Liberation?' [1996] CFLQ 137.

Bailey-Harris, R., 'Dividing the Assets on Breakdown of Relationships Outside Marriage: Challenges for Reformers', in R. Bailey-Harris (ed.) *Dividing the Assets on Family Breakdown* (Bristol: Jordans, 1998).

Dewar J., 'Land, Law and the Family Home' in S. Bright and J. Dewar (eds), *Land Law: Themes and Perspectives* (Oxford: Oxford University Press, 1998), 327.

Glover, N., and Todd, P., 'The Myth of Common Intention' (1996) 16 Legal Studies 325.

Hale, B. (Baroness Hale of Richmond), 'Unmarried Couples in Family Law' [2004] Fam Law 419.

Law Commission, *Sharing Homes: A Discussion Paper* (Law Commission, 2002).

Law Society, *Cohabitation: The case for clear reform* (London: Law Society, 2002).

Ancillary financial relief for adults: the courts

Introduction

On most family law courses, a fair amount of time is spent looking at financial relief for adults. This includes financial provision in the magistrates' courts, but the main emphasis will be on financial provision and property adjustment ancillary to divorce, nullity and (judicial) separation under the Matrimonial Causes Act 1973. In practice these ancillary matters, including the children's future, are where attention is now focused. The Child Support Acts 1991–2000 would seem to have complicated the issue by segregating child support (administrative and formulaic) from spousal provision (court-based and discretionary). In fact, in practice, the package negotiated will be built on the statutory amount required of the absent parent, and in the exam room ancillary financial relief questions may well be child-free, involve stepchildren only, or give the amount of child support required.

Some students seem to take an instant dislike to ancillary financial relief (and property matters generally) and exclude them from their revision programme without a second thought. Perhaps they find the amount of material daunting or wrongly think that it will involve some difficult mathematics. It is not easy at the highest level in practice (e.g. pensions) but if you can crack this topic it is bound to be on the paper, either on its own or with another topic, perhaps the ground for divorce. You will usually be given a lot of information, sometimes actual figures to work with: there is a lot of case law to use and good marks can be obtained. Our best hints are these: to consider the data in the light of the s. 25, MCA 1973 criteria for the court's exercise of discretion; and in 'Big Money' cases, that uneven divisions must be justified by those criteria (*White* v *White* [2000] 3 WLR 1571 (HL)). Future examiners may well wish to explore the possibilities inherent for lawyers and mediators in s. 328(1) of the Proceeds of Crime Act 2002: 'A person commits an offence if he enters into or becomes concerned in an arrangement which he knows or suspects facilitates (by whatever means) the acquisition, retention, use or control of criminal property by or on behalf of another person'. Because of the principle of full disclosure of finances, it is obvious to a family lawyer or mediator if a party has failed to declare income—'The money laundering rules are aimed chiefly at organised crime . . . but most reports from solicitors are coming from family lawyers' (*The Times*, 20 July, 2004).

There are three questions in this chapter, one on the magistrates' court and two on ancillary financial relief in the superior courts. All are problems. An essay title is possible (e.g. ' "It is difficult to reconcile fairness with predictability in our discretion-based ancillary financial relief system". Discuss.'), but problems generally provide both the examiner and the student with more scope.

Q Question 1

Terry has been married to Alison for three years. They have no children of their own although Sharon, Alison's seven-year-old daughter from her previous marriage lives with them. Terry left Alison three weeks ago when he discovered that she has been having an affair. He refuses to pay her any maintenance either for herself or for Sharon. Terry has a well-paid job. Alison does not work and is now receiving state support.

Terry has now received a summons from the magistrates' court in which Alison is claiming maintenance for herself and for Sharon.

Terry seeks advice on the extent of his liability for maintenance. He wants to know what factors the court will take into account when assessing maintenance and what the court's attitude would be if he failed to make any payments ordered.

Advise Terry.

Commentary

As questions go this is about as straightforward as they come. It is concerned with financial provision ('maintenance') in the magistrates' court, so if you know enough about the Domestic Proceedings and Magistrates' Courts Act 1978, you should be well placed. The 1978 Act provides a statutory procedure for financial provision during marriage. In practice, when compared with orders made on the ending of a marriage, it is little used, but the Act brought the family jurisdiction of the magistrates' court into line with the law administered in the divorce court and intended to counter the allegation that the magistrates' jurisdiction was 'a secondary system' of family law (Report of the Committee on One-Parent Families, Cm. 5629 (1974) (the Finer Report)).

During marriage, application for financial provision can also be made to the High Court or a county court with divorce jurisdiction under the Matrimonial Causes Act (MCA) 1973, s. 27 (as amended). On establishing the ground of failure to provide reasonable maintenance, the court has power to make periodical payments orders (secured or unsecured) and lump sum orders. As you are told in this question that a magistrates' summons has been received, there is no need to consider s. 27 here, but you should be aware of it as an option during marriage.

Your answer is virtually planned for you, as you are told that Terry wants advice on three issues: liability for maintenance, assessment criteria and enforcement of orders.

Stepchildren have escaped the clutches of the Child Support Acts 1991–2000, so apart from a brief mention to that effect, there is no need to explore that area. You will be expected, however, to deal thoroughly with the three areas referred to, so do not be tempted to do the question if, for example, you know nothing about enforcement.

- **Magistrates' court—DPMCA 1978**

- **Step-child**

- **Failure to provide reasonable maintenance**

- **Periodical payments and lump sums**

- **'All the circumstances'**

- **Enforcement measures—MCA 1980**

:Q: Suggested answer

We are asked to advise Terry, who has received a summons from the magistrates' court in which his wife Alison, to whom he has been married for three years, is claiming maintenance for herself and for Sharon, her daughter from a previous marriage. Basically Terry wishes to know what his maintenance liability is, how the maintenance will be assessed and what will happen if he refuses to make any payment under the court order.

At the outset it should be stated that as Sharon is Terry's stepdaughter she is not a 'qualifying child' within the provisions of the Child Support Acts 1991–2000, and a maintenance assessment cannot be made under that legislation against Terry as her stepfather. If he is to be made to pay maintenance for Sharon, it will have to be done by court order.

First, we turn to the extent of Terry's liability for maintenance. On the facts, Terry perhaps assumes that as Alison has been having an affair and Sharon is not his child, he does not have to pay maintenance for either of them. This, however, is not the case.

The relevant legislation is the Domestic Proceedings and Magistrates' Courts Act (DPMCA) 1978. For Alison to be able to claim maintenance for herself she must establish a ground under s. 1 of the Act. Of the four current grounds, the ones which she is most likely to use are that Terry has failed to provide reasonable maintenance for herself, and has failed to provide or make proper contribution towards reasonable maintenance for a child of the family, Sharon (s. 1(a) and (b)). The grounds based on failure to provide reasonable maintenance involve the application of an objective test. Non-payment need not be wilful and all the circumstances of the case, including the means and needs of the parties, will be looked at to determine whether there has been a failure to make reasonable provision. Terry, we are told, has a well-paid job whereas Alison is not in employment and is in receipt of state support. It is therefore the case that Terry has the means to make provision for his family but has refused to do so. Thus this ground could be established.

There is nothing in the given facts to indicate that the behaviour ground could be established. So far as the final ground is concerned, Alison would not be able to establish that Terry has deserted her, despite the fact that he left her three weeks ago, because as she has been having an affair, Terry had good cause for leaving (*Glenister* v *Glenister* [1945] 1 All ER 513) and thus one element of the 'offence' cannot be established.

Assuming that Alison successfully establishes that Terry is not maintaining her reasonably, the court will be able to make an order under s. 2 for financial provision for both Alison and any child of the family. To claim maintenance for a child, no ground needs to be established and maintenance would be available even if Alison's application were unsuccessful. However, Sharon is not Terry's natural daughter, she is Alison's daughter from a previous marriage, and it must therefore be established that she is a 'child of the family' before Terry will be liable to maintain her. 'Child of the family' is defined in s. 88(1) of the 1978 Act to include a child who has been *treated* by both parties to a marriage as a child of their family. The test is objective, there is no need for a link by blood or adoption to one of the parties; it is sufficient that both parties independently treat the child as one of the family, regardless of whether they are aware of all the material facts. Here, Terry has been living with Alison and Sharon for three years—it was a mere fortnight in *W* v *W* [1984] FLR 96—and therefore one assumes that Sharon has been treated as one of the family by Terry and is within the definition. He will thus be liable to make provision for her.

So what types of orders is the court likely to make? Under s. 2 the court could make a periodical payments order (PPO) for Alison and possibly a lump sum order (LSO) (to a maximum of £1,000—more if he consents!) to meet any liabilities and expenses she has reasonably incurred since the separation. The lump sum could be made payable by instalments. Unless the magistrates' court decides to make the PPO for a limited term only, on the basis that Alison should become self-supporting once she is back on her feet, the PPO will last until Alison remarries or until either Alison or Terry dies. It would also cease to have effect if she and Terry resumed cohabitation for a continuous period of more than six months (s. 25(1)(a), DPMCA). A PPO and/or an LSO could also be made for Sharon, the PPO lasting until she is 18, though it could continue beyond then if she was in continuing education or training. It would seem that Terry's liability for maintenance extends to both Alison and Sharon.

In deciding whether, and if so how, to exercise its jurisdiction, the court is influenced by a number of factors. The court will be assisted primarily by the statutory guidelines contained in s. 3 of the 1978 Act, which are virtually identical to those applicable on divorce. It should be noted however that, as in most cases in practice, the conclusive factor will be Terry's ability to provide for Alison and Sharon (*Stockford* v *Stockford* [1981] 3 FLR 58). Section 3 places a duty on the court to have regard to all the circumstances of the case, first consideration being given to the welfare, whilst a minor, of any child of the family who has not attained 18. Consequently the first aim is to ensure that Sharon is properly provided for and that Alison has adequate maintenance to fulfil properly her role as residential parent.

The court must then pay particular regard to a number of factors. On the given facts the income, earning capacity and financial resources of both Terry and Alison would be taken into account and the court would look to see whether it would be reasonable for Alison to take steps to acquire any increase in her earning capacity. Both parties' financial needs, obligations and responsibilities would be considered, plus the standard of living enjoyed prior to the separation. The fact that Alison and Terry have only been married for a short time is a relevant factor and, certainly if no children were involved, would be likely to lead to a limited term order.

Terry may feel that Alison's conduct should be decisive but conduct is only relevant if it is such that it would in the court's opinion be inequitable to disregard it. Case law has established that adultery *per se* is not sufficient: the circumstances must be such that to disregard the conduct would offend a reasonable person's sense of justice (*Robinson* v *Robinson* [1983] 1 All ER 391; *Kyte* v *Kyte* [1987] 3 WLR 1114). This does not appear to be the case here.

In assessing Sharon's maintenance her financial needs and resources will be relevant, as will the manner in which she is being educated, but the bottom line in practice is the financial position of her parents (s. 3(2)). As Terry is not Sharon's natural father and would not, in the absence of the wide definition given to 'child of the family', be under any legal obligation to make financial provision for her, additional criteria will be considered by the court (s. 3(4)), i.e. whether Terry has assumed responsibility for her maintenance and if so, on what basis and for how long; whether he assumed responsibility knowing that she was not his child; and the liability of any other person to maintain Sharon. We assume that Terry maintained Sharon during the three years of his marriage to Alison; and obviously knew that she was not his child. Her natural father, if still alive, would be liable to maintain her. These additional factors do not negate Terry's liability to Sharon but may affect the amount he is ordered to pay. Indeed, in *Leadbeater* v *Leadbeater* [1985] FLR 789, the court refused to order a husband to make payments to his stepdaughter on the basis that primary responsibility lay with her own natural father. On the other hand in *E* v *C (Child Maintenance)* [1996] 1 FLR 472 it was held relevant to consider what the Child Support Act assessment would have been.

Finally Terry wants to know what the court's attitude would be if he failed to make payments as ordered by the court. Terry may find that when the orders are originally made, the magistrates' court will order payments to be made by standing order or direct debit, or it may make an attachment of earnings order (Maintenance Enforcement Act 1991).

If he should subsequently default, then enforcement proceedings would be taken against him. The enforcement procedure is contained in the Magistrates' Courts Act 1980 and has been modernised by the Maintenance Enforcement Act 1991. The court may decide to enforce any arrears in total or to remit them in whole or in part, depending on the payer's financial position and all the circumstances of the case. The main methods of enforcement are: distress (little used); committal to prison; and the making of an attachment of earnings order (AEO) under the Attachment of Earnings Act 1971.

Terry should be warned that as an ultimate deterrent if he wilfully refuses or culpably neglects to pay the maintenance ordered, he could be sent to prison for between five days and six weeks according to the sum owed. He would only be committed after first being given the opportunity to pay off the arrears by instalments (by postponing issue of the warrant of committal) and if the court felt it inappropriate to make an AEO. As Terry has a 'well-paid' job, and assuming that he is not self-employed, an AEO would seem more appropriate. The order would be directed to Terry's employer who would be ordered to make deductions from Terry's earnings and remit them to the collecting officer of the court. The protected earnings rate would ensure that Terry's remaining income would be kept above subsistence level.

In addition to the above, Terry could be fined up to £1,000 for his default (s. 59B Magistrates' Courts Act 1980). He would thus be well advised to make any payments ordered as the court's attitude to default is not favourable.

Q Question 2

Richard is divorcing his wife, Hyacinth.

When they married five years ago Richard, a successful businessman, was 45 and Hyacinth 25. Hyacinth insisted at the time of their marriage that Richard should sell his bachelor flat and buy a house in their joint names, which he duly did. The house is now valued at £1,000,000 and there is no mortgage.

Richard earns £110,000 a year, and has further assets worth some £2.5 million. Hyacinth, a secretary and part-time model, has not worked since the marriage but was always happy to spend Richard's money. There are no children.

Last year Richard was diagnosed as having multiple sclerosis. Hyacinth's reaction was to tell him that she had no intention of spending her life looking after an invalid and that she was leaving him to go to live with Justin, with whom she had been having an affair for two years. When Richard said he did not know how he would carry on without her, Hyacinth said it would probably be best all round if he killed himself and then at least she could have the house.

Richard has now received a letter from Hyacinth's solicitor with a proposed financial settlement. Hyacinth wants half the value of the house, £3,000 a month maintenance and a lump sum of £50,000. Justin is a 'mature' student with no income and cannot support her.

Richard thinks that this is what the court might make him pay. Do you?

Commentary

You need to get to poor Richard quickly with some sound, informed, advice before he makes another big mistake.

Here, there is an offer of settlement on the table which Richard is considering agreeing to, as he thinks it is reasonable. But is it? You need to know your way around the relevant provisions of the Matrimonial Causes Act 1973 and, using the information provided in the question itself, hazard a guess as to how a court would be likely to exercise the wide discretion vested in it in such circumstances.

Note that the Code of Practice of the Solicitors Family Law Association states that: 'You should encourage your client to see the advantages to the family of a constructive and non-confrontational approach as a way of resolving differences. You should advise, negotiate and conduct matters so as to help the family members settle their differences as quickly as possible and reach agreement, while allowing them time to reflect, consider and come to terms with their new situation.'

Despite your need to disabuse Richard, both sides need to be kept informed of the costs, and that gaining a larger proportion of a smaller pot may mean less—even for the 'winner'.

- Ancillary financial relief—Part II, MCA 1973

- Periodic payments and lump sums

- Property adjustment

- 'All the circumstances'

- *White*: not half

☼ Suggested answer

One's sympathy is certainly with Richard. The immediate reaction, i.e. that what has been proposed cannot possibly be reasonable, must however be justified by looking at the relevant provisions of the Matrimonial Causes Act (MCA) 1973 (as amended by the Matrimonial and Family Proceedings Act 1984), and considering what the likely outcome would be if the court was asked to resolve the ancillary matters in the given circumstances.

Hyacinth is asking for half the value of the house (£500,000); £3,000 a month maintenance; and a £50,000 lump sum. But is she legally entitled to this?

The MCA 1973 gives the court very wide powers of financial provision and property adjustment, so that it is usually possible to achieve a fair, just and reasonable result (ss. 21–26). Financial provision orders available include periodical payments (secured or unsecured) and a lump sum order (LSO). As specifically provided in the Act an LSO may be made to enable the payee to meet liabilities and expenses already reasonably incurred, or it could be used to enable a wife to take a course of training. Such an order is only of any practical value where the payer has the necessary capital, which would appear to be the case here.

Richard is presumably living in the matrimonial home which, at Hyacinth's insistence, is in both their names. Hyacinth is asking for half the value, a sum to which as a joint tenant she is technically entitled. Courts with divorce jurisdiction however, have wide property adjustment powers and are not constrained by existing beneficial ownership.

How then will the court decide what is a fair and just settlement for Richard and Hyacinth?

The philosophy of the MCA 1973 (as amended) is to discourage the 'alimony drone' and to encourage women to be self-supporting and independent. In deciding what provision should be made for Hyacinth, the court will be assisted by statutory guidelines (s. 25). It might once have taken the one-third 'starting point' approach (*Wachtel* v *Wachtel* [1973] Fam 72), as per Hyacinth's 'maintenance' demand. But today, following the House of Lords decision in *White* v *White* [2000] 3 WLR 1571, and given that there is a surplus of assets over needs, the court will, if necessary, need to explain why it is not ordering an equal division. As there are no children, the direction in s. 25(1) to give first consideration to the welfare while a minor of any child of the family who has not attained 18, is inapplicable. The court is then directed to consider the specific matters listed in s. 25(2)—which create no hierarchy (*Piglowska* v *Piglowski* [1999] 2 FLR 763).

Sections 25(2)(a) and (b) are always very relevant, i.e. the present and future income and other financial resources of both parties, including any increase in capacity it would be reasonable to expect a party to take steps to acquire, and the present and future needs, obligations and responsibilities of each. Here, Richard is a successful businessman with an annual salary of £110,000, he has substantial savings, and may well have a pension (future resource). Hyacinth on the other hand has never worked since they married, preferring to spend Richard's money, though she is apparently a secretary and part-time model. Should she be expected to work? It is not enough to make general assertions about earning capacity, evidence is required that Hyacinth can in fact become self-supporting. Hyacinth is only 30 now, she has no young children to look after, has not been out of the job market for too long and would seem to have earning potential either as a secretary or model.

The fact that the marriage has been fairly short (five years) is also relevant (s. 25(2)(d)), as is the standard of living enjoyed by the parties before the breakdown of the marriage (s. 25(2)(c)). But Hyacinth cannot expect to be enabled to maintain the same standard forever, particularly now that the court need no longer attempt to keep the parties in the financial position they would have been in had the marriage not broken down (Matrimonial and Family Proceedings Act 1984).

Section 25(2)(e), MCA 1973, directs the court to have regard to any physical or mental disability of either party; the fact that Richard has multiple sclerosis will be regarded as significant. With regards to the contribution made by both to the welfare of the family, including looking after the home, one suspects that Richard has done most of the giving and Hyacinth all the taking. As a spouse she leaves a lot to be desired—a matter reflected in s. 25(2)(f), 'contribution to the welfare of the family'. In *Vicary* v *Vicary* [1992] 2 WLR 271 it was held that no distinction be drawn between the business-supporting wife and the home-maker. The 'non-working, happily-spending' Hyacinth has been neither.

Of particular significance in this case is the conduct of the parties (s. 25(2)(g)). Hyacinth's conduct certainly merits examination. First, she had been secretly having an affair with Justin for two years before she left Richard. Secondly, her reaction to Richard's illness was unforgivable. In *K* v *K (Financial Provision: Conduct)* [1988] 1 FLR 469 a wife helped her depressed husband with his suicide attempts, in order to set up home with her lover and to get as much from her husband's estate as possible. The court held that to ignore this conduct would offend right-thinking members of society. The facts are not dissimilar here. Hyacinth saw an opportunity to get the house, presumably for herself and her lover, and what happened to Richard was of no concern to her. In addition, her behaviour at the time of the marriage could be considered suspect; what were her motives for insisting on the flat being sold and a house bought in joint names? Did she never intend to stay long, but want to ensure half the house was hers, as in *Cuzner* v *Underdown* [1974] 2 All ER 351? It would appear that Hyacinth's conduct is such that to ignore it would offend a reasonable person's sense of justice and falls within s. 25(2)(g). In *Clark* v *Clark* [1999] 2 FLR 498, a wife who had induced her much older husband to buy property in her name had her conduct born in mind by the divorce court. Finally, and in view of Hyacinth's conduct, this is most certainly *not* a case in which the rich(er) spouse will have to struggle to show that he has made a 'special' contribution—as the millionaire solicitor failed to show in *H* v *H (Financial Provision: Special Contribution)* [2002] 2 FLR 1021.

Under the MCA 1973 (as amended) the goal now seems to be to make the parties self-sufficient. The court has a mandatory duty, when deciding whether to make financial provision, to consider whether it would be appropriate to terminate the financial obligations of the parties as soon after the decree as the court thinks just and reasonable (s. 25A(1)). The court will consider an immediate clean break or a limited term order.

One option available to the court in this case would be a deferred clean break. If the court considers it appropriate to do so, it may make a PPO in Hyacinth's favour for a limited term only to enable her to adjust without undue hardship to her change of status (s. 25A(2)). Here, as we have seen, Hyacinth has real potential for increasing her earning capacity and should be made to make adjustments to her life and attain financial independence as soon as possible. It would seem entirely appropriate to limit any PPO, even though Hyacinth does not have a job at present, particularly as the marriage was short, and childless (*Barrett* v *Barrett* [1988] 2 FLR 516). In addition Hyacinth should be debarred (by an order under s. 28(1A)) from applying for an extension of the term: if not, Hyacinth could at any time during its life apply for the period to be lengthened (*Richardson* v *Richardson (No. 2)* [1994] 2 FLR 1051). However, in the circumstances it would not seem inappropriate, unjust or unreasonable to effect an immediate clean break (s. 25A(3)) with no continuing obligations at all. Although there is no presumption that a clean break be ordered (*SRJ* v *DWJ (Financial Provision)* [1999] 2 FLR 1761), the trend in PPOs is to dismiss them—nearly one in three such applications in 2003 (*Judicial Statistics*, Cm. 6251, Table 5.7). Once again, the wife's conduct hardly permits her to argue that his earning capacity was a resource to be equitably shared (as noted in *J* v *J* [2004] EWHC 52 (Fam)). Property adjustment orders could be made and Hyacinth's claim for periodical payments dismissed. Hyacinth, as a joint tenant, is entitled to half the value of the house, but a court could well decide to reduce her share in the light of her conduct.

One suspects that Richard is likely to want to settle and, knowing what a court is likely to do post-*White* (HL, above), be confident in offering a one-off, unreopenable, capital pay-off, representing far less than 50 per cent of his assets (as has been the case with far more deserving spouses than Hyacinth, e.g. *Dharamshi* v *Dharamshi* [2001] 1 FLR 736). Let him offer £300,000, i.e. 10 per cent of his capital. This is a case for a once and for all settlement with all claims dismissed—given her behaviour and despite his income being significantly greater than their combined outgoings, this is light years away from the 'unusual' divorce case of *Mcfarlane* v *McFarlane, Parlour* v *Parlour, The Times*, 18 July, 2004, where the court had a duty to consider the *future* possibility of a clean break via a temporary periodical payments order.

Q Question 3

Victor and Margaret were married 25 years ago. The matrimonial home was bought in joint names.

Victor has been in index-linked pensionable employment in the public sector all his working life. Margaret was a secretary but gave up work early on in the marriage to run the home. She successfully completed a Cordon Bleu cookery course earlier this year.

Victor and Margaret had a daughter, Sarah, who died last year aged eight. Sarah was born with Down's syndrome and Victor could never cope with the fact that a child of his was handicapped. He found her an embarrassment and wanted her to go into a residential home. Margaret would not hear of this and three years ago Victor left the matrimonial home.

He is living in a comfortable flat owned by his father who is terminally ill. Victor will inherit the flat and a considerable sum of money when his father dies.

Since moving out Victor has paid maintenance for Margaret (and for Sarah until her death), together with all outgoings on the house. He has some money in a building society account.

Divorce proceedings have now been commenced. Margaret is claiming maintenance and wants to stay in the matrimonial home. Victor says she can have the house if she takes on all the outgoings, but he will not pay maintenance any longer, as he feels that she could now seek employment.

How is the court likely to resolve the ancillary matters and on what basis is any financial settlement likely to be made?

Commentary

To answer this question you need to remember that the court has a very wide discretion in such cases and will put together a 'package' unique to the couple involved: see how the outcome differs from that of the previous question. Ask yourself three questions: what is available under the Matrimonial Causes Act 1973?; what principles, statutory or otherwise, will influence the court's decision? and what should go into Victor's and Margaret's 'package'? Note that the Child Support Acts 1991–2000 are not relevant as there are no 'qualifying children'.

The actual terms of the settlement you decide on are not crucial, the examiner is not looking for a definitive answer, but you must show an awareness of the available options and relevant principles. As always, take your cue as to which aspects require emphasis from the information provided.

- Principles only, not amounts

- Powers—ss. 22–24, MCA 1973

- Criteria—s. 25(2), MCA 1973

- Property adjustment *and* periodical payments?

- Pension—'attach' or 'share'?

☼ Suggested answer

How is this likely to be resolved? On divorce the court has very wide powers under the Matrimonial Causes Act 1973 (as amended) to make arrangements which are, in all the circumstances, just and fair. The financial position of both Victor and Margaret will be considered as a whole, and any financial settlement will be a complete package unique to them. On the information provided, it seems likely that at least until Victor's father's death there are insufficient funds to prevent one or both of them from noticing the difference. This is not a *White* v *White* [2000] 2 FLR 981 situation: the problem is how best to share the loss, not the surplus.

Financial provision orders available under ss. 23, 24 MCA 1973 include periodical payments orders, secured or unsecured, and lump sum orders. Secured periodical payments would ensure that payments would not cease on Victor's death. If there are sufficient assets, a lump sum order might, even today, be made on the basis of a *Duxbury* ([1987] 1 FLR 7) calculation. This is a computer programme which produces 'capitalised maintenance' by taking into account variables, e.g. inflation, life expectancy and income tax.

In relation to the matrimonial home, the court has a wide discretionary power to adjust property rights (s. 24) and to make arrangements which are in all the circumstances just. Possible options here are a Transfer of Property Order (TPO) or a Settlement of Property Order (SPO). We know that Margaret wants to remain in the matrimonial home and, indeed, Victor says she can have it, but only on condition that she takes on all the outgoings. The house is in joint names and Victor could sign his half share in the home to Margaret. Indeed, even if Victor did not agree to this, a court could make a TPO to recognise that, although Margaret may not have made any financial contribution to the home, her efforts in the home have given Victor the freedom 'to feather his nest'. However, one must be realistic, and Margaret has not worked for over twenty years and has no income at present. Can she afford to run the house? Almost certainly not. Margaret would need financial provision orders to enable her to take over the outgoings.

One possibility would be for the court to make a Martin order (*Martin* v *Martin* [1976] 3 All ER 625), allowing Margaret to continue to live in the home (even though there are no relevant children) until she remarries, cohabits, voluntarily removes or dies. The house would then be sold and the proceeds divided. Martin orders avoid the disadvantage inherent in a Mesher order (*Mesher* v *Mesher* (1973) [1980] 1 All ER 126) in relation to the wife's ability to rehouse herself on the postponed sale taking place (*Clutton* v *Clutton* [1991] 1 All ER 340). With such an order, provision could be made for Victor to continue to contribute to the mortgage and other outgoings, or Margaret could be awarded an increased LSO or PPO so that she herself could make the payments.

Margaret is probably not going to be made to leave the house, but the court is going to have to decide on the best way to enable her to remain there. In deciding what provision to make for Margaret, the court will be governed by the legislative guidelines of s. 25. Section 25(1) directs the court to have regard to 'all the circumstances of the case' and to give first consideration to the welfare of any minor children of the family. Clearly the latter is not relevant here as there are no children under 18 to consider.

The court is then directed to consider the specific matters listed in s. 25(2). First, the income, earning capacity and other financial resources of each party now and in the foreseeable future, including any increase in earning capacity it would be reasonable to expect a party to take steps to acquire (s. 25(2)(a)). All Victor's assets will be taken into account. We are told that he has money in a building society account and also that he lives in a flat owned by his father, presumably rent free, thus freeing more of his income for possible maintenance payments. Inheritance expectations are rarely relevant because they are uncertain (*Michael* v *Michael* [1986] 2 FLR 389) but the court may take account of the likelihood that Victor will benefit under the will of his father who is terminally ill. We are told that he will inherit the flat and a considerable sum of money (future resources).

Also relevant under s. 25(2)(a) is Margaret's potential earning capacity. Victor thinks she should be self-supporting, particularly now that, tragically, she no longer has a young child to look after. But does Margaret in fact have any earning potential and is it reasonable to expect her to seek employment? Margaret is probably in her late forties, she has not worked for over 20 years and will undoubtedly find it very difficult to find a 'good' job. In *Leadbeater* v *Leadbeater* [1985] FLR 789, in not dissimilar circumstances, the Court of Appeal decided that it was not reasonable to expect the wife to 'familiarise herself with modern office technology'. The court will require evidence to prove earning capacity and is likely to take the view, certainly since *White* v *White* (2003, above), that after a long marriage (25 years) and having been a good mother and homemaker and also taking into account her age (s. 25(2)(d)), Margaret is entitled to more than just being able to survive (*M* v *M* [1987] 2 FLR 1). We do not know how useful Margaret's Cordon Bleu cookery qualification might be. Margaret and Victor's respective needs, obligations and responsibilities are also relevant. The parties' needs are often in practice the main factor and of course include accommodation. Here, Victor is living in his father's flat and Margaret is in the matrimonial home and wishes to stay there. Neither party is entitled to expect to maintain the standard of living which they enjoyed during the marriage, but adequate recognition should be given to it and after a long marriage, as here, the vulnerable party is entitled to the security of a reasonably decent standard of living.

The court cannot ignore the contribution made by Margaret to the welfare of the family by looking after the home and caring for the children, particularly Sarah. She has a real value as a housewife and her contribution may be relevant in assessing any LSO, on the basis that she could be said to have 'supplied the infrastructure and support in the context of which the husband was able to prosper and accumulate his wealth' (*per* Purchas LJ in *Vicary* v *Vicary* [1992] Fam Law 248). In addition, enhanced orders have always been available to compensate for the loss of the chance of acquiring any benefit such as a pension (*Richardson* v *Richardson* (1978) 9 Fam Law 96) and recent legislation has now addressed this problem more closely. Firstly, s. 25B(2) of the MCA 1973 (as inserted by the Pensions Act 1995) *requires* the court to consider whether to make a financial provision order when a spouse has a pension scheme. Section 25B(4) to (6) allows for 'attachment' whereby the pension fund manager could be ordered to divert some of the eventual payments from the pensioner to his divorced wife. Additionally, the 1973 Act has been further amended by the Welfare Reform and Pensions Act 1999. This allows for a 'pension sharing order' which directs the scheme's trustees to transfer a specified amount of one spouse's entitlement to the other on divorce.

It is unlikely that conduct will influence the outcome. Victor's attitude towards Sarah was not exactly exemplary, but he does not appear to have done anything that the court has so far thought inequitable to disregard within s. 25(2)(g).

Section 25A directs the court to the desirability of promoting severance of financial obligations between the parties. In all cases where a court is deciding whether to make financial provision, there is a mandatory duty to consider a clean break or imposing a time limit on financial obligations (s. 25A(1)). If the court decides that no continuing obligations should be imposed, it may effect an immediate clean break (s. 25A(3)). This would involve making property adjustment orders and dismissing any claim for periodical payments with a direction that no further application be made. But there is no presumption that a clean break must be ordered (*SRJ* v *DWJ* [1999] 2 FLR 176).

So perhaps Margaret is destined to receive one of the comparatively few PPO's currently being made (*Judicial Statistics, passim*). When considering making a PPO, the court must consider whether it is appropriate to make the order for a limited term, sufficient to enable Margaret to adjust without undue hardship to ending her dependence on Victor. Can and should Margaret find a way of adjusting her life to attain financial independence? In *Barrett* v *Barrett* [1988] 2 FLR 516 Butler Sloss LJ said that limiting an order was not appropriate in a situation where the wife had no job and where it could not be predicted whether she would ever have one. It would seem, therefore, that to terminate payments to Margaret would cause hardship, and it should be left to Victor to apply to have the PPO varied if and when she does become self-sufficient. In *Flavell* v *Flavell* [1997] 1 FLR 353, the Court of Appeal suggested that the termination of a PPO in favour of a former wife in her 50s would normally only be appropriate if she had a lot of capital and a good earning capacity. Although the amounts concerned do not appear to be as high as in the 'unusual' divorce case of *Mcfarlane* v *McFarlane, Parlour* v *Parlour, The Times*, 18 July, 2004, the court may, as there, consider itself to be under a duty to consider the *future* possibility of a clean break via a temporary periodical payments order from which Margaret can build up capital.

Most likely, a PPO would be made whether or not the house is actually transferred over to her by Victor, but particularly in the event of a *Martin* order, in which case she may also receive a lump sum to ensure the equitable redistribution of the available assets. Such measures could take appropriate account of Victor's testamentary and pensionary expectations. Let us hope that (perhaps with the help of mediation) the parties will be successfully encouraged to reach a settlement at, or before, a Financial Dispute Resolution appointment.

Further reading

Barton, C., and Hibbs, M., 'Ancillary Financial Relief and Fat Cat(tle) Divorce' (2002) MLR Vol. 65, p. 79.

Barton, C., and Bissett-Johnson, A., 'The Declining Number of Ancillary Financial Relief Orders' [2000] Fam Law, p. 94.

Bird, R., *Pension Sharing: The New Law* (Family Law, 1999).

Cretney, S., 'Trusting the Judges—Money after Divorce' (2000) *Current Legal Problems*, p. 286.

Davis, G., *et al*, 'Ancillary Relief Outcomes' [2000] CFLQ, p. 43.

Gilmore, S., 'Duration of Marriage and Seamless Preceding Cohabitation' [2004] Fam Law, p. 205.

Moore, P. and Frasier, C., 'NCIS or Ensnared—how the Proceeds of Crime Act 2002 Affects Family Law' [2004] Fam Law 885.

Watson-Lee, P., 'Financial Provision on Divorce: Clarity and Fairness' [2004] Fam Law, pp. 182, 348.

Child support: the state and the court

Introduction

This chapter is primarily concerned with the Child Support Acts 1991–2000, and if you are really sure there is not a question on this subject, you had better look at the exam paper again: they may have given you the wrong one. The 1991 legislation may not have received much attention when it was being promulgated but, as the 1993 implementation approached, family lawyers and separated parents alike were faced with huge changes in principle and practice. For practitioners, at least, it probably caused as big a shock as the Children Act 1989.

The basic idea is that a non-resident parent (some 90 per cent—but falling— are fathers) who does not pay is identified by the resident parent to the state, which finds him, uses a fixed formula to determine his liability, and then punishes him if he still does not pay. Resident parents 'on' benefit are penalised if they do not invoke this procedure. Men, the argument runs, are thereby made to face up to their financial responsibilities to their children, thus aiding the latter and their mothers and taking the weight off the taxpayer. There is no (discretionary) role for the court, and it is irrelevant whether the child is marital or not. Yet it soon became embroiled in a controversy, to put it at its lowest, and one which ironically made co-belligerents, if not allies, of the divided parents. Mothers agonised, e.g., about loss of benefit if they refused to name the father and fathers complained, e.g., that the formula made no allowance for their costs in maintaining contact with the child. Although the 1995 Act attempted to address some of these problems, the reality of the child support experience was the continuing (and well-documented) administrative incompetence of the Child Support Agency, which was created by the 1991 Act to run the—admittedly over-demanding—new system. Most recently, a third effort, the Child Support, Pensions and Social Security Act 2000, has dramatically simplified the formula, reducing from $c.$ 100 to 3 the amounts of information required for the assessment. Note that the 2000 reforms are now contained in amendments to the 1991 Act.

Where is it going to show in the exam? The following possibilities present themselves: a nice essay in evaluation of the system; a free-standing calculation, or at least the principle thereof, as part of a question on putative fathers; and as an aspect of ancillary financial relief in divorce. We suspect that the last type of question is engendering such disclaimers as: 'There are no children of the family'. We also suspect that many examiners will see their duty best done by dealing with the subject by essay. There is little tradition of calculating examples in LLB exams; consider, for example, revenue and welfare law.

Those comparatively rare family law courses which include detailed consideration of welfare benefits and personal taxation could generate further coverage of the child support legislation in those contexts.

Finally, do not forget what remains of the—now residuary—potential for private law initiatives under the Children Act 1989, the Matrimonial Causes Act 1973, and the Domestic Proceedings and Magistrates' Act 1978. Capital orders (lump sums and, other than under the 1978 Act, property adjustment) are still dependent upon such applications and step-children (and others over 18) are reliant upon them even for income (periodical payments). On divorce, the presence of under-age children of the family may well clinch a property adjustment order over the former home in favour of the resident parent.

Q Question 1

Why was the Child Support Act 1991 promulgated and how far have its shortcomings been ameliorated by the Child Support Act 1995 and the Child Support, Pensions and Social Security Act 2000?

Commentary

No hidden agendas here—go for it. Apart from being the best you will get on this difficult topic, the form of the question is one of the least threatening in the examiners' armoury. 'Review', 'analyse', 'critically consider', 'why', 'how far', are all just one gentle step up from mere description. This one does not involve any sums, is frozen in time and is likely to have been well-flagged during the course.

It is also likely that your lectures, or your tutorial reading, will have given you the appropriate pre-1991 background, laced with the necessary comment. You will find the best published account of that in Barton and Douglas, *Law and Parenthood*, 1995, chapter 9.

Ideally, you will need to know: the 'old' law (some of it still extant) on 'child support'; its undeniable shortcomings; some knowledge of the published Papers which preceded each Act; the shortcomings the Acts hoped to rectify and the improvements they hoped to achieve; and the misgivings which were expressed. You will want some numbers: how many one-parent families? how many non-paying absent parents? the cost to the public purse etc. Some politics will be useful (you will get at least one opportunity to say 'Thatcherism' and 'Blairite').

A prepared student should find it comparatively easy to achieve Upper Second standard, i.e. to display knowledge and assessment beyond that obtainable from any one standard text. One warning: do not do these 'background' questions merely on the basis of your knowledge of the current legislation. If you really do not know the history, leave them alone.

- **A decade of disaster?**

- **Pre-CSA 1991: feckless fathers?**

- **CSA 1991: martyred fathers?**

- **CSA 1995: more discretion**

- **CSPSSA 2000: simpler formula**

- **Out of the wood?!**

☼ Suggested answer

> The underlying message of the legislation is that the old law, administered by lawyers and the courts, was unnecessarily fragmented, uncertain in its results, slow and ineffective.

So said Stephen Cretney (of the 1991 Act) in the foreword to *The Child Support Act* by District Judge Bird (2nd edn, 1993). Before 1993 (when implementation of the 1991 Act began) statute provided three methods whereby a parent could be required to support 'his' child. Their shortcomings pointed the way to reform.

The three private law routes were: in matrimonial proceedings under the Matrimonial Causes Act (MCA) 1973; domestic proceedings under the Domestic Proceedings and Magistrates' Courts Act 1978 (both restricted to marital children); and by way of the Children Act 1989. By definition, their activation was dependent upon a private initiative, taken normally by the other parent. The powers of the court under each statute were governed by (similar) discretionary codes: under s. 25(3)(e) of the MCA 1973, for example, it was necessary to consider, *inter alia*, 'the standard of living enjoyed by the family before the breakdown of the marriage'.

It became extremely clear that these methods left many children in one-parent families (whether those families were created by divorce, separation of cohabitants, or by one-night stand) poorly supported by their fathers and that, in so far as the shortfall was being met, it was by the taxpayer mainly through the medium of income support. That such children were often poorly served, even where orders were actually made and paid, can be demonstrated by reference to the National Foster Care Association recommended scales. The philosophy of the fostering scheme is that it should not be undertaken for gain. Yet in a survey of 38 district judges, 14 were found to consider the NFCA rates 'unrealistically high': *Regulating Divorce*, John Eekelaar (1992). Furthermore, there was also evidence of a wide variety in the orders actually made.

A second set of figures concerned the non-compliance rate in the case of orders actually made. Edwards, Gold and Halpern ('The Continuing Saga of Maintaining the Family after Divorce' [1990] Fam Law 31) found that 55 per cent of orders made by one court were in arrears, and the White Paper, *Children Come First* Cm. 1264 (1990), found a DSS recovery rate of 23 per cent.

Perhaps it is not too cynical to suggest that it was the impact on the social security budget which finally galvanised the Government into action. The White Paper found that about two-thirds of single parents were dependent on income support in 1989. Crucially, less than one-quarter of these families were receiving maintenance in 1988/89 when the taxpayer was subsidising them in benefits to the extent of some £3.2 billion. These facts came to the attention of the Government of the day and might be said to have been anathema to the principles of 'Thatcherism' in that absent parents were, it was said, able to cast the financial burden of their children upon the state, and thus upon the taxpayer.

Children Come First Cm. 1264 (1990), set out the case for change and the proposals for reform. Only 30 per cent of lone mothers and 3 per cent of lone fathers received maintenance for their children. Child maintenance is normally an issue for 13 to 16 years of a child's life. During the short consultation stage and the subsequent passage of the Child Support Bill through Parliament, opponents imputed less worthy motives to the Government. Lord Houghton said:

> The Bill reflects the outburst of the former Prime Minister, Mrs Thatcher, whose concern for children came second to not allowing absentee fathers to get away with non-payment of maintenance.

Lord Simon (a former President of the then Probate Divorce and Admiralty Division) had a different objection, claiming that the maintenance formula was:

> as incomprehensible as the ancient Egyptian hieroglyphs must have been to an illiterate peasant in the Nile Delta.

The entire process, from the then Prime Minister's initial announcement to Royal Assent, took almost exactly one year: an indication of the force of the political will which drove it. The matter fell comparatively quiet for nearly two years, although concern was expressed about mothers having to name the potentially-violent absent fathers of their children on pain of reduced benefit. In fact this point became one of the Act's lesser difficulties, because s. 6(2) excuses her if she or her child is at risk of 'suffering harm or undue distress'. Yet post-implementation, a number of other, well-publicised objections arose. They concerned injustices wrought by: the formula itself, with particular reference to cases where there had been a pre-1993 'clean break' arrangement on divorce; the impotence of the courts; and by the administrative shortcomings of the Child Support Agency.

So far as the original formula is concerned, the 1995 Act (which was presaged by the 1995 Government White Paper, *Improving Child Support*, Cm. 2745) enabled, mainly by way of regulations, either parent to apply for a 'departure direction' in three 'cases'. The first involved 'special expenses' and covered costs incurred in travelling to work, maintaining child contact, and certain debts incurred before the marriage breakdown for the benefit of the family.

The second 'case' concerned 'property or capital transfers' made before the 1991 Act came into force. It was an attempt to address the resentment expressed by some fathers—and their new families—that these men would not have entered 'clean break' divorce settlements, under which they may have ceded the family home to their former wives, had they realised that the maintenance assessments subsequently calculated under the Act would be so high. Regulations under the 1995 Act provided a formula for calculating the 'equivalent weekly value' of the transfer, leading to a reduction in the maintenance assessment.

Although the absent parent/second family lobby was the more vociferous in the 1993–1995 debate, parents with care also had reason to complain. In *Phillips* v *Peace* [1996] 2 FLR 230 the father, who owned a company, lived in a £2.6 million house and had three cars was—rightly, the court held—granted a nil assessment by a child support officer on the basis that he had no income. 'Departure directions' under the 1995 Act included 'additional cases' which might lead to amended assessments. The relevant regulations covered a parent with: assets capable of producing income; a lifestyle inconsistent with declared income; and a parent who had 'diverted' income.

Yet the 1995 Act did little to redress the unease expressed about the non-paramountcy of the welfare of the child, the sidelining of the courts and—most emphatic of all—the administrative inadequacies of the Child Support Agency. Its low public and media image have been confirmed by a number of official reports (e.g. the Parliamentary Commissioner for Administration's 1995–6 *Investigation of Complaints Against the Child Support Agency*, HC 20) which have detailed its delays, errors, and failures to make the promised public savings. However, as is pointed out in *The Performance and Operation of the Child Support Agency* 1995–1996 (HC 50), the 1991 Act would have caused controversy because of the social change it produced even if the Agency's administrative performance had not been so 'dire'.

So for the third time in ten years the poisoned chalice was lifted again, this time by the new Labour—'Blairite'—administration. A 1998 Green Paper, *Children First: A New Approach to Child Support* (Cm. 3992), was followed in 1999 by a White Paper, *A New Contract for Welfare: Children's Rights and Parents' Responsibilities* (Cm. 4349). The proposals therein were intended to make the system fairer, simpler and faster, and have now produced the Child Support, Pensions and Social Security Act 2000. Most important of all, the basic child support formula is now much easier to understand. Gone are the references to 'net', 'exempt', 'assessable', and 'protected' income(s) and the concomitant deployment of over 100 pieces of information, preferably by computer programme. Instead, a non-resident parent (NRP) earning over £200 per week net will pay (the basic rate) 15 per cent of 'his' income for one 'absent' child, 20 per cent for two, and 25 per cent for three or more (a ceiling operates at a weekly net income of £2,000), although that same income will be notionally reduced by the same percentages in line with the number of children in his new family. To complete the picture, NRP's with net incomes between £100 and £200 per week will pay a reduced rate, those under £100 will pay £5, and such as 'children' (i.e. under 16) will pay nothing. These amounts are subject to change by regulation.

But, following the example of the 1995 Act, it is accepted that rigid application of a formula may bring injustice, so the 2000 Act reprises the 'departures' idea but under the new title of 'variations' (both up and down) and with some refinements, such as reductions for non-resident parents with overnight contact. Additionally, the Child Support Agency's role will be streamlined, with the resources formerly spent on calculation now being available for enforcement. Finally, the 2000 Act provides for tougher sanctions such as criminal prosecutions, late-payment penalties—and loss of driving licence.

Are we there? The Agency's work may be better than its media image, with its Annual Report for 2002 claiming a 71 per cent collection rate on maintenance due—and, surprisingly, 98 per cent of surveyed customers expressing satisfaction. Yet only in Utopia is the child support system admired by both the separated parents, their new families and the taxpayer, and already there are criticisms of this most recent effort: the formula is crude; it will reduce most payments (although the residential parent will receive up to £10 pw from the state on top of child support and the richer father will note that his duty is tied to his actual income and not to income support levels); it ignores the income of the resident parent; the attempt to encourage care-sharing may foment litigation over residence or contact; and the system is still dependent upon a shift to an efficient and friendly Child Support Agency. Finally, and on a related issue to that last point, successive Governments continue to put their trust in a non-discretionary, non-integrated, non court-based mechanism, yet in *R (Kehoe)* v *Secretary of State for Work and Pensions* [2004] EWCA Civ 225, it has now been held that there is no right to child maintenance enforceable through the courts, once it has been collected by the Agency. This puts the resident parent at the mercy of administrative incompetence, with only the possibility of judicial review to offer a glimmer of hope. This one will run and run.

Q Question 2

Critically consider the extent to which the Child Support Acts 1991–2000 have affected the family lawyer.

Commentary

Only a line and a half, but think carefully about where your marks are coming from. As an experienced student, you know that there will not be a 'good honours degree' in merely writing all you know about the legislation in question. In truth, it involves a three-point approach. One, how have the Child Support Acts *not* affected the family lawyer?, i.e. when does the old law still apply? Two, remembering that the new law was designed to exclude the discretionary jurisdiction of the courts and substitute an administratively applied formula, what role is there for lawyers? Third, so what? (i.e. the 'critically consider' element). The more you can integrate the last into your treatment of the first two, the better.

- Discretion v Formula—Courts v Clerks?

- Step-children

- Older children

- Capital

- 'Top-ups' and consent orders

- Legal aid

·Q· Suggested answer

It is fundamental to the Child Support Acts 1991–2000 that a state body, the Child Support Agency, will trace absent parents, establish the means at their disposal, calculate their liability to make child maintenance payments and then collect that amount, using enforcement procedures if necessary. These assessments are made by officials called Child Support Officers (CSO). Section 8(3)—all references are to the 1991 (as amended) Act unless indicated to the contrary—provides that '. . . no court shall exercise any power which it would otherwise have to make, vary or revive any maintenance order in relation to the child and absent parent concerned'.

It might seem, therefore that the answer to the question is: 'Deprived them of their previous work'. In fact, there remain a number of circumstances where the court's jurisdiction still applies and where the work of the family lawyer continues as before. In addition, the family lawyer will need to *understand* the legislation, and to be able to calculate the amount due, in order to consider the impact on the remainder of the financial package and to ensure that liability is met and Agency involvement pre-empted (s. 1(2) states that the absent parent shall be taken to have met his responsibility). These matters are not without controversy: only where (s. 2) the CSO is considering the exercise of a discretionary power under the Act, shall he '. . . have regard to the welfare of any child likely to be affected by his decision'.

First, then, when does the court continue to have jurisdiction? There are a number of such circumstances. The CSO may lack jurisdiction under s. 44 because one or more of: the person with care; the absent parent; and the qualifying child, is not 'habitually resident' in the UK (what constitutes 'habitual residence' itself may require legal advice): emphasis is given to the nature and degree of UK residence and intentions for the future (CS/7395/1995). Stepchildren—marital or otherwise—are not covered, and yet their numbers are on the increase: even when the 1990 Act was activated it had been estimated that there were over 1 million dependent children under 16 in step-families (Haskey, *1994 Population Trends*). And it is one of family law's great ironies that although second families are increasing in number, their separation and/or divorce rates are high.

By s. 55 the Act does not apply to children between 16 and 19 years of age who are not in full-time, non-advanced education, or to 'children' over 19, and so, if 'maintenance' is sought for such children it will be necessary to make application to the courts. If the child is non-marital, the Children Act (CA) 1989 will be the medium, but if the parents are, or have been, married to each other then proceedings may be under the 1989 Act, the Matrimonial Causes Act 1973, or under the Domestic Proceedings and Magistrates' Courts Act 1978. Not only do these avenues all require a private legal initiative, they all involve the use of discretion—the lawyer's friend.

Section 8 permits the court to make orders in respect of additional educational expenses (the 'school fees exception') and in respect of disabled or blind children. The rich are not only always with us, but are remembered by s. 8(6) as well. No matter how well-off the parents are, there is a maintenance ceiling for assessments made by the Agency. Section 8(6) therefore allows the courts to 'top up' payments after the maximum assessment has already been made under the Act. In *A v A (Minor: Financial Provision)* [1994] 1 FLR 657, a periodical payment of £20,000 a year was made even though the maximum child support assessment at that time would have been about £7,500. So some might say that lawyers have retained the lucrative end of the market which, since the Child Support, Pensions and Social Security Act 2000, means cases where the non-resident parent's net income exceeds £2,000 p.w. As this is a much higher ceiling than before, it would appear that s. 8(6) is rendered much less relevant.

Furthermore, s. 8(11) defines a 'maintenance order in relation to a child', as 'period-ical payments'. It therefore follows that the courts' power to make other forms of financial relief, capital orders, in effect, continues unabated. Although lump sums under s. 24(1), MCA 1973 are rarely made in favour of a child, the court nonetheless retains its jurisdiction. Nor have property adjustment orders been popular but, as the CA 1989 permits the court to make such orders against the putative father, men who lose their houses in such a way (after a one-night stand, perhaps) will no doubt '*encourage les autres*' to behave more responsibly. In *Phillips* v *Peace* [1996] 2 FLR 230, the Agency had made a nil assessment for maintenance but the court order required the father to settle sufficient capital on the child to provide a suitable home.

Three more court-based matters involve consent orders, variation of existing orders, and orders against the resident parent. The first is the most important. By s. 8(5), and by way of a major exception to s. 8(3) above, the court may make a maintenance order in favour of a child provided it is in terms agreed in writing by the parties. (These will normally be part of an overall package on divorce.) Similarly, such orders may be varied under s. 8(3A). Finally, if a little unrealistically, s. 8(10) permits court orders to be made against the parent housing the child. All in all, there were the not-inconsiderable total of 24,508 periodical payments made for children in the county courts in 2003 (Table 5.7, *Judicial Statistics* 2003)—good for lawyers, the parties, their children and society? Lawyers should, however, note that s. 4(10) of the 1991 Act as amended will permit resident parents with consent orders nonetheless to apply for an agency assessment after the court order is one year old. Do not forget to tell them.

So there are 'exceptional' circumstances in which nothing has changed. Even in accumulation they represent a considerable shrinkage of the old ways, as the Act intended, of course. Yet it would be a mistake to think that lawyers have lost out to Child Support Officers. In every parental divorce case, as we have seen, the court will need to know exactly what the CSA 1991 liability will be: s. 25, MCA 1973 will require the court to consider it as a 'liability' for one party and a 'resource' for the other in considering ancillary financial relief orders. So the family lawyer will need to be able to calculate it. Lawyers and others may well want to check the Agency assessments: failings identified by, amongst many others, the Ombudsman (*Investigation of Complaints Against the Child Support Agency*, Third Report, Session 1995–96) included mistaken identities, delays, confusion over jurisdiction, breaching confidentiality, slow enforcement and delay in passing on money received—fertile ground for the lawyer or so it would seem: yet under *R (Kehoe)* v *Secretary of State for Work and Pensions* [2004] EWCA Civ 225, child support cannot be enforced through the courts (although judicial review is available).

Even the most innumerate family lawyer will need to know the principles, at least, on which child maintenance is to be assessed. Challengingly, the original formula consisted of four key elements: the maintenance requirement; the parent's assessable income; the deduction rate; and the protected income. From an interaction of these figures (each of which was itself often arrived at by some complicated arithmetic) the absent parent's liability was calculated. Now, since CSPSSA 2000, a pocket calculator rather than a computer programme will normally suffice, as the only information that will usually be required is the non-residential parent's income, the number of 'qualifying' children, and the number of children in 'his' new family. [SEE ANSWER TO Q1 FOR DETAILS.]

To return to the reality of the question asked, it should be remembered that Green Form legal advice and assistance is available in relation to child maintenance and the Child Support Acts 'only to the extent that it constitutes the application of a matter of English law'. Completing the Agency forms will not, therefore, normally qualify. Civil legal aid, however, will be available for proceedings under ss. 20 and 27 of the Act. Section 20 deals with appeals against decisions made by CSOs. (The discretionary system of 'departure directions' introduced by the 1995 Act—but reduced by the 2000 Act under the new name of 'variations'– provides further scope for such appeals.) Section 27 deals with applications to the court for declarations of parentage. Civil legal aid will, of course, also be available for appeals to the Court of Appeal from the Child Support Commissioner on a question of law. The crucial point is that, reflecting the limited jurisdiction of the court, civil legal aid certificates for contested ancillary relief no longer cover representation for child maintenance, except in respect of stepchildren of the absent parent and where proceedings are concluded by a consent order which deals with child maintenance as part of a global settlement.

Where the CSO retains a discretion, such as reducing the mother's benefit if she refuses to recover support from the father, there will be opportunities for judicial review.

In conclusion, it should be remembered that for many years family lawyers (and their clients, and their clients' children) have had to respond to an ever-increasing rate of change. Perhaps this latest challenge was best put into context by Margaret Bonner, chairing the Solicitors Family Law Association Annual Conference 1993, who said:

> By the year 2000 will those of us who are still practising be first and foremost mediators and part-time computer operators? Will politicians decide that our skills training and experience be replaced by a purely administrative process? The prospects are daunting.

We are now well past the year that Ms Bonner could only imagine, yet 'the jury is still out' on her question.

Further reading

Bird, R., *The New Law*, 5th edn, (Family Law, 2002).

Burrows, D., '*Kehoe*: the CSA and the Child; Right to Maintenance' [2004] Fam Law 453.

Gillespie, G., 'Child Support—When the Bough Breaks' [2002] Fam Law 528.

Gilmore, S., *Re P (Child) (Financial Provision)* – Child Support from the Affluent to Fabulously Rich' (2004) 16 *Family Law Quarterly* 103.

Pirrie, J., 'Report of the Child Support Agency, March 2002' [2003] Fam Law 105.

Worwood, A., 'Countdown to "D-Day" for Fathers' [2003] Fam Law 191.

Domestic partnership contracts

Introduction

Why has this been left until the penultimate chapter? Why not start with the partnership at the beginning of the book? Perhaps there are two reasons. The first is that such contracts are mainly concerned with anticipating the aftermath of the relationship and are therefore better dealt with as a part of matters concerning property and support. Secondly, a knowledge of family law helps to suggest the possible content of such contracts and warns of the *status quo* which will otherwise apply. What might the couple not want to apply to them? How far are they allowed to choose their own regime?

Domestic partnering by private treaty is an enduring (if not, to some, endearing) idea which has re-surfaced from time to time in a number of jurisdictions. The present 'state of the art' requires a distinction to be made between cohabitation and marriage, an acknowledgement of the many uncertainties which currently obtain, and an understanding of the proposals for reform. For these reasons it may be particularly susceptible to coursework assessment.

Almost by definition 'contracts' (if that is what these agreements are) lend themselves to problem-type questions, perhaps as part of a wider treatment of financial relief or property rights. But given the still-tenuous nature of the subject, its uncertainty and need of reform, an essay approach is more likely. Of the standard texts, Hale and Pearl *et al*, *The Family Law and Society*, 5th edn, 2002, pp. 77–90, is the most helpful. Further reading might include: *The Marriage Contract: Spouses, Lovers and the Law* (L. Weitzman, 1981); *Cohabitation Contracts* (C. Barton, 1985); and *Cohabitation: Law, Practice and Precedents* (H. Wood *et al*, 2nd edn, 2001). The last three are the texts which re-discovered the topic in modern times. In its present reincarnation, the status of this topic seems to have shifted comparatively quickly from risibility to tentative usage—if not yet to the extent imagined by the media or hoped for by salivating practitioners.

Q Question 1

'It is not proposed in this paper to consider contracts drawn up between cohabitants— although these contracts often have very similar terms as marriage contracts and many, if not all, of the same reasons exist for their use.' 'Maintenance and Capital Provision on Divorce' (Law Society's Family Law Committee, 1991).

Consider the present law on pre-marital and cohabitation contracts respectively: how best might it be reformed?

Commentary

This is not too forbidding if you know the material. When examiners forsake mainstream areas they often compensate by asking comparatively easy questions. Furthermore, they may well have provided detailed notes during the course. 'Consider' is one of the milder commands.

Here, although there have been detailed proposals for reform (such as those proffered by the Law Society's Family Law Committee itself, *Supporting Families* (1998), and *Cohabitation: the Case for Clear Law* (The Law Society, 2002), it is quite possible to generate respectable *a priori* suggestions from a knowledge of the existing law. An Upper Second answer will include a comparison between the two sorts of 'contract': always relate the question asked to the quotation given. Intending cohabitants contract with one another in order to counter a vacuum, particularly post-relationship, whereas the affianced are attempting to avoid, or at least to vary, an imposed *status quo*. Are such 'contracts' binding? Should they be? What might they want to agree about? What is happening in other jurisdictions? What about children? What do wiser heads think?

- 'Contracting in' and 'contracting out'

- Two very old ideas

- Other jurisdictions

- Recent cases

- Official proposals for reform

:Q: Suggested answer

'Despite the prevalence of couples living together in England and Wales, agreements regulating cohabitation and its aftermath, are rarely found in practice. This is consistent with the general lack of attention to [the] possible consequences of transactions entered into between unmarried couples. [Yet] the effect of the court's redistributive powers on divorce have led to the emergence of pre-nuptial agreements' (H. Wood, *Cohabitation: Law, Practice and Precedents*, 2nd edn, 2001).

The essential legal difference is that the former involve 'contracting in' to a relationship, which would therefore be subject mainly to the common law and equitable remedies for breach, while those entering pre-marriage contracts, on the other hand, hope to 'opt out' of the—mainly statutory—matrimonial law.

There is certainly nothing novel about the idea. In *Bodley's Case* (1679) 2 Ch Ca 15, for example, the court was prepared to uphold a man's promise to make financial provision for his non-marital partner on the ground that it included support for their children. So far as 'pre-nuptial' contracts are concerned, the old Jewish marriage contract, the 'ketubah', contained the terms of the divorce settlement. Even today, s. 24(1)(c) of the Matrimonial Causes Act 1973 still envisages the possibility of 'ante-nuptial' settlements in its enumeration of property adjustments ancillary to divorce, etc. In *Sabira Begum* v *Mushtak Hussain* (1985, unreported) a woman who had married in Pakistan invoked s. 17 of the Married Woman's Property Act 1882 in order to resolve a dispute about the gold and jewellery which she had received under the 'marriage contract'.

Currently, however, the law has only just begun to formulate clear policy on 'forward-planning' for either medium of domestic partnership. (These developments are exclusively judge-made: despite a number of official proposals—see below—there has been no statutory intervention.) Given the established legal safety net which automatically underpins all marriages, an asymmetrical approach may prove necessary; the point being that a cohabitant, unlike a spouse, has no *ex hypothesi* right of support from 'her' mate during or after the relationship. It is equally fundamental that only a marital partner may invoke the divorce court's (discretionary) powers of financial relief under Part 2 of the Matrimonial Causes Act (MCA) 1973. Three cases in the 1990s involved pre-marital contracts entered abroad. In *F* v *F (Ancillary Relief: Substantial Assets)* [1995] 2 FLR 45, the couple had entered such agreements under German and Austrian law but Thorpe J held that they were of 'very limited significance' because our divorce law is intended to be 'of universal application throughout our society'. Yet two 1997 cases were prepared to give weight to such contracts. In *N* v *N (Foreign Divorce: Financial Relief)* [1997] 1 FLR 900, Cazalet J held that a pre-marital agreement (entered into in Sweden and by which the parties would not gain an interest in each other's property) would be a 'material consideration' here. In *S* v *S (Divorce Staying Proceedings)* [1997] 2 FLR 100 (a New York agreement), Wilson J held that 'escape from solemn bargains carefully struck by informed adults is [not] readily available here'. More recently, *N* v *N (Jurisidiction: Pre-Nuptial Agreement)* [1999] 2 FLR 745 held that the weight to be attached to such an agreement is matter for the divorce court in exercising its financial relief discretion under s. 25 of the MCA 1973, and in *M* v *M (Prenuptial Agreement)* [2002] 1 FLR 655, Connell J held that a 'pre-nup' could be relevant either as one of 'all the circumstances', or 'conduct inequitable to disregard'. These two cases also involved agreements struck abroad, but now, in *K* v *K (Ancillary Relief: Prenuptial Agreements)* [2003] 1 FLR 120, the court has taken a more encouraging approach to the home-grown variety An affianced couple agreed to limit her personal claim on his *capital*, each party having taken independent legal advice that this 'pre-nup' would not be binding, especially if children were involved. When the marriage broke down, it was held that whilst it would be unjust to ignore the arrangement, she deserved periodical payments in recognition of her child-caring duties. He also had to provide for a home for the child (although it would revert to him, the father, when the child's full-time education was completed).

As mentioned above, 'cohabitation contracts' have been known to English law since at least 1679. It might seem surprising, given the comparatively recent emergence of other forms of legal reaction to extra-marital relationships, that such arrangements have been known to the courts for so much longer than pre-marital bargains. *Weldrick* v *Essex & Suffolk Equitable Insurance Society Ltd* (1949) 83 Ll Rep 91 seems to take for granted the textbook perception of the old cases as invalidating 'sexually immoral' contracts, despite the fact that the woman won the day in about half of the fifty cases reported since *Bodley's* Case. Now, thanks to *Sutton* v *Mishcon de Reya and Gawor & Co* [2003] EWHC 3166, we have a modern view of the significance for contract law not merely of extra-marital cohabitation, but of sexuality, homosexuality—and of consensual master-slave domestic relationships. Two men agreed that one should exercise 'absolute power' over the other, and be given all his property, plus other gifts and payments. The defendant—the drafting solicitor—advised the 'master' that the deal might not stick. Eventually, 'master' and 'slave' entered into a separation deed under which the former returned 'their' London apartment to the latter. The 'master' then sued the solicitor for negligent drafting. Hart J drew a distinction between a contract *between* parties to a (non-criminal) sexual relationship (potentially legal), and one *for* such a relationship (illegal), placing the instant case in the latter category and thus finding for the defendant-solicitor whose advice was therefore correct and whose drafting had not contained any (other) flaws. Yet the judgment recognises that a cohabitation contract can be valid provided that it manifestly intends to create legal relations, there is no reference to payment for sexual services, and there are no other vitiating circumstances.

What terms might domestic partnership contracts contain? Might they be ambitious enough to provide for the working relationship? Professor Weitzman's *The Marriage Contract* (US, 1981) gives this famous example:

> Absent truly extraordinary circumstances we agree to spend at least one evening a week enjoying each other, alone together. An evening begins at 7 pm.

The more conservative Law Society's Family Law Committee, in the document cited in the question, has suggested (for pre-marital 'contracts') that the heads of agreement might include: ownership of income and assets acquired before the marriage; the barring of claims under statute; gifts and inheritances; ownership of personal items; liability for tax and debts; duration, variation and review; the proper law of the contract; severability; and methods for the resolution of any conflict. The Committee proceeded to recommend that each party should take independent legal advice as a condition precedent to validity and that events such as the birth of a child, or the onset of permanent disability or long-term unemployment should trigger an automatic revocation or review of the contract. But if the intervention principle is to apply, why not include good news, pools wins and the like? The suggestion that the reviews be legally supervised will provide further ammunition for the cynical. More recently, the Government's Discussion Paper, *Supporting Families* (1998) suggested that the lack of certainty may discourage such agreements—which could otherwise wean couples away from cohabitation and into wedlock, and which could be used to protect the children of an earlier marriage. The Paper recommended that an otherwise binding contract entered at least 21 days before the wedding (but after independent legal advice and full disclosure), should stick—provided that it would not cause 'significant injustice' to either of the parties or to a child of the marriage. But would not potential parties be put off by such a threat to their private arrangement?

The Cohabitation (Contract Enforcement) Bill 1991, introduced under the ten-minute rule by Teresa Gorman, MP, attempted to deal with what the Law Society's Family Law Committee, as the question reminds us, declined to incorporate in its own deliberations. Teresa Gorman's measure would have required such contracts to be written, signed and witnessed (but not preceded by independent legal advice). Consideration would not have been required and an intention to create relations would have been rebuttably presumed. The parties would have been permitted to agree that their private terms would survive any subsequent marriage between them. It might be remarked, however, that any definitive coverage would also have to deal with the homosexual couple or the already-married, for whom marriage itself—despite the Civil Partnership Bill 2004—is not (yet) an option: non-contractual private ordering by way of deeds and wills and such is the way forward for them. But now, the Law Society has taken an opposing stance to that of *Supporting Families* (above). *Cohabitation: The Case for Clear Reform* (2002) states that it is illogical to allow cohabitants to make enforceable contracts if married couples may not, and recommends that their evidential value should be the same.

Both sorts of domestic partnership contracts are currently on a legal footing in such countries as South Africa, Sweden and Germany, as well as in North America and Australasia. Part 4 of the Ontario Family Law Reform Act 1978 allows for 'domestic contracts' which include 'cohabitation agreements'. The parties are free to arrange for such matters as: property ownership; support obligations; and the education and moral training, but not the 'custody' and 'access' of their children.

To return finally to the quotation in the question, many of the policy arguments apply equally to each sort of contract: promotion of an equal partnership; privacy and freedom of relationships; the encouragement of diversity; and the opportunity to avoid what may be perceived as an imposed and inadequate regime. Many of those who wed each year, and the many more who are currently cohabiting, would surely welcome a clarification of the position. On second thoughts, perhaps only *some* of them: the potential for such contracts is probably greater when one or both parties are well-off, or destined to become so. Following the advantageous financial relief gained by the wives in *White* v *White* [2001] 1 AC 596 and *McFarlane* v *McFarlane, Parlour* v *Parlour, The Times,* 18 July, 2004, rich folk may prefer merely to cohabit—with or without contracts—or at least push for a pre-marital contract.

Q Question 2

Draft an examination-type problem-question involving a domestic partnership agreement, and any related matters, which:

  (a) is of 200–220 words in length;

  (b) includes provision for the working relationship; and which

  (c) is uncertain in its solution.

Commentary

This could be described as a case of 'the bitten to bite', although not as much as in some of the essay-bound social sciences, where the final question occasionally asks for an entire exam. Law exam problems are rather harder to draft and it is probably fairer to restrict this sort of question to coursework: easy to set, quick to mark and hard to do, despite being less than a fifth as long as the shortest of the other answers in the book. So the answer is a question, and the commentary is how to set it. Exchanging roles with the examiner on this occasion may make you better at answering questions in the future. Inductive reasoning will help with your powers of deduction.

The disciplined use of imagination is the most demanding part of this job but the examiner knows that and will have every sympathy for you provided you follow the instructions. Here, the topic is clearly stated, lends itself to the required uncertainty, and a term for the going concern can be imagined without too much difficulty. The length is surprisingly hard to get right. Overall, choose what laws you want to invoke and then imagine a story which does so. Avoid superfluous material as much as possible.

Applying all this to the present question, the first job is to choose between cohabitation and pre-marital contracts. Perhaps knowledge is best spread thin by opting for the former, but including a term purporting to allow for any subsequent marriage between the parties. Money and property is the guts of it, and you know a lot about that after a year of family (and other) law.

The reference to 'and related matters' should be exploited, e.g. deeds; financial relief on divorce. Be very careful with children as the Child Support Acts 1991–2000 and the Children Act 1989 have left little room for effective private treaty as regards, respectively, their financial support and upbringing. (One exception might be where a step-parent disallows potential liability for his wife's children in the event of divorce.) Imaginative as it might be to cast the couple as homosexuals, it does narrow any possible answer. You could, however, use the 'Would your answer be any different if . . .' device that you will have seen in law exams. If you have more than one part, you might give the mark allocation(s) for each. Use short names, perhaps the man's name beginning with 'M' and the woman's with 'W', and do not have too large a cast.

Remember that the examiners are not going to expect anything as good as they can do, particularly if you encounter this sort of thing in an unseen end-of-year-exam. The one below is the sort of thing for which we have, in the past, given students an Upper Second mark. The intention was to build in both cohabitation and pre-marital 'agreements'; a possible declaration of trust as a 'related matter'; a term about sharing the chores as one for the 'working relationship' (should it be included as a sign of its importance to the parties even if it might have no legal effect?); s. 4, Children Act 1989 'parental responsibility agreement' (or joint registration) should they produce a non-marital child; and a prospective attempt to limit any future ancillary relief by way of the agreement being seen as one of 'all the circumstances' which the divorce court has to consider under s. 25 of the Matrimonial Causes Act 1973. The word limit has been complied with: there are 217 words in the suggested answer.

- **Comply with the rubric and word limit**

- **Be imaginative**

- **Be holistic**

- **Beware children**

- **Money and property**

⬤ Suggested answer

Mark and Wendy intend to set up home together. For the time being, at least, they do not intend to marry as they are both divorced and are wary of repeating the experience. Neither of them has children.

They plan to live in Wendy's house and pay all bills, including the mortgage, *pro rata* to their earnings. Wendy is a doctor who earns four times more than Mark, a nurse. Wendy is adamant that Mark, unlike her ex-husband, will share all household chores equally with her. Both want to play a full part in bringing up any children they may have.

Their other intentions concern money and property, and they particularly want their wishes to continue to take effect should they eventually marry, and then divorce, each other. Their wishes are that neither one should be obliged to maintain the other, or have any (other) claim to money or property, with the exception that

Mark have a half share in the house. Wendy particularly wants to safeguard her entitlement to her recent £300,000 inheritance.

Mark and Wendy want to know how far you can help them to give effect to their wishes. Advise them (80 marks) and include a critical account of how the position would differ were they both of the same gender (20 marks).

Further reading

Barton, C., and Hibbs, M., 'Ancillary Financial Relief and Fat Cat(tle) Divorce' (2002) MLR Vol. 65, p. 79.

Bridge, S., 'Marriage and Divorce: the Regulation of Intimacy' in J. Herring (ed.) *Family Law: Issues, Debates, Policy* (Willan Publishing, 2001), pp. 24–29.

Francis, N. and Phillips, S., 'New Light on Prenuptial Agreements' [2003] Fam Law 164.

Miller, G., 'Pre-nuptial Agreements and Financial Provision' in G. Miller (ed.), *Frontiers of Family Law* (Ashgate, 2003), pp. 120–41.

Pavlowski, M., 'Cohabitation Contracts—the *Sutton* Case' [2004] Fam Law 199.

Q&A 16

Putting it all together

Introduction

In this chapter we consider areas of overlap in family law. Generally, in practice, the person who seeks your advice wishes a number of matters to be considered, for example divorce, financial matters and children. Here we provide six examples. As the questions may cover many areas you will not be able, in your answers, to cover each topic in the same way you would a single topic question but you should be able to display a command of a wide area of knowledge, not superficially, but incisively and with depth in the relevant area.

Q Question 1

Edgar and Fiona have been married for 12 years. They have two children, George aged 10 years and Harriet aged 8 years. Edgar's work takes him out of the country for six months out of every year. Fiona admits that she finds children 'tedious', and when Edgar is away, George and Harriet are mainly looked after by Edgar's mother.

Fiona has acknowledged that she has a drink problem and has joined Alcoholics Anonymous where she met Ivy who has moved in with Fiona while Edgar is out of the country. Ivy and Fiona are lovers. Ivy occasionally drinks heavily.

When Edgar returned home unexpectedly he found Ivy and her friend Jake staying at the house. Fiona told Edgar that Ivy is bisexual and that Jake and Ivy are lovers. Fiona, Ivy and Jake have decided to move to a commune and intend to take the children with them.

Edgar has confided his unhappiness to Kay, his personal assistant, and with her help and understanding he has accepted that his marriage to Fiona is at an end.

Edgar seeks your advice as he wishes to marry Kay as soon as possible. He has recently gained a promotion and his new job will involve no overseas travel. Edgar is of the view that he will be able to provide a more stable and suitable home for the children and the spouses have agreed that Edgar will buy out Fiona's interest in their house.

Advise Edgar.

Commentary

Divorce and s. 8 orders are a likely area of overlap.

The parties may have to be persuaded not to use the children as weapons in the adult conflict and to attempt to reach agreement regarding arrangements for the children. They should be informed of the no order principle and advised not to make unnecessary s. 8 applications.

It is possible where the behaviour fact is being relied on in divorce that the respondent may feel constrained to defend the petition so as to prevent the petitioner using the same information to show that the respondent is an unfit parent and therefore should not have residence or contact.

Answer plan

- Divorce—Matrimonial Causes Act 1973. Sole ground—irretrievable breakdown, s. 1, MCA 1973. One of five facts, s. 1(2).

- Edgar wants a divorce as soon as possible—behaviour, s. 1(2)(b). Explain why not adultery, s. 1(2)(a). No-fault fact—1(2)(d)?

- Parental responsibility Children Act 1989.

- Residence order, s. 8, CA 1989.

- Welfare principle, s. 1. Checklist, s. 1(3)—apply to facts.

·☼· Suggested answer

Edgar and Fiona appear to be on the verge of a rancorous divorce, and although we are Edgar's champion—indeed *because* we are Edgar's champion—we should start by advising him that a 'private' resolution of their disagreements would probably redound to the good of all concerned, save money, and best serve his desire to marry Kay 'as soon as possible'.

Although Edgar must understand that his divorce, his children, and the potential conflict about them will all be legally linked—and the more so the less he and Fiona can agree about the children—we will start with the divorce. (Edgar should none-theless know that the children's living arrangements are matters for freestanding application under s. 8 of the Children Act 1989 which can be made by either him or Fiona at any time.) As there is nothing to suggest that the marriage between Edgar and Fiona is void (s. 11, Matrimonial Causes Act (MCA) 1973) or voidable (s. 12, MCA 1973) Edgar must bring his marriage to an end by divorce.

No petition for divorce can be presented within the first year of marriage (s. 3, MCA 1973 as amended by s. 1 Matrimonial and Family Proceedings Act 1984). Edgar and Fiona have been married for twelve years. Edgar must present a petition to the divorce county court showing that his marriage has broken down irretrievably, this being the sole ground for divorce (s. 1(1), MCA 1973). Irretrievable breakdown must be shown by one or more of five facts, namely, (a) adultery together with intolerability, (b) behaviour, (c) desertion, (d) two years separation and the respondent consents to a decree being granted and (e) five years separation (s. 1(2)). As Edgar wishes to marry Kay as soon as possible only the first two 'facts' will be considered at this point as they offer a quicker way out of the marriage than the last three 'facts'.

To petition on the first fact Edgar must prove that Fiona has committed adultery and that he finds it intolerable to live with her (s. 1(2)(a)). Adultery is voluntary sexual intercourse between a man and a woman who are not married to each other but one of whom at least is married (*Clarkson* v *Clarkson* (1930) 143 TLR 623). The requirement of one man and one woman will rule out Fiona's relationship with Ivy as the basis for an adultery petition, although it may be considered as 'behaviour'.

To petition on the second fact the petitioner must satisfy the court that the respondent has behaved in such a way that the petitioner cannot reasonably be expected to live with the respondent (s. 1(2)(b)). Behaviour has been defined as 'action or conduct by one spouse which affects the other' (*per* Sir George Baker, P in *Katz* v *Katz* [1972] 1 WLR 955.) Evidence of Fiona's relationship with Ivy (*Coffer* v *Coffer* (1964) 108 SJ 465) and possibly her drink problem may be sufficient behaviour to satisfy the district judge that Edgar is entitled to a decree.

Edgar must show that as a result of Fiona's behaviour he cannot reasonably be expected to live with her. The test is a cross between a subjective and an objective test. 'Would any right thinking person come to the conclusion that this husband has behaved in such a way that this wife cannot be expected to live with him, taking into account the whole of the circumstances and the characters and personalities of the parties?' (*per* Dunn J in *Livingstone-Stallard* v *Livingstone-Stallard* [1974] 2 All ER 766). The court will look not only at Fiona's behaviour but also at Edgar's behaviour (*Ash* v *Ash* [1972] Fam 135; *Hadjimilitis (Tsavliris)* v *Tsavliris (Divorce: Irretrievable Breakdown)* [2003] 1 FLR 81); is he particularly sensitive, is he a drunken petitioner objecting to a drunken respondent? If Edgar can show a disparity in behaviour he should commence divorce proceedings immediately based on the behaviour fact.

Even though Edgar may wish to marry Kay as soon as possible, he should at least give some consideration to 'the divorce by consent fact'—that is that the parties have lived apart for a continuous period of at least two years immediately preceding the presentation of the petition and the respondent consents to a decree being granted (s. 1(2)(d)). This could allow Edgar and Fiona to bring their marriage to an end with minimum distress to themselves and to their children.

Fiona wishes to take the children to a commune whilst Edgar thinks he can provide a more stable home. As married (or even divorced) parents of these children, they each have parental responsibility for George and Harriet (s. 2(1), Children Act 1989) and each may exercise that responsibility independently (s. 2(7)). In the absence of any order there is nothing Edgar can do to prevent Fiona taking the children to the commune and nothing Fiona can do to prevent Edgar taking the children to his home.

Edgar should apply for a residence order. A 'residence order' means an order settling the arrangements to be made as to the person with whom a child is to live (s. 8(1)). Although Fiona has said that she finds children to be tedious, she has expressed a desire to take the children to the commune, so it would seem highly likely that she will dispute Edgar's application and, presumably, will make an application herself.

Where divorcing parents can make their own arrangements as to where the child is to live, then the court will not intervene (s. 1(5)). As there is a dispute the court will need to consider the arrangements for the children. The welfare of George and Harriet will be the court's paramount consideration when deciding where the children should live (s. 1(1)). Where the making of a s. 8 order is opposed the court is to have regard to the welfare checklist (s. 1(3)). The factors to be taken into account are not given any order of importance, nor is it stated that the factors are to be given equal importance. It is not always necesary for the court to consider all seven items: *H* v *H (Residence Order: Leave to Remove from Jurisdiction)* [1995] 1 FLR 529.

The court should have regard to the ascertainable wishes and feelings of the children, considered in the light of their age and understanding (s. 1(3)(a)). For young children the court will need to rely on the welfare officer's report. The wishes of an intelligent 10- or 11-year-old can be given considerable weight (*M* v *M, The Times*, 12 August 1992 see also *Re S (Contact: Children's Views)* [2002] 1 FLR 1156). The court will not be constricted by the child's wishes and should disregard them if the child's future welfare appears to diverge from his express wishes. It is the decision of the court and not the child (*Re P (A Minor) (Education: Child's Views)* [1992] 1 FLR 316). The wishes of George and Harriet will be taken into consideration along with the other factors on the checklist.

The children's physical, emotional and educational needs will be noted. Their physical needs may be better catered for by Edgar. The welfare officer's report would discuss details of the physical environment in the commune and compare that with the chidren's present home and the accommodation that Edgar is offering. Fiona does not appear to have made a major contribution to the children's emotional or physical development. Wherever possible brother and sister should be brought up together so that they are an emotional support to each other (*C* v *C (Custody of Children)* [1988] 2 FLR 291). Under s. 1(3)(c) the court must have regard to 'the likely effect . . . of any change in the circumstances'. With Edgar, they would stay in their lifelong home (where his mother may still be available).

Fiona's drink problem and lesbian relationship with Ivy (*C* v *C (A Minor) (Custody: Appeal)* [1991] 1 FLR 223 and *B* v *B (Minors) (Custody, Care and Control)* [1991] 1 FLR

402) will be factors the court will take into account, but what is more likely to cause concern is the fact that Fiona, who has not been a devoted mother, wishes to take the children away from a familiar background into the uncertainty and possible instability of the life of the commune, with what the court may view as unsuitable companions (capability of the parents and any other person of meeting the child's needs (s. 1(3)(f))). The court may decide that the children would be at risk of suffering harm if they went with Fiona (s. 1(3)(e)) and today there is no presumption that young children (or girls approaching puberty) should live with their mother: *Re S (A Minor) (Custody)* [1991] 2 FLR 388. (However, see comments by Bracewell J that there is a perception that courts rubber-stamp care to the mother and marginalise the father *(V v V (Children) (Contact: Implacable Hostility)* (2004) *The Times*, 28 May.)

In the circumstances it would appear unlikely that the court would grant a residence order to Fiona. If Edgar can show that he is capable of providing for the needs of the children, although he cannot show a stable home at this stage, the court may make a residence order in his favour while giving directions as to how the order is to be effected (s. 11(7)). Overall, perhaps, the case with most relevance to this dispute is *May* v *May* [1986] 1 FLR 325. The father attached importance to discipline in the home; the mother and her cohabitant did not.

The Court of Appeal declined to interfere with the trial judge's decision that the children should live with their father. Edgar can be advised that he will, if necessary, be granted a residence order.

Q Question 2

Amanda married Barry over two years ago when she was six months pregnant. She admitted to Barry, before their marriage, that she was not sure whether he, Barry, was the father of the child or whether it was Cliff. Barry, who was jealous of Cliff, had attempted to impress Amanda with stories of his famous and wealthy relatives. The stories were untrue.

Shortly after the child, Desdemona, was born Amanda resumed her affair with Cliff. Barry knew of the relationship but continued to live with Amanda in the hope that the affair would end.

Last week Amanda told Barry that she was taking Desdemona and going to live with Cliff as he was now free to marry her.

Barry regrets marrying Amanda and has no wish to live with her any more. He has grave doubts as to whether Desdemona is his child, as she bears a striking resemblance to Cliff.

Advise Amanda who states that she wishes to marry Cliff as soon as possible and does not care how the marriage is brought to an end, nor by whom.

Commentary

An overlap of nullity and divorce is something you should expect. In a family law examination, or in practice, it is unlikely that you will be able to consider nullity in isolation without considering divorce, although the reverse situation does not necessarily apply. If you are asked to advise one of the parties you will need to consider not only the availability of the remedies but also the advantages and disadvantages of particular proceedings. In nullity, for example, the parties will normally have to appear in court whereas in an undefended divorce the procedure has become something akin to an administrative process with no necessity for the parties to give evidence in court.

Answer plan

- Nullity—define void/voidable marriages. Void grounds, s. 11, Matrimonial Causes Act 1973. Voidable, s. 12.

- Apply voidable grounds to the facts.

- Establishing paternity.

- Bars to voidable marriages, s. 13.

- Divorce—s. 1, MCA 1973. Sole ground irretrievable breakdown, s. 1(1). Which of the five facts applies to the facts?

☼ Suggested answer

Amanda wishes to be free to marry Cliff as soon as possible. If her marriage to Barry were so faulty as never to have existed then she would be free to marry Cliff right away, but nothing in the facts suggests that Amanda's marriage to Barry is void *ab initio*. A void marriage is one that will be regarded as never having taken place and can be so treated by both parties to it without the necessity of any decree annulling it: a voidable marriage is one that will be regarded as valid until a decree annulling it has been pronounced (*per* Lord Greene MR in *De Reneville* v *De Reneville* [1948] P 100). A marriage will be void if the parties lack capacity to marry or have not complied with the necessary formalities (s. 11, Matrimonial Causes Act 1973). If the marriage is not void then it must be brought to an end by annulment on a voidable ground, or by dissolution by divorce before Amanda can be free to marry Cliff.

Amanda has said that she does not care how the marriage is brought to an end, nor by whom and Barry has stated that he regrets marrying Amanda, so it would seem that either party would be prepared to initiate nullity or divorce proceedings.

Potentially there appear to be grounds on which the marriage may be voidable (s. 12). The non-consummation grounds can be ruled out as can mental disorder, a Gender Recognition Certificate, venereal disease and lack of consent due to duress, as there is no information to suggest that any of these grounds apply. Amanda may claim that she did not validly consent to the marriage due to mistake (s. 12(c)). Clearly, she was not mistaken as to the nature of the ceremony; Amanda was aware that she was exchanging marriage vows with Barry (unlike *Mehta* v *Mehta* [1945] 2 All ER 690, where there was a mistaken belief that the ceremony was one of religious conversion). Before the marriage Barry had attempted to impress Amanda with stories of his famous and wealthy relatives; it has now transpired that these stories were untrue. Mistake as to identity will make the marriage voidable only where one party fails to marry the individual whom he or she intended to marry. Mistake as to attributes (*C* v *C* [1942] NZLR 356) or the other party's fortune (*Wakefield* v *Mackay* (1807) 1 Hag Con 394) will not invalidate the marriage. Therefore Barry's tall stories will not make this marriage voidable.

The marriage might be voidable if at the time of the marriage the respondent was pregnant by some person other than the petitioner (s. 12(f)). Desdemona may be Barry's child although she bears a striking resemblance to Cliff. Any child born to a wife is presumed to be the child of the husband although this presumption may be rebutted by evidence which shows on a balance of probabilities the child is not the child of the husband (s. 26, Family Law Reform Act 1969). The court may direct scientific tests under s. 20 FLRA 1987. The court is allowed to consent to the taking of a sample in the child's best interests (s. 21(3) Family Law Reform Act (FLRA) 1969 (as amended by the Child Support, Pensions and Social Security Act 2000) see *Re O and J (Children)* [2000] 2 All ER 29). As Amanda wishes to end the marriage it is to her advantage to undergo DNA testing herself and allow Desdemona to be tested. Barry and Cliff should have no objection to being tested; Barry regrets the marriage and does not believe Desdemona to be his child, Cliff wishes to marry Amanda and presumably would be delighted if Desdemona were proved to be his child (better to know the truth *Re H and A (Paternity: Blood Tests)* [2002] 1 FLR 1145). Were any of the parties to refuse to undergo blood tests the court is empowered to draw such inferences as it thinks fit (*Re A (A Minor) (Paternity: Refusal of Blood Test)* [1994] 2 FLR 463); *Secretary of State for Work and Pensions* v *Jones* [2004] 1 FLR 282 and s. 23(1) FLRA 1969). If Desdemona is Cliff's child Amanda would have been pregnant by another at the time of the marriage. Nonetheless a decree will be refused by the court unless it is satisfied that the petitioner was, at the time of the marriage, ignorant of the facts alleged (s. 13(3), MCA 1973). Barry's knowledge that Amanda was pregnant is not in itself a bar; he must also know that she was pregnant by someone other than himself (*Stocker* v *Stocker* [1966] 1 WLR 190). Amanda had admitted to Barry that she did not know whether he or Cliff was the father of her child, so there was uncertainty. At the time of the marriage Barry did not *know* that Cliff was the father; if he had such knowledge that would be a bar to a nullity decree, but can it be said that he was ignorant of the facts alleged? Would the court be satisfied?

Amanda is unlikely to raise any bar based on the petitioner's conduct (s. 13(1)) as she wishes to end the marriage. Nullity proceedings based on s. 12(f) should be brought within three years of the marriage (s. 13(2)), although leave may be granted for proceedings to be brought out of time in certain cases of mental disorder (s. 13(4)). The marriage took place over two years ago so no time should be wasted in presenting a petition. Legal aid is available in nullity proceedings.

If Desdemona is proved to be Barry's child there would be no grounds for nullity proceedings, or the child may be Cliff's but the court may have applied the bar in s. 13(3) and not granted a nullity decree. If either situation applies the parties would have to end their marriage by divorce.

Divorce proceedings may not be started within the first year of marriage (s. 3(1), Matrimonial Causes Act (MCA) 1973). As Amanda and Barry have been married for over two years the bar does not apply.

The sole ground for divorce is irretrievable breakdown of the marriage (s. 1(1), MCA 1973). However the court cannot hold that the marriage has irretrievably broken down unless the petitioner satisfies the court of one or more of the five facts set out in s. 1(2). The last three facts were discounted as Amanda wishes to marry Cliff as soon as possible and it would seem that s. 1(2)(b), the respondent has behaved in such a way that the petitioner cannot reasonably be expected to live with the respondent, would not be the most obvious fact to choose as Amanda has committed adultery. For Barry to petition on this fact he must prove that Amanda has committed adultery and he finds it intolerable to live with her (s. 1(2)(a)).

Adultery is voluntary sexual intercourse between a man and a woman who are not married to each other but one of whom at least is a married person (*Clarkson* v *Clarkson* (1930) 143 TLR 623). Proof of adultery will be satisfied by Amanda and Cliff admitting adultery in the acknowledgement of service of the petition (*Bradley* v *Bradley (Queen's Proctor intervening)* [1986] 1 FLR 128). In addition Barry must prove that he finds it intolerable to live with Amanda, it is not necessary for the adultery to be the cause of the intolerability (*Cleary* v *Cleary* [1974] 1 All ER 498, followed in *Carr* v *Carr* [1974] 1 All ER 1193). The test for intolerability is a subjective one (*Goodrich* v *Goodrich* [1971] 2 All ER 1340). Barry regrets the marriage and does not wish to live with Amanda, this would appear to satisfy the test. If the court is satisfied that the s. 1(2) fact has been proved then, unless it is satisfied on all the evidence that the marriage has not broken down irretrievably, it shall grant a decree of divorce (s. 1(4)). It is not necessary for Barry to prove that the irretrievable breakdown was caused by the adultery (*Buffery* v *Buffery* [1988] FCR 465). In *Stevens* v *Stevens* [1979] 1 WLR 885, it was the petitioner's own behaviour that had caused the breakdown.

For the purposes of his divorce petition Barry cannot rely on adultery committed by Amanda if, after the adultery became known to him, they lived together for a period or periods together exceeding six months (s. 2(1)). This is an absolute bar (*Court* v *Court* [1983] Fam 105). Where the parties have lived together for periods not exceeding six months, after discovery of the adultery, then this shall be disregarded in determining whether the petitioner finds it intolerable to live with the respondent

(s. 2(2)). Where the respondent commits adultery on more than one occasion time does not begin to run until after the petitioner learns of the last act of adultery. Although Barry knew of the relationship he continued living with Amanda; this state of affairs continued throughout their married life. Amanda is living with Cliff; presumably the adultery is continuing therefore s. 2(1) will not be a bar. This route out of the marriage would appear to be the most certain and speedy and would not involve the parties in a court appearance.

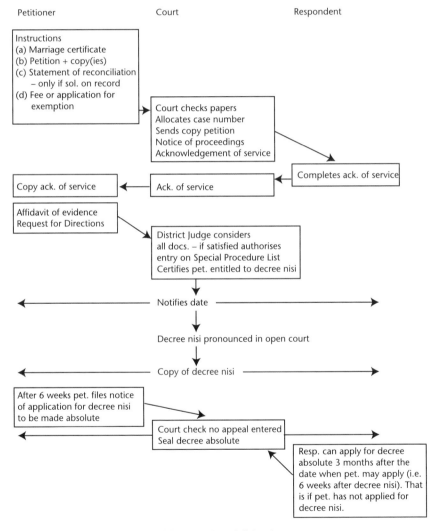

Special procedure undefended divorce (no children)

Q Question 3

Ursula, an unmarried mother, has a daughter, Victoria, aged four. Ted, Victoria's father, spends most weekends with Ursula and his daughter. Ted wishes to marry Ursula but she has told him that she does not wish to 'sign her rights away' either by marriage or by signing documents stating that he is Victoria's father.

William, Ursula's brother, emigrated to Australia five years ago. Ursula is dissatisfied with life in England and believes that schools and career prospects would be much better for them in Australia. Ted does not wish to leave England. William has sent tickets for flights to Australia for Ursula and Victoria; he wishes them to take a holiday to coincide with his birthday in two months' time.

Ted informs you that he wishes to be formally acknowledged as Victoria's father, however, at the moment, he admits his relationship with Ursula is 'rocky'. Although he is concerned that Ursula and Victoria may not return to England, he does not wish to prevent them taking a holiday. Ursula says that he is over-reacting and assures him that his concerns are unfounded. Ted does not wish to create a problem where none exists. However, he is worried that once they are out of the country he may not be able to get Victoria back.

Advise Ted.

Commentary

In any answer it may be reasonable to point out that more information is needed, but do not say that there is not enough information in the question for you to be able to answer it. There are a number of explanations for lack of information; it may not be relevant, or it may be relevant but the examiner wants you to consider all the options available in different circumstances and does not wish to signpost every step of the way for you; in other words credit is to be given for recognition of potential problems and solutions.

Answer plan

- Parental responsibility Children Act 1989. Acquisition of PR by non-marital father, s. 4.

- Proof of paternity.

- Prevention of removal of child from jurisdiction. Child Abduction Act 1984.

- Removal—Child Abduction and Custody Act 1985—Hague Convention.

- Prompt return/age of child/habitual residence/wrongful removal/retention/ Art. 12/Art. 13 etc apply to facts

Suggested answer

There are two main issues of concern to Ted: his parental responsibility for Victoria and international child abduction. Where parents are unmarried the mother acquires automatic parental responsibility whereas the father must take action to acquire it (s. 2(2), Children Act 1989). Parental responsibility means all the rights, duties, powers, responsibilities and authority which by law a parent of a child has in relation to the child and his property (s. 3). Ursula has sole parental responsibility. Ursula and Ted may enter into a parental responsibility agreement which would provide for Ted to have parental responsibility for Victoria (s. 4(1)(b)), this will last until discharged by the court (s. 4(1)(3)). The agreement will only take effect if it is made in the form prescribed by the Parental Responsibility Agreement Regulations 1991 (SI 1991/1478) and filed with the Principal Registry of the Family Division (approximately 4000 agreements during 2000). It would appear at this stage that Ursula may be unwilling to enter into such an agreement, in which case, Ted should apply to court for a parental responsibility order (s. 4(1)(a)).

Section 111 of the Adoption and Children Act 2002, which came into effect on 1 December 2003, amends s. 4 of the Children Act 1989. It provides that a father who is not married to the mother at the time of the child's birth is to have parental responsibility if registration or re-registration of the birth takes place according to the provisions of the Births and Deaths Registration Act 1953. Both parents have to register the birth of their baby together in order for the non-marital father to gain parental responsibility. The provisions are not intended to be retrospective and will apply to births registered on or after 1 December 2003. It is not possible for a birth to be re-registered if the father has already been correctly registered.

Any child born to a wife is presumed to be the child of the husband, however, cohabitation, in itself, does not raise such a presumption. If Ursula and Ted had jointly registered Victoria's birth and had Ted's name entered as the father of the child this will be *prima facie* evidence that he is the father (s. 34(2), Births and Deaths Registration Act 1953; *Brierley* v *Brierley and Williams* [1918] P 257). Accordingly, the burden would fall on Ursula if she wished to rebut the presumption. If Ted's name does not appear on the register he may wish to prove that he is Victoria's father by using DNA tests which provide 'a more accurate (although not conclusive) way of establishing parentage' (*per* Balcombe LJ in *Re F (A Minor: Blood Tests: Paternity Rights)* [1993] 1 FLR 598). Ursula may decide to oppose his application for tests. Under s. 20(1) of the Family Law Reform Act 1969 the court has a judicial discretion to direct that blood tests be taken to seek to determine paternity. The court will refuse to direct a blood test to be carried out against the will of the parent who has since birth had sole parental responsibility for the child and where the putative father had no relationship with the child (*Re F (A Minor: Blood Tests: Paternity Rights)* above). The circumstances are different in this case as Ted would appear to have established a relationship with

Victoria. A test will not be ordered if it is not in the best interests of the child but sought merely to satisfy curiosity (*Hodgkiss* v *Hodgkiss* [1984] FLR 563). Where the truth as to the child's paternity would be beneficial, a direction should be made (*S* v *McC, W* v *W* [1972] AC 24; *Re H (Paternity: Blood Test)* [1996] 2 FLR 65). Increasingly, the courts are taking the view that justice is not served by impeding the establishment of truth. Samples cannot be taken from a person without his consent (s. 21(1), FLRA 1969). However, should any of the parties refuse to undergo blood tests the court is empowered to draw such inferences as it thinks fit (s. 23, FLRA 1969; *Re A (A Minor) (Paternity: Refusal of Blood Test)* [1994] 2 FLR 463; *Secretary of State for Work and Pensions* v *Jones* [2004] 1 FLR 282). In *Re H and A (Paternity: Blood Tests)* [2002] 1 FLR 1145 the Court of Appeal asserted that the paternity of any child was to be established by science and not by legal presumption or inference. Together with the new s. 21(3) of the Family Law Reform Act 1969 (amended by the Child Support, Pensions and Social Security Act 2000), which enables a court to consent to the taking of a sample in a child's best interests, this should see the end of secrecy and (sometimes) self-deception as seen in *Re F* (above).

If Ted were able to prove paternity he could apply for a parental responsibility order (s. 4(1)(a)) (9,524 PR orders were made during 2003, *Judicial Statistics*, 2003, Table 5.3). In considering whether to make such an order the welfare of the child will be the paramount consideration (s. 1(1)) and the no order principle will apply (s. 1(5)). The court will consider the level of commitment to, and involvement with the child, and whether making an order could destabilise a new family unit (which would not apply in this case) and whether it would be justifiable to equate Ted with a married father (*Re H (Illegitimate Children: Father: Parental Rights) (No. 2)* [1991] 1 FLR 214; *Re H (Parental Responsibility)* [1998] 1 FLR 855; *Re P (Minors) (Parental Responsibility Order)* [1997] 2 FLR 722; *Re P (Parental Responsibility)* [1998] 2 FLR 1996; and *Re J-S (Contact: Parental Responsibility)* [2003] 1 FLR 399).

If Ted were to be successful in obtaining a parental responsibility order then he will acquire, amongst other rights, the right, in relation to Victoria, to object to the provision of, and removal from local authority accommodation (s. 20), also his consent must be sought or dispensed with under the Adoption Act 1976. More to the point here, Ursula could not remove Victoria from the UK without the consent of all those persons with parental responsibility. Even if Ursula has a residence order in relation to Victoria, no person may remove her from the UK without the written consent of every person who has parental responsibility for her, or the leave of the court (s. 13(1)). Section 13(1) does not prevent the removal of a child, for a period of less than one month, by the person in whose favour the residence order is made (s. 13(2)). If there is no residence order in force this does not mean there is no restriction on Ursula taking Victoria out of the country. The Child Abduction Act 1984 makes it a criminal offence for anyone with parental responsibility for a child under 16 to take the child out of the United Kingdom without the consent of all those with parental responsibility, or without the leave of the court. The crime is not committed by a person with a residence order who takes the child out of the UK for less than one month unless it is done so in breach of a court order under Part II, Children Act 1989.

As a parent of Victoria, Ted may apply as of right for any s. 8 order (*Re C and another (Minors) (Parent: Residence Order)* [1993] 3 All ER 313; s. 10(4)(a)). If Ted feared that Ursula intended Victoria's permanent removal from the UK, he could apply for a specific issue or a prohibited steps order. However, if Ted's fears are merely a product of his over anxious imagination, with no foundation in reality, then such an application would be inappropriate and may produce an undesired reaction by Ursula.

Ted may find some consolation in that if the worst were to happen, that is, Ursula and Victoria settling in Australia, then he could invoke Part I of the Child Abduction and Custody Act (CACA) 1985 which incorporates the Hague Convention on the Civil Aspects of International Child Abduction 1980 into UK law. Every Convention country (Australia is a contracting state) has a Central Authority which deals with the administrative action required to operate the remedies under the Convention. Central Authorities must co-operate with each other to promote the objects of the Hague Convention, one of which is to secure the prompt return of children wrongfully removed to or retained in any contracting state (Art. 1).

Ted, as a non-marital father, would be disadvantaged, in that his family life is not protected by the Hague Convention unless he had taken steps to acquire parental responsibility (see House of Lords in *Re J (A Minor)(Abduction: Custody Rights)* [1990] 2 AC 562, *sub nom C* v *S (A Minor)(Abduction)* [1990] 2 FLR 442. However, in the Court of Appeal in *Re B (A Minor)(Abduction)* [1994] 2 FLR 249, terms such as 'rights of custody' have been held to be capable of describing inchoate rights of those who are carrying out duties and enjoying privileges of a custodial or parental character, which may not yet formally be recognised or granted by law (see *Re C (Child Abduction) (Unmarried Father: Rights of Custody)* [2003] 1 FLR 252). The importance to non-marital fathers of having parental responsibility in cases of potential or actual child abduction was emphasised by the Court of Appeal in *Re J-S (Contact: Parental Responsibility)* [2003] 1 FLR 399). This factor provides further incentive to Ted to acquire parental responsibility. Ted may contact the Central Authority in the UK, in turn, it would deal with the Central Authority in Australia, in an attempt to secure a voluntary return of Victoria to the UK. However, if Ursula would not agree to a voluntary return then the Central Authority would initiate proceedings. Should the Convention apply to Victoria's circumstances, the courts could not investigate the merits of the case and must order her return unless one of the grounds in Articles 12 or 13 applied. 'The courts of the country of habitual residence should determine their future . . . The interests of the child in each individual case are not paramount since it is presumed under the Convention that the welfare of children is best met by return to their habitual residence' (*Re M (A Minor) (Child Abduction)* [1994] 1 FLR 390).

The Hague Convention applies where a child under 16 who is habitually resident in one contracting state is wrongfully removed to, or retained in, another (Art. 4). The question of a child's habitual residence has been established as one of fact (*Re M (Abduction: Habitual Residence)* [1996] 1 FLR 887). When a child lives with his parents, the child's habitual residence will normally be that of his parents (*Re A (Wardship: Jurisdiction)* [1995] 1 FLR 767). There can be no dispute that, immediately before any retention in Australia, Victoria was habitually resident in the UK. Where both parents have parental responsibility, neither can unilaterally change the child's habitual residence (*Re B (Minors) (Abduction) (No. 2)* [1993] 1 FLR 993). Where a child has been wrongfully removed or retained for less than a year the court must order the return of the child (Art. 12). Even where a year has elapsed such return is mandatory unless it is demonstrated that the child is 'settled in its new environment' (Art. 12). However, Art. 13 gives the court a discretion whether to order return if the person who opposes the return can establish that the applicant, at the time of the removal or retention, was not exercising custody rights or consented to it, or subsequently acquiesced, or there is a grave risk of physical or psychological harm if the child is returned, or a mature child objects. There is a heavy burden on a person alleged to have abducted a child if she is to bring herself within the provisions of Art. 13 (*Re H (Abduction: Grave Risk)* [2003] 2 FLR 141). It would need to be an exceptional case for the child's return to be refused. In exercising its discretion the court must give due weight to the primary purpose of the Convention. A less stringent approach would undermine the spirit and purpose of the Convention, which is the speedy return of children so that a court in the country of their habitual residence can decide what is best for them. However, in exercising their discretion, the courts have been influenced by the fact that a child returned to the country of habitual residence would be more than likely to be allowed to leave again by a court of that country (*Re A (Minors) (No. 2) (Abduction: Acquiescence)* [1993] 1 FLR 396); (*Re K (Abduction: Consent)* [1997] 2 FLR 212).

It is to be hoped that Ursula will relent and enter a parental responsibility agreement with Ted. If not, Ted should apply for a parental responsibility order, as it can be seen above that a parental responsibility order provides him with rights in relation to Victoria, notably that his consent must be sought in certain matters and, potentially of importance here, gives him rights under the Hague Convention.

Q Question 4

Ruby, aged eight, was taken into care last year and has settled down well with her foster parents, Simon and Trish. Ruby's parent's, Violet and William, were divorced two years ago. Violet's behaviour, which had become increasingly bizarre, culminated in her being committed to a mental hospital last year. By then William had left the area and could not be traced.

As Violet's condition was thought to be improving, six months ago she entered a programme at the hospital, which has the aim of rehabilitating her into the community. Trish told Violet that she was welcome at their home any time. At first the visits went well; Violet would call soon after Ruby returned from school and would take tea with Trish and Ruby, leaving before Simon returned from work. On one occasion two months ago Simon returned early and since then Violet has visited the house every evening, waiting for Simon's return. When he insisted that she should limit her visits to seeing Ruby and leave before his return, she declared her undying love for him and has since then pestered him with phone calls during the day at his place of work and throughout the night and weekend at his home. She has delivered letters and presents to his home every day. So far Simon and Trish have been able to shield Ruby from this behaviour.

Last week William called at the house. He wants Ruby to live with him. He has remarried and his wife, Yasmin has said that she would love to have Ruby come and live with them.

Advise Simon and William.

Commentary

This question illustrates a situation where family law alone cannot provide a remedy. Here the overlap is between family law and the law of tort.

Answer plan

* Simon and Violet are not associated persons—Part IV, Family Law Act 1996 does not protect Simon.

* Tort—trespass? nuisance? Protection from Harassment Act 1997?

* Injunction appropriate?

* Care order, s. 31, Children Act 1989. Threshold. Effects of care order.

* Contact with child in care, s. 34.

* Residence order/discharge of care order/supervision order. Welfare of child.

:Q: Suggested answer

Although Simon is being pestered in his own home he will be unable to invoke the protection the court can give under Part IV of the Family Law Act 1996. The 1996 Act protects 'associated persons' (s. 62(3)) from molestation (s. 42). Simon and Violet are not 'associated' therefore Simon must seek a remedy in tort.

It would seem unlikely on the facts that Simon would wish to apply to the county court for a residence order (s. 8, Children Act 1989) so that he could ask for a non-molestation injunction ancillary to those proceedings (s. 38, County Courts Act 1984 (as substituted by s. 3, Courts and Legal Services Act 1990). Molestation or harassment can be forbidden where the behaviour complained of amounts to an established tort. Simon has limited Violet's visits to his property; if she comes on to his land outside the time allowed she will be a trespasser.

Besetting a person's house, by conduct which seriously interferes with the ordinary use and enjoyment of the house beset, can support an action for nuisance (*J. Lyons & Sons Ltd v Wilkins* [1899] 1 Ch 255). It was decided in the Appellate Division of the Alberta Supreme Court that a legal owner of property can obtain an injunction on the grounds of private nuisance, to restrain persistent harassment by unwanted telephone calls to his home (*Motherwell v Motherwell* [1976] 73 DLR (3d) 62). Nuisance is not actionable per se, damage has to be proved. The law expects the ordinary person to bear the mishaps of life with fortitude and customary phlegm (*Bourhill v Young* [1943] AC 92) but can it expect Simon to tolerate such behaviour? If he is suffering from 'stress' at this point, the continuation of Violet's campaign could lead to physical or psychiatric illness.

The Protection from Harassment Act 1997 may provide Simon with an effective remedy against Violet's campaign of adoration. A person must not pursue a course of conduct which the person knows or ought to know amounts to harassment of another (s. 1). This involves conduct on at least two occasions, and conduct includes speech (s. 7). The court may award damages and it may grant an injunction restraining Violet from any conduct which amounts to harassment (s. 3). No power of arrest can be attached to the injunction but a warrant of arrest may be applied for if breach is alleged. It is an offence punishable by up to five years' imprisonment to do anything, without reasonable excuse, prohibited by the injunction (s. 3(6)).

The court may take the view that an injunction is an unsuitable remedy against Violet. In *Wookey v Wookey* [1991] 2 FLR 319, the Court of Appeal said that a person who was incapable of understanding an injunction could not be guilty of contempt by disobeying it. When it appears that a person who is molesting the plaintiff may be suffering from a mental disorder, the Official Solicitor should be notified as soon as possible if an application is to be made to a court for an injunction and the possible need for a guardian *ad litem* should be addressed. If the court has evidence to show that Violet is capable of understanding an injunction, then it should be expressed in words she would be able to understand readily. If she is not capable, then the appropriate way to deal with her would be under the Mental Health Acts 1959 and 1983.

Simon could not apply for a prohibited steps order while Ruby is in the care of the local authority (s. 9(1), Children Act 1989). Even if Ruby were not in care a prohibited steps order (s. 8) could not be used to prevent contact between Violet and Simon as such contact does not relate to a parental responsibility; Ruby is not aware of Violet's pestering (*Croydon London Borough Council v A* [1992] 2 FLR 271).

Ruby was taken into care last year. To make a care order the court must have been satisfied that Ruby was suffering or was likely to suffer significant harm and that such harm was attributable to a deficiency of reasonable parental care, or Ruby being beyond parental control (s. 31, Children Act 1989). The local authority will have acquired parental responsibility on the making of the care order (s. 33(3)) and will share that responsibility with Violet and William (s. 2(6)).

It is the general duty of every local authority to promote the upbringing of children by their families so far as that is consistent with the duty to safeguard and promote the welfare of children who are in need (s. 17). In furtherance of that duty the authority is required to allow Ruby reasonable contact with Violet (s. 34). The authority may refuse contact for no more than seven days in an emergency if they are satisfied that it is necessary for Ruby's welfare (s. 34(6)). Refusal of contact for any longer period must have the court's authorisation (s. 34(4)). When exercising its power the court must apply the welfare principle (s. 1(1)) and will have regard to the welfare checklist (s. 1(3)). Would Ruby's welfare benefit by refusal of contact or would it simply be more convenient for Simon? Contact could take place at some place other than Simon's home. The local authority could move Ruby to other foster parents but this would be another disruption for Ruby, particularly since she has settled down well with Simon and Trish. Violet's behaviour may cause the local authority to re-evaluate any plans it may have had concerning returning Ruby to her mother's care.

Even though Violet and William are divorced William will retain parental responsibility for Ruby; during the life of the care order the responsibility will be shared not only with Violet but also with the local authority. William could apply for a residence order (s. 8) and if that were to be granted the care order would be discharged automatically (s. 91(1)). William could apply for the care order to be discharged (s. 39(1)). The court may choose to substitute a supervision order for the care order (s. 39(4)). While a supervision order is in force it is the duty of the supervisor to advise, assist and befriend a supervised child.

In the circumstances the no order principle should prevail; the court could choose not to discharge the care order. It may be better to allow Ruby to get to know her father again; two years apart is a long gap in the life of an eight-year-old child. In addition, although Yasmin wishes Ruby to live with them a phased relocation may be preferable to a sudden disruption. This would also allow time for assessment of the new arrangements and a welfare officer's report. In any proceedings in which any question with respect to the upbringing of the child arises, the court must have regard to the general principle that any delay in determining the question is likely to prejudice the welfare of the child (s. 1(2)). Nevertheless if the delay is purposeful it should be encouraged (*C* v *Solihull Metropolitan Borough Council and Others* [1993] 1 FLR 290).

Q Question 5

Mark received a copy of his wife's petition for divorce based on his violent behaviour. On reading the petition and in a fit of temper he beat Naomi, his wife, causing extensive bruising and a broken rib. Last month Mark gave an undertaking to the court not to molest Naomi. Naomi has left the matrimonial home with their children, Olga, aged six, and Poppy, aged four.

Mark is due to have a sex change operation next week and he wishes to know whether or not this will make the marriage null and void. He acknowledges that the marriage is over but feels that an annulment would reflect the reality of his situation more than a divorce.

Although Mark no longer wants Naomi and the children to live with him, he does wish the children to continue to regard him as a parent and Naomi to treat him as a sister; Naomi thinks this will be too confusing for Olga and Poppy. She is frightened for her own safety and wishes to bring the marriage to an end and make a new start for herself and the children. The matrimonial home is a rented local housing authority property.

Naomi would like to change her daughters' surname to her own maiden name.

(a) How, if at all, may the undertaking be enforced? [6 marks]

(b) How may the local authority respond to Naomi's plight? [4 marks]

(c) Will the marriage be void after Mark's sex change operation? [4 marks]

(d) Is Naomi free to change the childrens' surname? [6 marks]

Commentary

Too far-fetched you think? The product of a fevered imagination? You may think you have heard it all before; but for practitioners of family law all human life is there, with all its frailties, and it never ceases to amaze.

You are directed to answer specific questions; keep to the point. Clearly indicate to the examiner which part of the question you are answering; do not throw in all the information for the examiner to sort out; you will not endear yourself to him or her. Start your answers with the letters corresponding to the questions. The hope that the examiner will do the work for you by extracting relevant information from a mass of irrelevance is a forlorn one. Follow the structure imposed on you by the examiner, it will save you time.

Answer plan

• Domestic violence—orders—Part IV, Family Law Act 1996. Power of arrest. Undertakings. Breach.

- Local authorities—duties—powers- homeless persons.

- Void marriage—s. 11, Matrimonial Causes Act 1973.

- Voidable marriage—s 12 MCA 1973.

- Gender Recognition Act 2004.

- Parental responsibility. Residence order. Children Act 1989.

- Change of name—if residence order—s. 13—if no residence order then applications under s. 8—specific issue or prohibited steps. Welfare principle. Checklist.

☀ Suggested answer

(a) If the court makes a non-molestation order or an occupation order and it appears to the court that the respondent has used or threatened violence against the applicant or a relevant child, it must attach a power of arrest to one or more provisions of the order, unless it is satisfied that in all the circumstances of the case the applicant or child will be adequately protected without such a power of arrest (s. 47(2), Family Law Act 1996). No power of arrest may be attached to an undertaking (s. 46(2)). Therefore, as the court accepted an undertaking from Mark it would appear that it believed that Naomi would be adequately protected without a power of arrest. A breach of an undertaking is contempt of court and punishable by committal to prison. To enforce the undertaking Naomi must apply for an order committing Mark to prison for breach. In family cases committal to prison was regarded as a last resort in *Ansah* v *Ansah* [1977] 2 All ER 638. However, in some cases committal may be necessary, in *G* v *G* [1991] 2 FLR 506 the Court of Appeal upheld a sentence of 16 months' imprisonment where the husband had persistently breached a non-molestation order. In *A* v *D (Contempt: Committal)* [1993] Fam Law 519 it was no defence that this was the first breach of the order; the respondent was given a sentence of three months for one violent breach of a non-molestation order (see *Wilson* v *Webster* [1998] 1 FLR 1097). The main reason for bringing Mark back to court is to make sure he obeys the order in the future. The view of Hayes and Williams ('Domestic Violence and Occupation of the Family Home' [1992] *Fam Law* 297) is that undertakings are treated as of less significance and, when broken, are likely to lead to the imposition of an order on similar terms, rather than committal for breach. If that were the case here, Naomi could apply for a non-molestation order (s. 42) and for an occupation order as an entitled person (s. 33). As violence was used by Mark on this occasion a power of arrest should be attached to one or more provisions of the orders. If a power of arrest is attached to an order, a constable may arrest, without a warrant, a person whom he has reasonable cause to suspect is in breach of any such provision (s. 47(6)).

(b) Local housing authorities have statutory duties and powers towards homeless persons under the Housing Act (HA) 1996. The Act acknowledges that it is not reasonable for Naomi to continue to occupy accommodation if it is probable that this will lead to domestic violence against her. Domestic violence in relation to Naomi means violence from a person with whom she is associated, or threats of violence from such a person which are likely to be carried out (s. 177(1) HA 1996 as modified by the Homelessness Act 2002). Those who are married to each other, Mark and Naomi, are included in the definition of associated persons (s. 178(1)). (The definition is the same as that under Part IV of the Family Law Act 1996.) As Naomi has dependent children living with her she will have a priority need (s. 189); some local authorities require sight of a residence order (s. 8, Children Act 1989) (Law Com. No. 172, para. 3.2). Where an applicant may be homeless, eligible for assistance and have a priority need, an authority has an interim duty to provide accommodation pending a decision as to whether any duty is owed to the applicant (s. 188 HA 1996 as modified by the Homelessness Act 2002). If Naomi does not wish to return to the matrimonial home she may think that an occupation order is unnecessary, but if she fails to take steps to regain possession of the matrimonial home the local housing authority may decide that she is homeless intentionally.

(c) Is the marriage void? The answer to that is 'no'. A marriage is void if the parties are not respectively male and female s. 11 (c) Matrimonial Causes Act (MCA) 1973. A marriage will be regarded as void or non-existent if the parties did not have the capacity to marry. The court will consider capacity at the time of the marriage. At the time of the marriage of Mark and Naomi the parties were respectively male and female.

The Gender Recognition Act (GRA) 2004 provides that a person of either gender who is at least 18 may make an application, to a Gender Recognition Panel (GRP), for a gender recognition certificate (GRC). This is on the basis of living in the other gender, or having changed gender under the law of a country or territory outside the United Kingdom (s. 1(1)). The GRP must grant the application if satisfied that the applicant—

(a) has or has had gender dysphoria (that is—gender dysphoria, gender identity disorder and transsexualism),

(b) has lived in the acquired gender throughout the period of two years ending with the date on which the application is made (in the first six months of the Act coming into force, the two-year period would be increased to six, to deal with the anticipated backlog of applications. Gender dysphoria is estimated to affect 1 in 10,000 people. It is believed that there are some 5,000 people in the UK who could qualify for GRCs under the new legislation see Hanson, N., 'It's Law in the Genes' (2004) 101(21) *LSG* 30) , and

(c) intends to continue to live in the acquired gender until death (s. 2(1)).

The applicant must provide the information by way of a statutory declaration and medical evidence in support (s. 3).

If a GRP grants an application it must issue a GRC to the applicant. Unless the applicant is married, the certificate is to be a full GRC. On the issue of a full GRC, the person will be entitled to a new birth certificate reflecting the acquired gender (provided a UK birth register entry already exists for the person) and will be entitled to marry someone of the opposite gender to his or her acquired gender.

A married applicant, such as Mark, would receive an interim GRC, which would make the existing marriage voidable (s. 12(g), Matrimonial Causes Act (MCA) 1973 (as amended by Gender Recognition Act (GRA) 2004)). A decree would not be granted on the s. 12(g) ground unless proceedings were instituted within six months of the issue of the interim GRC (s. 13(2A) MCA 1973 as amended by GRA 2004)).

The court granting the nullity decree under s 12(g) must issue a full GRC. If the marriage ends for any other reason, i.e. divorce, nullity on any other ground or death, the applicant with an interim GRC may apply, within six months of the end of the marriage, for a full GRC. The fact that a person's gender has become the acquired gender will not affect Mark's status as the father of Olga and Poppy.

(d) Where a residence order is in force with respect to a child, no person may cause the children to be known by a new surname without either the written consent of every person who has parental responsibility for them or the leave of the court (s. 13(1)(a)), Children Act 1989). If Naomi has residence orders with respect to Olga and Poppy she will need Mark's permission, as he has parental responsibility (s. 2(1)), or the leave of the court to change the girls' surname. In view of Mark's stated wish to continue to be regarded as a parent it would seem unlikely that he would agree to such a change. Where there is no residence order in force he should apply for a specific issue or a prohibited steps order (s. 8) to prevent a change of name (*Dawson* v *Wearmouth* [1999] 1 FLR 1167. The court regards a change of surname as an important matter, not to be undertaken lightly (*W* v *A (Child: Surname)* [1981] 1 All ER 100). The court will take into account all the circumstances of the case, including any embarrassment which may be caused to the children by not changing their name, the long-term interests of the children and the importance of maintaining links with the paternal family. Where an application is made either under s. 13 or s. 8 the court must apply the welfare principle (s. 1(1)). Additionally, in a contested s. 8 application the court must have regard to the statutory checklist (s. 1(4)). Although it is not mandatory for the court to apply the s. 1(3) welfare checklist in a s. 13 application, it has been acknowledged that it provides a useful *'aide-mémoire'* (*Re B (Change of Surname)* [1996] 1 FLR 791). Are the circumstances sufficiently exceptional or embarrassing to permit a change of name? Where there was 'stigma' attached to the father's surname and because the child was said to 'utterly depend on her mother' the court permitted a change to the mother's maiden name (*Beech* v *Beech* (1987) 27 March (unreported) CA (Lexis transcript)). (See *Re W, Re A, Re B*

(Change of Name) [1999] 2 FLR 930 and *Re R (Surname: Using Both Parents')* [2001] 2 FLR 1358.)

Q Question 6

H and W have lived together for 25 years. They are both writers. They married each other three years ago after W's previous husband died. There are no children.

W bought their house in her sole name 20 years ago for £25,000, paying £4,000 cash and raising the rest on a mortgage. They agreed to take equal responsibility for household expenses (excluding the mortgage instalments which W paid) and maintenance costs. The cooking, cleaning, gardening and such have always been equally shared.

Their relationship began to founder two years ago when W at last wrote a best seller. She has since neglected H emotionally and financially, had a number of short-lived affairs, and she and H's brother (a famous thriller writer) now wish to marry each other as soon as possible. Her latest novel is widely seen as a thinly veiled mockery of H.

The house is now worth £400,000. W has £200,000 saved and is currently generating an annual income of £80,000. H's brother is worth nearly £2 million.

Advise H, who wants as much as he can get by way of financial relief ancillary to divorce. (You do not need to advise him about the divorce itself.) How, if at all, would your answer differ were H and W never to have married?

Commentary

Well, you will need to read it all the way through. The (very possibly unwelcome) twist in the last paragraph of the question means you need to know the contents of two different chapters, often situated some way apart from one other at that. The topics here involved are, of course, ancillary financial relief in the divorce court and declaratory property rights respectively. The good news is that the necessary length and breadth can only be achieved at the expense of depth. This is one for the fast, legible handwriters.

As well as saving their nasty surprise for a throwaway line at the end, the examiners have given no express indication as to how the marks are to be allocated. This may be the saving of the reluctant chooser to whom the last sentence came as a spoiler. This is because the examiners are unlikely to restrict the spouses-only answer to half-question status. All the data, both money and property, can be related to financial relief, whereas only some of it, i.e. the house, has relevance to the cohabitants. So there is more to be said when H and W are spouses. On the other hand, the candidate who only knows about property rights, i.e. the couple as cohabitants, may well be doomed to a fail mark, no matter how well it is done.

It is probably better to segregate the two 'halves' in your answer. Integrated treatments are often the passport to the highest marks, but here the law treats the two situations so asymmetrically that it is both conceptually appropriate and more convenient to deal with them in turn. The situation as a married couple should be dealt with first.

- **Marriage better for poorer partner!**
- **Ancillary financial relief on divorce**
  - **MCA 1973—discretionary adjustment**
  - **'All the circumstances'; fairness**
  - *White*—**not half?**
- **Declaratory approach for cohabitants—not much**

☀ Suggested answer

This question neatly encapsulates the radically different positions of married and unmarried couples as regards their financial and property positions on relationship breakdown. It is only married couples who may obtain a divorce and thus make applications for ancillary financial relief under Part II of the Matrimonial Causes Act (MCA) 1973. Although not unlimited, the divorce court's power of redistribution over the family wealth is enormous. In *Hanlon* v *The Law Society* [1981] AC 124 Lord Denning MR said: 'The court hands out . . . according to what is the fairest provision for the future . . .', an approach now confirmed by Lord Nicholls in *White* v *White* [2000] 3 WLR 1571: the implicit objective must be 'to enable the court to make fair financial arrangements'. Yet the 'rights' of the 'unmarried househusband' amount to little more than orthodox principles for the determination of beneficial interests in property, principles which, ironically, were developed in disputes between spouses before the divorce court was granted its modern adjustive powers.

Turning first to H and W as a married couple, the court's powers are to be found in ss. 21–26 of the MCA 1973. These are maintenance pending suit, financial provision (periodical payments secured and unsecured, together with lump sums) and property adjustment (most notably property transfers). The criteria for the operation of these powers are to be found in s. 25. There is no sex discrimination, H will be relieved to hear (*Calderbank* v *Calderbank* [1976] Fam 93). In *Browne* v *Browne* [1989] 1 FLR 291 a wife was ordered to pay some £175,000 to her former husband, Butler Sloss LJ remarking that it was '. . . not in any way an unusual application'. More recently, Lord Nicholls in *White* (above) pointed out—no doubt with wives in mind—that although the traditional division of labour 'is no longer the order of the day, who plays what role should prejudice neither spouse'.

H has 'no money of his own', W has, and H should know that under s. 22, MCA 1973, on a petition for divorce, the court may make a 'reasonable' order for 'maintenance pending suit'. In *Re T (Divorce: Interim Maintenance: Discovery)* [1990] 1 FLR 263, an order of £25,000 per year was made—we need not mention to H the £360,000 p.a. order made in *F* v *F (Ancillary Relief: Substantial Assets)* [1995] 2 FLR 45.

So far as the other orders are concerned, the fact that there are no children means that the 'first consideration' specified in s. 25, MCA 1973 may safely be overlooked, and that the Child Support Acts 1991–2000 are inapplicable. Today, the law has no ultimate objective, no 'minimal loss' principle of the sort that obtained until the Matrimonial and Family Proceedings Act 1984. First, s. 25 requires the court to consider 'all the circumstances of the case', before specifying a number of them. One unspecified circumstance relevant here is the fact that nearly 90 per cent of their relationship was pre-marital. Now that pre-marital cohabitation is no longer seen as (so) aberrative perhaps greater weight will be attached to it on divorce. This could be crucial to H, whose marriage is childfree and 'worked' only for about a year: he will be pleased to hear that in *GW* v *RW (Financial Provision: Departure from Equality)* [2003] 2 FLR 108 it was held unrealistic to treat the periods differently where a relationship moves 'seamlessly' from cohabitation to marriage. A similar approach was taken in *CO* v *CO* [2004] EWHC 287—but as part of 'all the circumstances of the case', rather than under the 'duration of the marriage' (s. 25(2)(d)).

Sections 25(2)(a) and (b) are equally significant. They refer to the parties' past and present resources, needs and liabilities. H has nothing, for the moment at least, whilst W is loaded and about to marry his brother who appears to be very well off (whose riches are relevant, *Macey* v *Macey* [1981] 3 FLR 39, in that they reduce her needs). Section 25(2)(c) mentions the standard of living enjoyed by the family before the breakdown of the marriage: not such good news for H, as W's long-awaited success seems to have arrived contemporaneously with the breakdown. We are not told how old they are (s. 25(2)(d)), but on the timescale given they must be middle-aged, at least. Should H be over 60 he may fall foul of *A* v *A (Financial Provision)* [1998] 2 FLR 180 (20 per cent reduction for reduced expenditure needs) and, if over 70, of *A* v *A (Elderly Applicant: Lump Sum)* [1999] 2 FLR 969, where the husband's low life expectancy ensured that he saw very little of his wife's £1 million assets on their divorce. As already stated, s. 25(2)(d) also mentions the duration of the marriage and in *Attar* v *Attar* [1985] FLR 649 a single capital payment of £30,000 was thought sufficient after a six-month marriage to a very rich man.

Section 25(2)(f) refers to contributions to the welfare of the family, such as looking after the home. This seems to have been a matter of equality here.

Section 25(2)(g), however, seems particularly significant. It refers to 'conduct . . . that . . . would . . . be inequitable to disregard'. W has had a number of short-lived affairs, neglected H financially and emotionally, has taken up with H's brother and then finally mocked him in a novel. In *Baillie* v *Tolliday* [1982] 4 FLR 542 the wife's affair with her father-in-law was held relevant: surely W's not dissimilar behaviour, coupled with all the rest, must trigger s. 25(2)(g)?

So what, to take H's instructions, is 'as much as he can get'? In truth, and in the absence of an arithmetical approach to financial relief, or even an abstract criterion since the 1984 Act, it is difficult to say. It must be remembered that, since the 1984 Act, the court must encourage 'self sufficiency' (s. 25, MCA 1973 as amended) by, for example, the duty to consider whether any periodical payments order should be for a fixed term. H's likely age and dubious future earning prospects apart, this case may well be best suited to capital settlements rather than on-going income support, certainly after the maintenance pending suit has run its course. H's strong cards are W's riches and her conduct (there is no suggestion that he has helped her to her present professional eminence) and the more recent decisions on pre-marital cohabitation. Here the assets probably exceed the amounts required for the parties' respective financial needs in terms of housing and income. Since *White* (above) the court must therefore explain, by reference to the s. 25(2) factors, why it is departing— as it usually will—from a 50–50 split. Given H's lack of contribution to W's success, and despite her income being significantly greater than their combined outgoings, this does not seem to be on a par with the 'unusual' divorce case of *McFarlane* v *McFarlane, Parlour* v *Parlour, The Times*, 18 July, 2004, where the court had a duty to consider the *future* possibility of a clean break.

H must have somewhere to live, although not necessarily a £400,000 former marital home all to himself. Perhaps his best legitimate expectation would be for a clean break consent order of some one quarter of the £600,000 capital represented in the house and W's bank account. Despite the strictures in *Lambert* v *Lambert* [2003] 1 FLR 139 as to the need to limit the concept, W's literary success (coupled with H's failure) is surely a 'special contribution' (as per, e.g., *L* v *L (Financial Provision: Equality)* [2002] 1 FLR 642), and thus sufficient to imbalance the 50–50 approach.

H as unmarried partner to W epitomises the value of marriage to the economically weaker party to a broken relationship. With no marriage, there can be no divorce, and no financial relief. There is absolutely no question of tapping in to W's income or savings in which H has no claim under ordinary principles of ownership. The only possible avenue here is to the house, by way of implied, resulting or constructive trust, W having bought it 'in her sole name'. By s. 53(2) of the Law of Property Act 1925, the normal requirement of a deed or conveyance for the creation of any legal estate does not affect the creation of such trusts.

H will need to show a common intention that they should both be beneficial owners and that he relied on this to his detriment. He did not provide any part of the purchase price, unlike the contributor in *Sekhon* v *Alissa* [1989] 2 FLR 94 who was subsequently held entitled to an interest in equity in the property by way of resulting trust. We are expressly told that he did not help with the mortgage. In *Re Gorman (a Bankrupt)* [1990] 2 FLR 284, such help did permit the court to infer the necessary intention.

Perhaps there is hope for H in such old-ish cases as *Cooke* v *Head* [1972] 1 WLR 518 and *Eves* v *Eves* [1975] 1 WLR 1338, where non-financial contributions went some way towards providing evidence of the necessary intention. Yet there the claimants, who were women, wielded a sledge hammer and cement mixer in the former, and did similar heavy work in the latter. But more recently, the woman in *Burns* v *Burns* [1984] FLR 216 lived with her man for 19 years, gave up her job to look after him and their two children, bought consumer durables for the house and laid half a patio—and got nothing. (A far cry from waiting for the muse, which is how H seems to have spent most of his time.) In *Lloyds Bank* v *Rossett* [1990] 2 FLR 155, Lord Bridge was 'extremely doubtful' that anything other than a direct contribution to the purchase price (whether initially or by payment of mortgage instalments) would suffice.

The disdain felt for these last two cases has increased in line with the growth in extra-marital cohabitation. Sadly for H, this will not help him any more than will the many ameliorating proposals which have since been laid on the table. But does *Le Foe* v *Le Foe* [2001] 2 FLR 97 offer him a glimmer of hope? There, the court held that a common intention could be inferred from indirect contributions, because the family economy had depended upon them. Furthermore, it is now clear from *Oxley* v *Hiscock* [2004] EWCA Civ 546 that where there was evidence as to intention, but none as to the intended respective proportions, the latter need not be assumed to be pro rata to their actual contributions, as the court must look at the entire course of dealing. But perhaps H (as cohabitant) might be better advised to consider a libel action.

Further reading

Hale, B., Pearl, D., Cooke, E., and Bates, P., *The Family, Law & Society*, 5th edn (London: Butterworths, 2002).

Cretney, S. M., Masson, J., and Bailey-Harris, R., *Principles of Family Law*, 7th edn (London: Sweet & Maxwell, 2002).

Probert, R., *Cretney's Family Law*, 5th edn (London: Sweet & Maxwell, 2003).

Index